# OFF THE BEATEN TRACK IN SUSSEX

BEEDING LEVEL.
*By Fred Davey.*)

THE GATEWAY, MICHELHAM PRIORY (page 316).

(By A. S. C.)

# OFF THE BEATEN TRACK IN SUSSEX

BY
ARTHUR STANLEY COOKE
WITH ONE HUNDRED AND SIXTY
ILLUSTRATIONS BY SUSSEX ARTISTS

IN CUCKFIELD PARK
(*By Walter Puttick.*)

HERBERT JENKINS LIMITED
3 YORK STREET ST. JAMES'S
LONDON S.W. 1 ❀ ❀ MCMXXIII

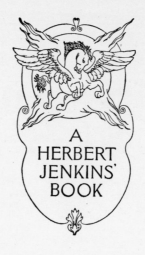

A
HERBERT
JENKINS'
BOOK

*NEW EDITION*

*Wyman & Sons Ltd., Printers, London, Reading and Fakenham*

BOSHAM (page 176).
*(By Hubert Schroder, A.R.E.)*

# PREFACE

IF this volume tends to make our varied and beautiful county better known, " it shall do well "—especially if it gives pleasure to those unable to take such walks. If it has, here and there, a thought or an idea not generally obvious, it may perhaps be forgiven the repetitions which are inevitable in describing similar details—forgiven the recital of familiar facts, whether historical, archæological or natural—forgiven, where, by the light of later or expert knowledge, errors are apparent.

Some of these blemishes are consequent on the passage of time necessary to cover so large an area by frequent personal visitation. Some thirty-seven rambles are described, about equally divided between the east and west divisions of the county. Although indications of route are given, chiefly for the benefit of strangers, it does not claim to be a guide-book. Its size would preclude such a use. Neither does it pretend to be exhaustive. Much more remains to be dealt with.

Sincere acknowledgments are due to the various sources from which information has been gathered, the Sussex Archæological Collections, as usual, having been largely drawn upon.

Much of the interest of the book will be due to the number and variety of its illustrations, by twenty-five different pens. They are all reproduced from original black-and-white drawings. My thanks are specially given to the members of the Brighton Arts Club, present and past, no less than twenty of whom have contributed sketches. One of the past members, Mr. Arthur B. Packham, has been most generous with his work.

A. S. C.

vii

The sheets of the one-inch Ordnance Map of Sussex are fourteen in number, running thus (parts, of course, dealing with Kent, Surrey and Hampshire) :—

| 300<br>Arlesford. | 301<br>Haslemere. | 302<br>Horsham. | 303<br>Tunbridge Wells | 304<br>Tenterden. |
| 316<br>Fareham. | 317<br>Chichester. | 318<br>Brighton. | 319<br>Lewes. | 320<br>Hastings. |
| 331<br>Portsmouth. | 332<br>Bognor. | 333<br>Worthing. | 334<br>Eastbourne. | |

COTTAGE AT ALBOURNE.
(*By the late Joseph Diplock.*)

TROTTON BRIDGE (page 160).
(*By Arthur B. Packham.*)

# CONTENTS

## WEST SUSSEX.

ix

WEST SUSSEX—*continued.*

SALVINGTON MILL.

*(By A. Jobson Brown.)*

# ILLUSTRATIONS

# ROUTES WEST OF BRIGHTON

BEEDING FROM BRAMBER IN 1891.

(*By A. S. C.*)

# OFF THE BEATEN TRACK IN SUSSEX

## CHAPTER I

### BRAMBER TO SHOREHAM (5 MILES)

#### BY RAIL TO BRAMBER

WITH ILLUSTRATIONS BY FRED DAVEY, BROOK HARRISON, ARTHUR B. PACKHAM, H. S. PERCIVAL AND A. S. C.

IT was in the early spring that the Artist and the Man with the Camera—hereinafter called " T'other "—climbed the castle-hill at Bramber. The castle (what remains of it) is probably well known. The church is not—at least, inside. The door is invariably locked, and although the key has been traced on one or two occasions by specially gifted and tireless enthusiasts, the effort has robbed them of all courage to remount the hill, so that the interior has not often echoed the sound of week-day footsteps.

The Artist told T'other that he once caught the sexton at the church by mistake, and had a glimpse of the four Norman arches supporting the low, massive tower, those to the west having curiously carved capitals. These arches and the whole of the tower-chancel were decorated in a somewhat trivial style about thirty years ago, with stencilled bands and ornament. But Norman architecture does not lend itself to the pretty in Art. Nothing but its own rugged, deeply-cut zigzag, tooth or billet mouldings and the like have any part in its sombre magnificence. Surface patterns, or smooth finish, rob it of half its charm. This is probably why so much imitative modern work in the Norman style so utterly fails to convince. Nearly all old work shows the chisel marks, even on small pilasters.

This tower and a short nave are all that remain of a once larger church. Cromwell's Ironsides are credited with its curtailment, as well as with the destruction of the castle ; but it is doubtful if Time, or the needs of the neighbouring community in the matter of ready-made, well-squared masonry, had not more to do with the latter. The collapse of the roof of a little-used transept or aisle probably accounts for the shrinkage in size of the church, following on a decrease in the population of the village, when the castle was destroyed.

BEEDING BRIDGE.
(*By H. S. Percival, A.R.E.*)

The village has much to commend it, and had more before motor-cars arrived. Sussex villages, with their almost universal characteristic of one long street, are singularly ill-adapted for this modern application of the whirlwind to daily life. Dustless roads may result from the scourge, but villages are almost unbearable now.

Of old houses, Bramber has its fair share, one being particularly beautiful, both in build and position. It is greatly favoured by artists. One and all they seize upon the view on entering the village from Beeding, looking up the street to the background of the wooded castle-hill. The Artist ventured to think that the view given here with Beeding Mill and the distant downs was the finer subject, if less popular. The mill, alas, has since been blown down, and the elm trees shading the beautiful old timbered house, which were superb in stature and shape, have also been " topped," destroying much of its charm.

This old house (St. Mary's), together with Amberley Castle, has its tradition of a night spent by Charles in his flight from Worcester, and a frescoed, or painted room is shown as his ; but the only thing that is certain, is that the fugitive King passed by on his way through Beeding.

Beeding is scarcely a stone's-throw from Bramber, but when the floods are out, is very effectually cut off, except for vehicular traffic, or by boat. It is of high antiquity. Beida, one of the Saxon invaders, gave it his name, and it is expressly mentioned in King Alfred's Will, bequeathing it to his nephew Æthelm.

OLD BARN AT BEEDING.
(*By Fred Davey.*)

The bridge, with its long causeway approach, probably occupies the site of the Roman ford across the estuary. Both bridge and village are favourites with painter-folk, and the churchyard, with its melancholy cypress avenue, has an inexpressibly solemn air, heightened by seclusion. It is a long step by the river-bank to the church, which stands on a promontory looking out over the level. In early days this was an estuary of the sea as far as Steyning, by whose quays ocean-going vessels used to discharge their cargoes.

Inside the church, "restoration" has made "all things new," and the most interesting fragment is a Transition double window in the south wall of the chancel, with angle shafts, and a door of similar style. Adjoining, stood in former days, the Priory of Sele, of which no vestige remains. Braose of Bramber gave to the

Abbey of St. Florence of Salmur, his own church of St. Nicholas, that of New Shoreham, and St. Peter de Veteriponte. Some Benedictine monks came over to found the Priory. Its endowment was small, only sufficient for the Prior and four or five brothers. It was also kept poor, being taken, in common with the possession of all the alien priories, into the King's hands during the wars with France, or made to support French prisoners. It was thus taxed by Edward III £10 yearly, for the maintenance of Robert d'Artoys.

At the base of the hillock on which the church stands, a stream runs, and from this there are several charming views of Bramber hill and castle. To-day, however, the objective was Coombes, so recrossing the bridge and following this west bank of the river, they came to Botolphs, which some learned men vow is identical with the Roman Veteriponte, and others equally "larned," declare is nonsense!

BEEDING—THE RIVER BANK.

(*By Fred Davey*.)

" St. Botolph's is a half-way 'house of God,' within whose walls one is well content to rest awhile." This was the Artist's sentiment, but it was spoiled by the sequel—a locked door and a lost key! Lost, at least, to them. "The key be over at Coombes," was the answer a passing native gave to anxious inquiries. " No one looked after the church now," he thought. " Well, it's old enough to look after itself," grumbled T'other, as he flattened his nose against the low-side chancel window, and peered in ; and was again obliged to be content with description.

" If we had been able to get in," said the Artist, " it would have been interesting to hear your opinion of it. We are so apt to be influenced by the first general appearance of a place, that I should not be surprised if more than this impressed itself on your mind : viz., that it has a neglected, Sunday to Sunday kind of look, with the dust of several days on everything, and perhaps a want of repair about the floor and seats ; with nothing remarkable in the architecture ; a very low chancel arch ; evidence of a north aisle now in ruins and the arches blocked up ; dust, as before mentioned ; damp, of course, and therefore rather ' smelly ' ; and you are outside again, the door locked and the poor old place, with its dead within and around it, soon left far behind.

" One cannot complain at this. It is the natural result of impressions received from without rather than from within. It was the fashion of fifty years ago to call all architecture ' mean,' which did not evince the matured styles. (Dallaway and Horsfield dub St. Botolph's and Coombes, ' small and uninteresting ' : ' of mean architecture.') ' Is anything " mean " that pious hearts and earnest hands have raised to the glory of God ? ' was the Artist's question. ' Primitive, heavy, rude—ugly, may be ; but wholly beautiful in His eyes Who sees not as man sees, and beautiful even in man's eyes, if sentiment and reverence for age have any place in his heart. Look you now ! If those who so lightly appraise and dismiss the recollection of the place from their minds, had been born in the parish, and spent

ST. BOTOLPH'S.

(By Arthur B. Packham.)

boyhood's days about it, some affection would exist for its ancient walls and modest air. But even such would have to hark far back into the past to realise what it meant—the raising of these flint walls, tiny tower, nave, chancel and aisle in the time, maybe, of Rufus, or an earlier king.'

" If any score of families living now within an average mile of any given spot, were without a church, I wonder if one half so worthy as St. Botolph's would be the result—without aid from other parishes, or kindly well-wishers—or would there be a church at all ?

" I never yet found a village church in Sussex that had not the keenest interest for me, even if it were plain almost to dullness. Such an one, perhaps, is St. Botolph's. And yet, if instead of large, sweeping glances which take in everything and retain nothing, we bring our eyes to look for the detail which may repay study, we shall see that the chancel arch is rude enough to have been the work of an ancient Briton.  A rough rib runs up under the plain soffit of the arch, starting from corbel-capitals of the simplest form, indented with one of the earliest known embellishments, an uneven tooth ornament.

" All honour to the man who turned its somewhat doubtful semi-circle ; who had none but the most elementary ideas of ornament, yet gave of his best.  He had seen that the point of a trowel impressed into mortar or clay took away the reproach of its being an unmeaning mass of matter ; and that a second and third gave it (save the mark) distinction !  A poor, pitiful discovery, the very glimmerings of enrichment and ornament—but he meant well. So he carved the capitals of his arch of this rude pattern, and He, Whose House it is, accepted, and has preserved it, while many a noble pile, such as Battle Abbey, raised in a spirit of vaunting pride, has crumbled into dust and desolation.

" How can anyone stand in these holy places, simple and rude though they be, unmoved ?  Consider the large piety which built these small churches !  The population of Coombes is given in Domesday at 47.  Its church will hold a hundred now, and *was* larger !  What self-denial is here !  What an example for us ! "

Thus the Artist ; while T'other set up his camera and took a view similar to the one given here.

" Then our care for sacred places," continued the Artist, " has been apt to err too much on the side of neglect.  The ruined aisle of St. Botolph's proves this.  When it was better cared for, its worshippers took pride in enriching it, and although their ways were not at all admirable, the balance was in their favour.  Thus we read that John Slutter, in 1520, bequeathed his body to be buried ' in the Church of Botollys,' and ' to St. Peter's lyght ; item, to the lyght of Our Ladye and the lyght of St. Botollys in the same Church, to either of them, a yewe sheep.'  Richard Ockenden, 1535, wished his body to be buried ' between ye door and ye sant.'  To this day, stone brackets on the north and south walls show where these ' lyghts ' were kept burning.

" Nor is this all.  There is more to be seen, but only the antiquarian—who recks not whether the dust of ages adorns his clothes, or the beams they sweep so unwontedly clean—has courage enough to scale the tower and make an examination of the three old bells, which for the last three hundred and seventy years have called the living to church and tolled the dead to rest.  On the waist of each bell is a large floriated cross in relief, and under it in Old English lettering, but in Latin, ' John Tonne made me.'  One has : ' sancte pe tre ora pro nobis ' ; the second : ' of your charity

St. Botolph's Church.

*(By Fred Davey.)*

prai for the soulles of John Slutter, John hunt, willem slutter ' ;
and the third : ' Jesu thes belles were made in the yer of God,
mdxxxvi.' Each has also in relief a coin, a Tudor rose, and a
small medal of Henry VIII, as well as an initial cross before each
inscription.

" It is interesting to see that the good man who endowed the
' lyghts,' is partly responsible for the gift of these bells also, which
are among the oldest dated bells in the county, and yet are youthful
compared with that at Duncton, which bears date 1369, and came
from abroad. This is probably the earliest dated bell in the whole
of England. Hawies says there are very few bells extant earlier
than 1400.

" The house near by is the Priest's house, as modest and unassuming as the church."

On their way to Coombes, the Artist again took up his parable
and said :

" Five houses and the little church comprise the village of
Coombes. It is the place for a pastoral poet to dwell, if peace and
unbroken solitude are what his soul delights in. The very road
towards it gets grass grown and uncertain where to trend, and
finally decides to leave it lying undisturbed in its hollow. If seclusion means peace, surely this is the home of peace. But Coombes
has not always been so productive of quietude as it would seem.
Strife and envy have wrestled over the possession of this tranquil,
almost unknown spot. Its name is derived from the Saxon for a
deep valley, ' an expression perfectly suited to its situation.'
Domesday records, ' William Fitz-Norman holds Cumbe of William
(of Bramber).' Absorbed by the vigorous Saxon, the name of
Fitz-Norman was soon lost in that of *de Combe*. ' Hugh Norman
de Combe ' appears in a charter of Stephen's reign.

" Few spots in Sussex have been more fruitful of ' law ' and license
than this. John de Combe had to defend his right to give his
daughter Agnes to whomsoever he or she would ; Robert le Sal-
vage, of Broadwater, claiming the disposal of the lady. Mazeline
de Cumba and her sons were fined one mark ' to have an inquest
to find whether they were accused for the death of a man, who was
found dead upon Mazeline's lands, justly, or out of hate or envy.'

" Early in the reign of Henry III, Sybill, wife of Richard de
Cumbe, was accused of attempting to divert the succession of
certain lands. In 1279 Robert de Combe tried to establish his
claim to Coombes against the holders, William de Braose and
John de Combe ; but the jury, ' upon their oaths ' say that
Robert was not ' disseised ' and Bob was accordingly ' amerced '
(i.e. left at the mercy of the Court) for making a false claim.

" But the most interesting event in the annals of Coombes

OLD CLERGY HOUSE, COOMBES.

(By A. S. C.)

occurred in 1259. Sir John de Gaddesdon, of Broadwater, was sheriff for three years in Henry III's reign. His exalted office, however, did not deter him from an outrage peculiarly ' characteristic of that barbarous age.' He invited Michael de Combe to his house at Broadwater, ' made him very drunk, conveyed him home to Coombes, where he was shut up, drunk, half dead, and not *knowing good from evil.*'

" Sir John then took Michael's seal, affixed it to a ' deed ot feoffment,' by which he obtained possession of Michael's manors and lands by fraud, appropriated the corn and hay, removed goods from the manor, and even robbed the little church of its chalice, ornaments and vestments. He defended himself at the trial in 1261, but a verdict of the jury compelled him to disgorge his ill-gotten gain—an eloquent proof that even at this early date the judgment of ' twelve good men and true ' was given without fear or favour. Truly—however the Law may have failed—even-handed justice was generally meted out when a jury had a voice in it.

" Perhaps it is not surprising that the daughter and heiress of this ' unjust judge ' leaves an equally shameful record behind her.

" In 1400 the family name of Combe changed (by marriage), and the Manor was conveyed to Sir John Halsham ; but the validity was doubtful, until upheld at two inquisitions held at West Grinstead and at Shipley in 1405 and 1410.

" Our chief seat of learning had an interest in little Coombes, for in 1288 the Prior of Merton recovered the demand he made of Thomas de Marve for the rent of ' one messuage and six virgates of land.' Thomas had to ' pay up and look pleasant,' and to find securities for future probity.

" The little church could hardly be older, being Saxon or very early Norman. The chancel arch and the blocked up window are like those at Ovingdean, except that the latter has a triple arcade to its sanctuary. The south and priest's doors, and the font, are all Norman. Perpendicular windows have been inserted, and there is a circular low-side or ' leper window,' splayed internally eastward, so that the altar could be seen. On the priest's door are circular marks which may be sundials, and there is some old stained glass. The chalice is dated 1588, and the register goes back to 1538, a very early date.

" Bishop Bower at his visitation (MSS.) says :

' In a window over the communion table lye two brass figures taken off some tomb, or gravestone. The one a man in armour (with a two-hilted sword) in a praying attitude, the other is a woman in a close dress and praying posture.'

"Needless to say, this brass, like those it recorded, is 'departed' too."

\*　　　\*　　　\*　　　\*　　　\*

As of old, Coombes caused or saw strife, so did it now. The manner of it was as follows. The old clergy house was the subject the Artist sat down to sketch, and T'other prepared to photograph. The light, and the patience of both, were getting exhausted. He of the pencil groaned at the detail in those trees, and T'other sighed for a gleam of sunshine, for the sky was " black with clouds." At the latter's earnest desire—and to escape the trees—the Artist went up the hill, and in answer to the anxious call said that " the heavens were as lead above him—and were likely to continue so ! " But " all things come to him who waits," and when hope was well-nigh gone, a patch of sunlight, not twenty yards in breadth, came rapidly down the long coombe, across the churchyard, passed over the old house, and over that alone, for it did not extend five yards to right or left. A greater change than it caused would be difficult to conceive. In a twinkling, T'other had removed the cap, and captured the view and the visitor in his " trap to catch a sunbeam."

A merry laugh was the reward of that sun-ray, and as it had

COTTAGES BY THE " SUSSEX PAD."
*(By Arthur B. Packham.)*

happiness in its ring, the ray was probably as well pleased with the part it had played as was any ray that day. (This was how the Artist put it, and was wroth when his companion robbed the thought of its poetry by declaring that the clouds had more to do with it than the ray. T'other offered to make amends by writing some verses embodying both ideas, and was wroth in turn when the Artist declined the honour of the dedication, on the ground that the only part worth reading would be the title—" The Ray and the Rift ! "—The quarrel is not yet " composed.")

   *        *        *        *        *

Crossing a pleasant open space which might be a village green, were the village existent, and where a caravan takes up its position every summer, " to fleet the time carelessly," the road is gained once more, and it winds along with a runnel by it, in a delightfully

casual way to Applesham Farm, standing on a gentle rise. As
with many of these byways, the road has wide grassy margins on
either side, and little, inconsequent pathways trodden by footsteps
straying off the track to feel the grass under foot, or gain the shade
of the trees.

Beyond Applesham Farm there is a beautiful valley with a
plentiful spring. This is called by the pretty name of " Ladywell,"
and there is a track from here across Steepdown, and up to Cissbury
Camp, which tradition says was regularly used by the Roman
soldiery to fetch water. The remains of a Roman villa were found
on the hill above Lancing by the side of this track ; but of this
" more anon."

On the opposite side of the valley rises the great Chapel of Lancing
College. It is built on a scale which dwarfs the rest of its own
college pile.

OLD SHOREHAM FROM THE MARSH.
(*By Fred Davey.*)

Unless Time
alters the im-
pression given
now, it seems
out of harmony
with its im-
mediate neigh-
bourhood.
Not that it
dominates the
Downs as a
range. There
are many hills
from which
one may look down on it, but their line and slope in the vicinity
are so gradual and suave, that the sudden altitude of this
building rather does violence to one's ideas of proportion. What
shocks await the æsthetic sense should the tower and lantern ever
be erected, will probably—and fortunately—fall on the next generation, or our grandchildren, judging from the rate of progress made
since I was a boy.

After all, this leisurely pace is only following the methods of our
forefathers, with this probable advantage : that our want of originality in evolving a new style of architecture, will admit of there
being but one style in Lancing College Chapel, which was by no
means the case where many of our churches were concerned—even
little Coombes !

Inside, the Chapel is, or will be when finished, of truly magnificent, cathedral-like proportions and grandeur. It is 86 feet to the
groining.

Crossing the Ladywell stream by a little bridge, on which one lingers to look at the valley and river, the road turns east for a while, and where it bends southwards again, a short cut can be made along the river-bank to Old Shoreham Bridge. In olden days there was no bridge, but only a ferry. The ferry dues were part of the endowment of Hardham Priory, and though might was often right in those troublous times, yet we find " the Earl of Arundel or the ferryman " his tenant, " for setting up a rival ferry," was made to pay an annual rent of £10 for his usurpation.

Old Shoreham Bridge is one of the few remaining wooden structures which yet defy the ravages of Time. The reason the old

OLD SHOREHAM BRIDGE AND CHURCH.
*(By Brook Harrison.)*

bridge-keeper gives—and he stakes his existence, almost, on the truth of his dictum—is that the piles are of winter-cut oak, that is, trees felled before the sap has risen. However this may be, long may it stand ! It would be a keen, personal loss to many hundreds of artists. With the church and wooded slope of Old Shoreham on the east, Lancing College and Downs to the west, and from the river-banks and levels north and south—in all and every case it seldom fails to compose well. But what is, perhaps, of greater moment, it is in itself a really beautiful structure by reason of its modest simplicity and unassertiveness.

If we say this of the bridge, what shall be said of the old Norman fane which does so much to enhance the prospect—Old Shoreham Church ? Description is apt to express too much, or too little, according as it presents itself to men of different tastes.   Therefore, to the artist, let the view speak for itself.   But let him, if he can, see it from the west of the bridge, when there is one of those yellow sunsets which herald the end of summer, and when the tide is near the full !

It is difficult in our northern clime, to believe such a feast of colour possible, as suffuses the water and landscape from Old to New Shoreham in such a sunset.   Swinburne must have seen such an effect when he wrote so lovingly and melodiously :

" Winds are glancing from sunbright Lancing to Shoreham, crowned with
    the grace of years ;
  Shoreham, clad with the sunset, glad and grave with the glory that death
    reveres."

\*              \*              \*              \*              \*

Of this walk (which is said by a Sussex man of my acquaintance, and no mean judge, to be the most beautiful short walk in the county) there is a variant.   It is by the lane on the left of Bramber Station westward for a while, then turning south through Annington Farm by St. Botolph's, and on as given in the preceding pages.

\*              \*              \*              \*              \*

There is yet another path, which turns in just below " St. Mary's House " at the bottom of Bramber Village, and skirting the water-meadows comes out by Annington Farm.   This is also charming, but not quite so easily followed.

# CHAPTER II

## STEYNING TO BUNCTON AND CHANCTONBURY (7 MILES)

### WITH ILLUSTRATIONS BY ARTHUR B. PACKHAM, BROOK HARRISON, GORDON C. GALSWORTHY, AND A. S. C.)

WHEN one regards the Steyning of to-day—little more than a large village—it seems difficult to believe that it was once a place of much importance, and of considerable size. Even at the Conquest it was larger than either Southampton, Bath, or Northampton! True, none of them, including Steyning itself, were big places at that date, but one is not quite prepared for the fact that the latter had 123 houses, and the three former, 84, 64 and 60 respectively! Steyning increased rapidly, and during the reign of the first Henry was flourishing and important.

Then, again, it seems difficult to realise Steyning—rural, and nestled far inland under the hills—as a seaport; yet it is undoubtedly a fact that what are fat pastures and marshlands, were once, and at no very distant date, an estuary of the sea, which flowed sufficiently past Bramber to enable the shipping of mediæval days to reach Steyning. In nothing has "the mighty main" shown its power to kill "or make alive" more certainly than in its neglect or patronage of harbour towns.

If places so moribund can be said to be "living examples" of this, Winchelsea and Rye are in evidence, and the struggles of Shoreham to keep access to the ocean are continuous to this our day. Of all "the spoils to the victor" those of the dredger are surely of the least value, and could well be spared. Certainly, it requires an effort of the imagination to see in Steyning the characteristics of a maritime port. It is not even within sight of the "restless blue of ocean," and a calm more profound than ever glasses the summer sea, has settled down on its whilom industries and bustle.

Yet it has "a proper pride," has Steyning. Its noble Church, its Brotherhood Hall, and the sort of county town expression of its High Street, are evidences of past greatness too important to be lightly overlooked. If it has seen better days, it does not wear

31

STEYNING CHURCH—INTERIOR.
*(By Gordon C. Galsworthy.)*

a charity garb to accentuate the fact, but relies on its own self-
sufficiency, and points to a history of more than respectable
celebrity.   A philosophic student of times past might call attention
to the fact that its prosperity in days gone by was largely artificial,
due to the solicitude of too many " nursing fathers and nursing
mothers "—especially fathers !   For Steyning was, in a special
sense, under the ægis of the Church.   There is a phrase in the
Particulars of Estates of Brotherhood Hall, 1548, which exactly
hits off the condition of mediæval Steyning.   It mentions " half
an acre of meadow lying in Munkery."   " Lying in Munkery " is
good—is very distinctly good !   No better description of the clerical
shadow that hung over the demesnes of " Staenyngas " could
be penned.   Not that its influence partook of the nature of
miasma, with
resultant tor-
por.   It was
rather of the
pet - dog type
of solicitude.

As early as
the Confessor's
reign the codd-
ling began.
That distribu-
ter of spiritual
temporalities
on all and every
of the Churches
—provided only
they were other

**BROTHERHOOD HALL, STEYNING.**
*(By Arthur B. Packham.)*

than Saxon—could not withstand the temptation to present the
estates of the Great Alfred in Steyning, which happened to revert
to him, " to the Holy Minister at Feskamp, after Bishop Ælfwine's
day, with sac and with soc, so fully and freely as it at first and at
the best stood him in hand."   The fact that Ethelwulf, the father of
Alfred, was buried in the Church, would make the gift to the foreigner
particularly pleasing to the crank bias of the too generous Edward.

The great Earl Godwin had no such illusions.   His influence compelled the monk-king to revoke the gift almost as soon as made,
in 1052 ; but the Conqueror confirmed the original charter and
added to its privileges.   He had " votively " presented it before
he sailed for England.   " If England to itself had been but true,"
this reckoning of unhatched bantams would have miscarried.   It
succeeded, and so did the subsequent " quarrelling among thieves."
De Braose, of " Brambroughe," and the Abbot measured legal

swords for the best part of fifty years, but the Churchman won all along the line. An interesting recrudescence of the dispute, like a spark from grey ashes, arose in 1791, when a Parliamentary Committee found that only the properties held in descent from the Abbots by Sir John Honeywood carried the right to the franchise, and not those held by the Duke of Norfolk from the De Braose family.

The Abbot had " royal liberties in Steyning." He could punish felons, hang murderers ; divide their chattels among his men ; fine his people ; also " all liberty, customs, and all judgments of all his matters and things which may happen, without usurpation of the King's rights."

Such were the powers held by the Fecamp Abbots, that they held their own even against archiepiscopal jurisdiction in 1290. These powers were often questioned, but unsuccessfully. Whatever wrong came of it, right also had " a look in." William de Molend and William de Veske were fined and compelled to amend their ways : the one for encroaching on the waste places by the highway ; the other for raising two shops in the middle of Steyning Market Place.

The first was a sort of equivalent to our modern " Pathways Preservation Societies."

Whether it is good for a locality to be under such stringent, if fatherly, government, is difficult to decide. Certainly Steyning prospered under the outstretched hand of Fecamp. But just as certainly was the possession of such absolute privileges unlikely to last. The first Edward found much virtue in a study of the word " aliens," and by passing a law that property could not be held in England by such, he transferred the rights of Fecamp in Steyning to the Abbey of Our Lady of Sion. This was the last blow to Steyning's prosperity. Forsaken by the sea, and divorced from its wealthy patrons, its star began to wane—and Steyning is now what it is—a pleasant, if sleepy country town.

Nevertheless, independence would seem to have been instilled into the Steyning Burgesses by these ancient powers. There is a letter from the Earl of Arundel, *circa* Charles I, to the Burgesses, beginning with his " very harty commendations," and ending " soe I rest your loving friend " ; but between these fair words is a very different strain. He had recommended two gentlemen to them as Members of Parliament at the previous election. Steyning " would have none of them." He, being " given to understand that it proceeded more out of ignorance than neglect towards him," thought good to again recommend the two worthies, and accompanied it with a bribe, " that he would undertake that they shall not require any Parliament wages." It is refreshing to see that

Steyning promptly returned two other gentlemen, for neither of the names the Earl gave appear in the list of its members. It would also appear from the above that it was not uncommon for burgesses to pay their Members of Parliament.

The early history of Steyning is practically that of the legendary St. Cuthman. Like the Wise Men, he came from the East—not, however, from the Orient. He is the pattern of filial affection, for rather than forsake his old and crippled mother, he trundled her before him in a sort of barrow, in his search for a spot to settle in. The rope suspended from his shoulders, to carry part of the weight, breaking for the second time at Steyning, or what is now

HIGH STREET, STEYNING.
(*By Brook Harrison.*)

its site, he took up his abode there, and built him a church. One other legend describes him as drawing a circle with his pastoral staff round his flock of sheep, and on returning from absence, the gentle creatures had not strayed beyond its limits. If this was prophetic of later realities, it is borne out by the circle of clerical power drawn round the town by the Abbots of Fecamp ; a surround of such potent influence that not only could those inside not get out, but those outside failed to get in ! That Steyning under Fecamp rule was " lying in Munkery " is best proved by the fact that the Abbots had power to sentence to death.

*      *      *      *      *

As we stood and looked along the original of which the sketch gives a pleasant reminder, I remarked to T'other that " nearly every old town has its High Street.   Situation probably had more to do with its christening, for, like Lewes High Street, they generally climb as far towards heaven as the rising ground will permit." T'other, who is nothing if not argumentative, reminded me that the gaol, and not the celestial regions, is to be found at the top of Lewes High Street   This is like him, for when I gently proceeded, " however that may be in one instance, the fact remains that their tendency is upwards," he rudely hinted that it all depended from which end one started.   I lost patience at this and told him it was well that its sponsors were in the habit of looking up rather than down, or " Low Street" would be its present designation, and probably better suited to his taste and quality.   Whether this made him thirsty, I am not sure, but he made off, and left me to sketch.

How alike these streets are in general, and how different in detail!   Taking the name at its full value, they usually centre in themselves the prosperity and much of the aristocracy of each little country town.   Here the *White Hart* or the *Chequers*, old-time houses of call, look like what they were intended to be, viz., hostelries and not mere drinking shops.   In the High Street, too, the Court House, or the little Town Hall, rears its modest tower and red-brick front to grace and mark the view.   The doctor's well-built and comfortable house, and the lawyer's trim Georgian-windowed abode are quietly conspicuous from the rest ; and many a plain, almost ugly " front " is but the rough rind to a sweet and pleasant interior.   Happily, the Gothic craze—which some of our recent great men, including even Ruskin, have advocated unreasonably—has passed away.   It is realised now that much that used to be called " debased," when applied to ecclesiastical architecture, is both useful and appropriate in a domestic sense.   First " Queen Anne " architecture began to revive, and the once despised " Georgian " has come to be copied in its best features.   The uses to which a domestic habitation is put, renders the severity of the Gothic style, even when most ornamental, unsuitable for lay purposes, just as the " Queen Anne" mode, except for small private chapels, is wanting in nobility and grace when used for churches.

Our High Streets, therefore, are likely to retain their composite character of Old English, Queen Anne, Georgian, and other hybrid styles, and our churches, their purer Gothic.   Long may the diversity exist !   We do not want our houses to look like conventual buildings, nor our churches to be as glorified County Courts.   Long may we gaze upon such pleasant High Streets as that of Steyning, and see its charming irregularity a matter of fixed principle, however much individual buildings may alter !

" Thank Heaven," I said, as T'other came strolling back from his voyage of discovery, " that in architecture the general trend of taste in our day is good, whether it be shown in building country cottages or houses in High Streets."

Even T'other agreed and said " Amen " to this.

Steyning Church is beautifully situated and the view from the west is attractive, albeit the tower is somewhat clumsy and out of keeping with the rest, being five hundred years later than nave and chancel. The modern lichgate is substantial and well-designed, and when the elm trees were of full stature, the whole was a favourite subject with artists. But elms, when in decadence, are dangerous. There was nothing for it but to top them, and the view has, therefore, suffered.

The Church is one of the finest and most interesting in Sussex. The part which may be St. Cuthman's are the plain arches at the east end of the aisles, but the greater portion is late and richly elaborate Norman. The chancel arch is the finest in the county, and the nave arches are also the richest in carving of many varieties. The capitals are also beautiful. Until recently the whole effect of the interior was spoiled by galleries which are now removed. This veritable " restoration " seems to have been carefully done, and the stonework generally looks as if it were untouched, which is satisfactory. Parts of a previous renovation are not so pleasing, for instance, the inappropriate tower arch ; and even the chancel strikes one as unconvincing. In style it is neither broad enough nor simple enough to keep company with the glorious Norman nave. The present building is supposed to be only a portion of the original church. I have heard that foundations have been found west of the tower.

The fine clerestory over the nave arcades gives a most distinguished air to the whole, and one feels that there is too little length to the Church. It calls aloud for westward extension.

\*     \*     \*     \*     \*

A path by Steyning water-mill at the extreme west end of High Street—just by an interesting old timbered house—will bring you to Wiston. On the way there is a well under the bank, supplying water to a hamlet, which is quaint, if not old. It may be ancient, but the moulded flat arch springs from rough pier and square abacus, unlike the work of our forefathers. It is, however, picturesque, Time giving it the touch of age, in colour and greenery about it.

This walk to Wiston is beautiful, the view always bounded by Chanctonbury, and always charming, whether on a day of clear sunshine or broken sky, but especially in September, when the sun sets behind the hill, and it is finely silhouetted against the bars of colour and cloud.   Whether Mr. Charles Goring (then a youth of 17) who planted the ancient camp on the hilltop with beech and other trees in 1760, was inspired by the prescience of the artist, and foresaw the beauty and dignity it would add to the range of downs, certainly that consummation has been abundantly fulfilled.   From few points in the county is it invisible. Majestic and solitary, it seems to be the one touch of beauty which only genius in art or design knows how to imagine and to place. It might well be called " Crowned Chanctonbury."

The camp itself is supposed to be originally Neolithic, flint implements having been found in it, as well as Roman coins and pottery, showing that its importance as a stronghold was realised by the latter people also.

Wiston House, a Tudor building, with a fine hall, lies under the shadow of Chanctonbury.   It has a beautiful park with deer, and lovely views of the Downs as far as Wolstonbury on the east, and especially one from the lake towards the hill. Near by, in 1848, the foundations of a small building, with hypocaust, probably a guard-house for the Roman soldiery, were uncovered.

The Church has suffered more than most from the rage of the restorer, not even the monuments being allowed to remain where they were originally placed, and the result is peculiarly exasperating. A fine brass to Sir John de Braose, 1426, is powdered over with fleur-de-lys and the words " Jesu Mercy."   This and the tombs of the Shirley family, of whom Fuller in his " Worthies " gives a quaint account, are the only interesting things, unless it be the coats of arms in the east and west windows.   Over the interior, Stucco in its dull grey robe, reigns supreme.

Although the park is private, there is, either by courtesy or right of way, a path across the grass coming out on the high road not far from Buncton Chapel, a genuine Norman and Transitional chapel-of-ease to Ashington, and is far older and more interesting than the mother church.   It stands on " the hill of Biohcandoune " —a name now vulgarised into " Buncton "—of which hill we have documentary evidence as early as A.D. 791 as being the spot where Adelwulf, the titular King of the South Saxons, granted a wood for the use of St. Andrew's Church at Ferring, and marked the deed with the Holy Cross, in the presence of Offa, King of Mercia, his over-lord, and Wethun, the Bishop.   So that the little Chapel stands on ground which had " a local habitation and a name " when more famous places were unregarded tracts of forest or bare earth. And if the Roman tiles built into its walls tell any tale, they point to an even earlier dwelling-place.

In the choice of the summit of a hill for this solemn function, one seems also to see the survival of old rites, which began in pagan times, and did not entirely change with the advent of Christianity. It was in matters spiritual rather than temporal, that the Church at first sought to win for Christ, and not by too drastic change of sacred customs. Without subscribing to the revolting theory that the altar-slabs of Christian churches were originally sacrificial stones on which human beings were immolated in Druidical days

INTERIOR OF BUNCTON CHAPEL (UNDER CHANCTONBURY).
*(By A. S. C.)*

—one may regard the hill-top as being as near to Christ as to Wodin. The spirit of the worship was essential. Very few sites have been chosen for religious purposes that had not been so used for many years previously. On this hill there may well have been a preaching station, perhaps an altar, or even a wooden church for worship.

The monks of Sele, near Beeding, are supposed to have built the Chapel, about 1150, as there was a dispute with Ashington as to jurisdiction. It is of nave and chancel only, the latter apparently shortened when the decorated east window was inserted, probably replacing double or triple lancets. The two doors (one blocked up) are characteristic of an even earlier date. They have horizontal lintels, over which is a semicircular arch filled with rough masonry. There is a Saxon door of the same type at Eartham. It seems to me to be exactly suited to modest structures such as this. The usual tiny round-headed windows, high up, splayed internally, light the nave. Fitted with a wooden shutter, they were " wind-doors " indeed in winter.

The arcading in the exterior walls of chancel is both interesting as well as puzzling. That on the south is much obstructed by that which "sticketh closer than a brother," namely, the ivy, but taken together with the one on the north side, I believe the whole series were originally plain intersected arches. The intersections have disappeared in the others, which are carved with pellets and pomegranates on a kind of strap moulding of the most ingenuous type as shown by the casual spacing of the straps.

The interior is plain, and raises a protest that in these days of artistic ideas, no other mode of decoration could be found than a universal coat of blue-wash, smothering walls and stonework— thus freely applied some three years ago—unless, being cerulean in hue, it is supposed to add point to the exposition of heavenly things !

The west window is a rather uncommon treatment of two long lancets divided by a narrow mullion. The chancel arch is Norman, recessed on the west side with pillars, and on the abacus of one is a rudely sculptured figure, with pomegranate and other markings, surmounted by a chequer. There is a large fourteenth century aumbry with a shelf, and an elegant " Fenestella," trefoiled and moulded, beneath which is a piscina.

Altogether, it is in intention, simplicity of design, loftiness and general dignity, exactly what a chapel should be. Would it were better known and studied by architects to-day ! It stands on the edge of a hollow through which runs the stream that rises under Chanctonbury—this, if I remember aright, the imagination of Blackmore turned into a river in *Alice Lorraine*. It passes the rose-covered cottages at their very doors, and feeds a road-side fountain built of old stonework from Wiston House, sur-mounted by a natural slab, reminding one of a broken-down gentleman wearing a battered hat !

You can return to Steyning by the road which runs under the hill, a very ancient way. Although links are missing westward, it probably skirted the whole range. It is very prolific in sudden gradients and twists, but is an artist's road from end to end.

*      *      *      *      *

If you choose to climb Chanctonbury, the reward will be ample in the views it has to offer. Near the clump is one of the famous dew-ponds of which Kipling sings—

> " We have no waters to delight
>     Our broad and brookless vales—
> Only the dew-pond on the height,
>     Unfed, that never fails."

These ponds are of great age, probably contemporary with the various earthworks, and designed to supply them with water.  All honour to the Neolithic man who solved the problem of water supply on these waterless downs.  Simple, of course, like all great ideas, they are yet constructed on a scientific basis, which would have shed lustre on any age.

The brothers Hubbard in their work on *Neolithic Dew-ponds and Cattle-ways*, write thus of them ; and as it is always a puzzle to strangers, and even to Sussex folk why, in the hottest summer, they are always full, I cannot do better than quote the following :—

" Dew-ponds were invented to give water to the great earth-works such as Cissbury, for man and beast.  There is still in this country at least one wandering gang of men (analogous to the mediæval bands of bell-founders, masons, etc.) who will construct for the modern farmer a pond which, in any situation in a suffi-ciently dry soil, will always contain water, more in the heat of summer than during winter rains.

" This water is not derived from springs or rainfall, and is speedily lost if even the smallest rivulet is allowed to flow into the pond.

" The gang of dew-pond makers commence operations by hollow-ing out the space of earth far in excess of the apparent requirements of the proposed pond.  They then quickly cover the whole of the hollow with a coating of dry straw.  The straw in its turn is covered by a layer of well-chosen, finely-puddled clay, and the upper surface of the clay is then closely strewn with stones.  Care has to be taken that the margin of the straw is effectively pro-tected by clay.  The pond will gradually become filled with water, the more rapidly the larger it is, even though no rain may fall."

The technical explanation of how these ponds fill is as follows : " If such a structure is situated on the summit of a down, during the warmth of a summer day the earth will have stored a con-siderable amount of heat, while the pond, protected from this heat by the non-conductivity of the straw, is at the same time chilled by the process of evaporation from the puddled clay.  The consequence is, that during the night the moisture of the com-paratively warm air is condensed on the surface of the cold clay. As the condensation during the night is in excess of the evaporation during the day, the pond becomes, night by night, gradually filled. Theoretically, we may observe that during the day the air, being comparatively charged with moisture, evaporation is necessarily less than the precipitation during the night. In practice it is found that the pond will yield a supply of the purest water."

" The dew-pond will cease to attract the dew if the layer of straw should get wet, as it then becomes of the same temperature as the surrounding earth, and ceases to act as a non-conductor of heat. This, practically, always occurs if a spring is allowed to flow into the pond, or if the layer of clay (technically called the ' crust ' is pierced."

" Dew-ponds were originally made by that wonderful being, prehistoric man."*

I think it is well to say that the above theory of the construction and maintenance of dew-ponds has its unbelievers. These deny that dew has any material effect on the body of water. They give the credit to the heavy winter rains. It would seem an easy thing to determine, but in any case, the opposing opinions are sufficiently strident to form very windy argument.

I may here point out the artistic possibilities of these tiny pools when the sheep come up to drink. They group themselves naturally, but the composition of the picture is more difficult, seeing that the dew-ponds are usually on the summits of the Downs.

*    *    *    *    *

From Chanctonbury you can follow one of the ridges or valleys south-west to Findon, and catch a bus which will take you to Worthing Station ; or you can make for Bramber by traversing the perfect sward of the great ridge eastward till you come to a track winding down into a lane which debouches on the road between Steyning and Bramber.

* From *Neolithic Dew-ponds and Cattle-ways*, John Hubbard, M.D., and Geo. Hubbard, F.S.A., F.R.I.B.A.

# CHAPTER III

## SHIPLEY, THAKEHAM AND WEST CHILTINGTON (11 MILES)
### BY TRAIN TO WEST GRINSTEAD

WITH ILLUSTRATIONS BY H. S. PERCIVAL, A. R. E., AND A. S. C.

THE road leads directly west through an undulating country, fairly open, with wide fields bordered by hedges and trees and long strips and clumps of woodland, eminently a hunting district ; and, as if to prove it, on this winter day of chequered sunshine and cloud, a moist west wind "proclaimed a hunting morning "—nay, not only the weather, but the road also. All the country-side seemed, either mounted or afoot, in dog-cart, car, or on cycles, to be gathering at Knepp Castle, the ugly modern house, near which the remains of the Norman fortress of the Braoses stand—if such fragments may be said to stand. Dwellers in towns scarcely realise the attraction the " meet " has for the rural mind. In the three miles to Shipley, not a single person set his face westward. Every one you met seemed in a hurry, looked good-tempered, and among the country-folk " passed the time o' day " almost to a man.

From another point of view, that of the artist, it adds greatly to the charm of the landscape. He can find variety of colour where colour-blind or indifferent folk (it is practically the same thing) see only a dull grey cheerlessness ; but the life that the red coat of the huntsman, and the horses and dogs give to the prospect is one of those things which must be seen to be appreciated, and which few paint successfully. Horses and dogs are not easy drawing at any time, but the hunt in full cry finds out the weak spots in draughtsmanship sooner than any other subject.

Shipley lies to the south on a by-road, and is pleasantly placed on slightly rising ground on the banks of the Adur, which is here but an inconsiderable stream. From the south-west it " composes well "—as the artist says. Not that the church, which is a prominent object, is altogether beautiful. Its massive, high-shouldered tower rises but little above the lofty roofs of the nave and chancel. One sees at a glance how near akin the Norman church is to the Norman castle. I doubt if this view of Shipley

SHIPLEY CHANCEL.
(*By A. S. C.*)

44

is much changed since the days of the Knights Templars who built the church in the twelfth century. True, there is a windmill close by, but windmills were invented about the same time, or earlier, and there may have been one even then. Nearly every village had its mill, water being generally the motive power, but here apparently the ground did not lend itself to that method. Neither does the mill detract from the antique appearance of the place. It has a stunted, pyramidal cap, not unlike the helmet and gorget worn by the Templars themselves.

The severe lines of the church are characteristic of its builders. Shipley was one of two places in Sussex (the other being Saddlescombe, below the Dyke) where the Templars had their " grange " of habitation. No trace of it, or of the chivalrous Order which made Europe ring with its exploits, remains. They grew, prospered and passed away, with the growth, eminence and subsiding of the wave of enthusiasm which the Holy City and Sepulchre inspired.

Philip de Harcourt, the Dean of Lincoln, afterwards Bishop of Bayeux, granted " to the Blessed Mary, and to the Soldiers of the Temple of Solomon, *for ever*, in perpetual alms . . . the land of Heschaplia, with all its appurtenances, and the church in the said vill," about 1125. This is the form of most bequests in those days. It is enough to make the pious donors turn in their graves to see how little their pious emphasis availed.

The Order grew in power and wealth, but when in spite of the efforts of Crusaders and Templars the Holy Land was lost, the forced inactivity of this military Brotherhood prompted the French King, Philip, and later the Pope, Clement V, to plot their overthrow, the former from covetous greed, and the latter because Rome could brook no independent authority. Foul charges of vice and idolatry were brought against them, and after unheard-of cruelties and indignities, the Order was dissolved in 1312, after nearly two hundred years of brilliant and faithful service. They stand for all time as the pioneers of chivalrous adventure and high courage in a sacred cause.

Edward II visited Shipley in 1324 in his progress through Sussex. These royal condescensions were often as great a misfortune as a bad harvest, or a devastating fire. Some of the luxuries unobtainable, except in London, were brought by the royal retinue, but much was expected of the locality honoured.

Owing to its being so out of the way, Shipley Church is but little known by Sussex folk ; yet it is one of the finest Norman buildings we possess. The sketch will give a general idea of it, but it deserves a closer acquaintance. So much solicitude and money have evidently been spent on its restoration, it seems ungracious to suggest that it presents a rather " brushed and combed " appearance, destroying the marks of age. I also deem it unfortunate that Early English should have been chosen when the aisle was added about 1850. I know the probable reason, viz., to dispense with the more massive piers or pillars of the Norman style. Then why not have decided on Transition and thus have retained the circular arch ? West Wittering chancel or Boxgrove would have provided an object lesson. The contrast between the chancel and the pointed arches of the aisle is too marked, especially as the whole of the church is Early Norman, of a particularly austere type. Only the chancel arch and the west door are at all ornamented. A good idea of the massive character of the structure is provided by the tunnel-like entrance from the outside, entirely comprised in the thickness of the tower wall, as also is the newel staircase to the bell-chamber on the opposite side.

A Jacobean tomb of 1616, with a quaint inscription to Sir T. Caryll, and memorial windows and good modern carving should be noted.

As at Rustington, there seems to have been two ancient porches, one at least being fourteenth century, and a very fine example. The other is relegated to the use of the sexton in a corner of the churchyard.

I did not see the ancient gilt and enamelled reliquary supposed to have been brought from the East by the Knights Templars, which is kept in one of the aumbries. It is Byzantine and the subjects are the Crucifixion and Angels. In these days it is a more priceless possession than when it was deemed more precious, which seems paradoxical, but is nevertheless true.

On the south side of the churchyard a path leads to a footbridge over the river, and up the field to the high road which goes south-west to Thakeham, a good four miles distant. You must not forget that you are in the Great Wealden area, where villages are comparatively few and far between. A glance at the map will show how sparsely the Andredsweald was peopled. Large areas—one sixteen miles by ten—can be seen to possess only hamlets or farms to greet the wayfarer. The Domesday map of Sussex, by F. E. Sawyer, has but a dozen name-places in the northern half of the county.

Although the country around Shipley is of one type, the walk to Thakeham is never uninteresting, because of Chanctonbury and the line of the Downs to the south. Thakeham lies on high ground, and as you near it, the dark pine woods east of Storrington, which add so much to the landscape, come into view. The proximity of these belts of sand to the chalk hills is not the least remarkable of the natural features of this part of Sussex, and tend to that variety for which our county is noted. There could be no greater contrast in colour or form than that presented by these sombre pine woods set against "the line of the Downs, so noble and so bare."

Thakeham has a very Saxon ring to its name, and is finely placed

THAKEHAM STREET.
(*By H. S. Percival, A.R.E.*)

on the south side of a ridge. The view on entering the village, or that from the street across to the church, with some old timber-framed houses on the right, is distinctly good. Several fine old chimney-stacks are to be seen among the irregularly placed dwellings. The village generally is attractive. Thakeham Place, an old manor-house, is no longer existent, I regret to say.

The church is large and lofty. Except for one Norman window

remaining of a previous building, it is Early English, with a fine Perpendicular tower. This has a roof of the chicken-coop order, a shape very frequent in Normandy, but seldom seen here. The Apsley family—a branch of which resided at New Place, Pulborough, is commemorated by several tombs and brasses of the sixteenth century. One, an altar-tomb, is of alabaster, and the effigy of a knight in full armour is incised on the slab, and the grooves are filled with pitch—a form of engraving rare, if not unique. At each corner is a shield of arms.

Besides two fine piscinæ with trefoiled canopies, there is a squint, as in many Sussex churches. They vary from the simple aperture to the arched opening, and some have a centre pillar of chaste design. The squint was a concession to the desire of communicants to see the elevation of the Host ; or evidence of wisdom on the part of the ecclesiastical authorities, who realised the force of what Tennyson, long years after, put into words—

" Things seen are mightier than things heard."

Perhaps the sixteenth-century porch is the most attractive feature, with its elegant roof-timbers—unless it be an old door in the tower, which has a slight ridge in the centre of each slab of oak, the space between forming a shallow depression. Nothing could be more simple, nor more effective ; but had that door been made now, very flat and uninteresting boards, smoothly planed and immaculately joined, would have been the result, unless it had been too elaborately carved. Simplicity, not baldness, nor too much ornament, seems to be the great want of to-day.

Retracing your steps up the village street you will come across a derelict farmstead just north of Thakeham. The gate opens on to a track leading across the fields to West Chiltington, saving a long detour ; but before leaving Thakeham, a note should be made of the intimate connection William Penn had with the parish and with Sussex. He married Giulia Maria, daughter of Sir Wm. Springett, and one of his children, a daughter, is buried in the Friends' Meeting House graveyard, near Conyhurst Common. I am told that the little chapel still stands. If the fact were better known, there would be many Americans who would be pilgrims to the spot.

West Chiltington is quite out of the way, but is set in beautiful surroundings. The rock crops out and upward, and heather and bracken is plentiful on the higher ground where stands a tower mill. The village boasts of those quaint relics of justice—the stocks—and the church is celebrated for its mural paintings. These are usually of three colours—red, black and yellow, but the nameless artists who limned these in the twelfth and fourteenth centuries, like those of to-day, rejoiced in a richer palette. The building, also, is of more liberal extent than usual, the Transition arches in the nave and the north door being of good design. The pulpit is ancient, and an exterior stoup would seem to point to a chancel aisle.

" Death, the Comforter " is seldom acclaimed in epitaphs. Here he would appear to have been welcome. On a tomb, a singular inscription ends, " Now perjury and forgery can hurt no longer."

The church is pleasantly placed apart from the village, and its shingled spire of the favourite type—an octagon rising from a square base—is lofty enough not to be dwarfed by the fine trees by which it is neighboured.

Quite three miles remain to be covered before reaching Pulborough. Should the very long street of that very straggling village get on your nerves by reason of its rather utilitarian aspect, look southward across the marsh to the Downs, the fine woods of Parham, and the river winding its way to Amberley, and these will make amends.

Should it be winter, the floods will probably be out, and then a good idea of what prehistoric Sussex may have been will greet your eyes. It is supposed that most of the river valleys and hollows at the foot of the Downs were lakes or lagoons.

HANGLETON PLACE.

# CHAPTER IV

## HANGLETON TO POYNINGS AND EDBURTON
### (8 MILES)

#### WITH ILLUSTRATIONS BY THE LATE JOSEPH DIPLOCK AND A. S. C.

THE road north from Portslade Station brings you to Hangleton Place, a once fine Tudor mansion of the Bellinghams' lying in a broad valley which winds away to the Dyke. Our illustration is of the rear of the house, and represents it as it was in 1843, and as it was in 1907. Our old townsman, Edward Fox, had sketched it sixty-four years ago, and I have added the bell-turret, which did not always adorn the roof, and which is again absent in this year of grace 1911. Should anyone be curious to know what changes the passing years bring to an old building, let him take this book, and see for himself. All that is not there now was existent then—and how little it has changed!

Nestled in a hollow amid ancient elms it is but seldom visited, and yet it is a fine old house. Those desirous of knowing its history will find it in Mr. Clayton's exhaustive paper in vol. 34 of the Sussex Archæological Collections. Here we can only touch its fringe. Unlike the building the name shows fourteen variations, but as the first—in Domesday—" Hangeton," differs in only one letter from its present title, I leave the rest for the curious reader to find for himself. Domesday, that model book of brevity, tells its tale in a few lines—so many hides of land, ploughs, villeins and bordars (cottagers). So many acres of wood with pannage for so many hogs. The worth of the whole, past and present—and there an end. As for the " wood for 3 hogs," it has now disappeared, except a few very ancient elm trees. Whether the descendants of its then inhabitants are still to be found in this ancient wood at Hangleton, history—which has a lot to say about less useful creatures, such as the phœnix and dragon—does not say. History, in fact, says but little about Hangleton. Its secluded position accounts for its blessedness in this respect. One of its owners was Sir Philip Sidney—" the jewel of her Dominions," as Queen Bess called him. It is pleasant to think that the gallant

51

knight lived awhile in the old house. Of course it was larger
then. All these Down homesteads were, but it is no mean heritage
now. Its Saxon owners bore Saxon names without doubt. Turgod,
Cola and Azor have that about them which is *not* Norman. What
a bitter trial the Norman rule must have been to the conquered
Saxons. "William de Wateville holds Hangeton of William."
These are the first words Domesday has of this and nearly every
other place in England. They epitomise the Conquest.

The present kitchen of the house was most likely the hall at
one time, and has a panelled oak screen with fluted pilasters and
carved capitals. On it are cut the Ten Commandments, with the
quaintest of variations in the text. "D. R." in a paper in the
16th vol. of Suss. Arch. Coll. says this was followed by a curious
distich—

> "Persevere, ye perfect men,
> Ever keep these precepts ten."

Except in compliment to Queen Elizabeth, as in so many verses
of the day, the critical mind is apt to wonder why sense should
have been sacrificed in order that the vowel *e* should have entire
control, why men that are perfect need persevere. But what is
more disquieting is the fact that the distich "has no place" at
Hangleton now, and its historian could not hear of its existence.
Oh, "D. R.," hast thou mixed thy memories, and said that which
is not? Or—miserable thought—was it there when you went,
and absent when you left? Is it possible you deemed this "eleventh
commandment" unnecessary, and showed your zeal by its removal?
Or did you wish to give a practical turn to its advice, by "keeping"
as much of these precepts as you could conveniently carry away?
Speak to us "across the intervening years" and quiet our "troubled
breasts," O antique "D. R."!

The original entrance of the house faces west. The pretty
dovecote is on the east. A few years ago an old hunting-lodge
owned by the Coverts, of Slaugham, stood on the hill-side to the
west, called Benfields, which had a row of shields with coats of
arms just beneath the eaves. This has given place to a typical
specimen of the labourers' dwellings of to-day!

A grassy rise of a quarter of a mile brings you to the simple little
church, which until recently stood quite alone—except for a barn.
It is so old and rude in style that one associates it with the Saxon,
or Early Norman. Unconsciously the name of one of the Saxon
owners of "Hangeton" comes to mind, and one murmurs—"Turgod's work"! As if to be in harmony with its surroundings, there
is a strange unknown tomb in the chancel. One would scarcely
expect the dedication to have survived in so lonely a spot, yet it

has, and it is to a famous queen of old—St. Helen. In the solitary, exposed churchyard is a handsome altar-tomb (to Dr. Kenealy of Tichborne fame) with mosaic borders. It may certainly be said of him that " after life's fitful fever he sleeps well"—if quiet peaceful situation has anything to do with it.

Speaking of Dr. Kenealy, it may not be generally known that the Willett Collection at the Brighton Museum contains Caldecott's inimitable caricature of the principal actors in the famous trial.

HANGLETON DOVECOTE.
(*By A. S. C.*)

With master hand, in clay, Judge Hawkins as a hawk, the Claimant as a tortoise, Kenealy as a rooster, are hit off to the life. The latter's audacious manner and side whiskers are most cleverly indicated.

The village of Hangleton has disappeared. It was just north-east of the church. From here you can follow the ridge and join the Dyke Road, but I always prefer to wander as best I may over the cultivation, and follow the windings of the Benfield valley to the Dyke Station, or the farm close by it.

On reaching the grass turn down to the right, and descend the Dyke itself by the old thorn trees to the source of the mill stream— a beautiful spot, but less so than before the upper mill was burnt down. The iron wheel, gaunt and rusty, only remains. The hollow above was full of water then, but is now filled by willow growth among which the tiny stream trickles down to form a mill-pond for the older mill below Poynings.*

POYNINGS FROM THE DYKE.
(*By A. S. C.*)

Poynings is one of the places in our county towards which we may all be said to have a soft spot in our hearts. This may be because of the natural beauty of its situation—its proximity to that wonderful coombe, the Dyke—or on account of its fine four-teenth-century church, which is complete in itself, the work of its

* This hollow is again filled with water.

designer and builder, and has not been overlaid with later and baser styles. Each of these things may beget the liking we have for it, but, after all, the human interest is that which has made the name of Poynings famous, and has given distinction to the spot, and this is felt in a dim way even among the " unlearned and ignorant," much as a perfume borne across the fields, will be apparent to the senses, although the source is far away.

And like a sweet savour the memory and deeds of the Poynings of Poynings reach us across the years gone by, albeit " their place knows them no more."

In the history of men and families, Sussex has her full share of honour as a county, and of her early sons none shine more worthily than they. Whatever the Poynings motto may have been, Duty was with them a watch-word, and in performing it, life and leisure were rendered cheerfully to its call. The first Baron Poynings became so on his summons to Parliament in 1294. His " name-place " is mentioned in King Eàdgàr's charter to Wulfric in 960 as " Puningas," and it is worthy of notice in passing that where Saxon names are in question, the local rendering is most likely to be the correct one, although it may not commend itself to our somewhat superior sense of hearing.

Thus " Hoove " is the correct name of our neighbour town. " Hors-ham " and " Bos-ham " should be pronounced as here divided ; and that " Punnings " is the yokel's justification, this old charter proves. The document itself deals with the restoration of Wulfric to his lands—or his lands to Wulfric—and is sufficiently interesting to quote here. It quaintly gives the reason for the previous divorce of proprietor and property as " some slight offence," and is at pains to accurately describe the domain, and to call down an imprecation on all or any who should disregard its behests. One feels that here, at least, the generous thing is being done, and done handsomely, until the " cloven hoof " is seen in the ransom of " 120 marks of the most approved gold " ! A later King showed a similar desire of possession so strong, that for a good Norway goshawk, he granted the holding of Crawley Market to Michael de Ponynges.

Domesday, with characteristic and comprehensive simplicity, " lumps " together " church, 2 ministers, 2 mills, 50 acres of mea-dow, and a wood of 40 hogs " !

Tracing the family down, we find Thomas Poynings was among the slain in the sea fight off Sluys, and in commiseration, and as a reward for his bravery, his infant son was given immediate seizin of his titles and estates. This son, Michael, attended the King in all his foreign wars, was present on the glorious fields of Crecy, Poictiers, and at the surrender of Calais. For all his adventurous life, he yet died quietly in his bed at Poynings, and it is to him and his wife that we owe the possession of the beautiful church. They were its founders, and his son Thomas built it, with the counsel of his master, John de Worle, of Tarring.   In his will Michael bequeaths to his son " a ruby ring, which is the charter of my heritage of Poynings, together with the helmet and armour which my father demised to me."

Michael and his wife lie buried in the chancel, and this son Thomas directed that wherever *his* body might be buried, " ten Annets and Trentals should be said yet for his soul in Poynings and Slaugham Churches within one year of his death."   This is eloquent testimony to the uncertainty of affairs in his day.   It is not certain where his body rested. His brother Richard, who succeeded him, was called to attend the Black Prince and John o' Gaunt into Spain to restore the deposed King of Castile to his throne   The object was achieved, but at what a cost! The army, composed of the flower of English nobility, being decimated by disease. But when he was again called to " perform the same risque," he made his

POYNINGS CHURCH.
(*By A. S. C.*)

will at Plymouth on the eve of embarkation.   It is a pathetic document in the tone of farewell pervading it, and in the care shown in its drawing.   One can well believe the good knight thought it all out on the long marches from Poynings to Plymouth.   His foresight was that of presentiment.   He fell a victim to the burning suns and swamps of Leon.

It is a commonplace of history that good qualities, whether of heart, mind, or body, are to be looked for in the sons of worthy sires, and Robert Poynings, a boy of seven when his father died in Castile, " soon showed that his blood was fetched from fathers of war-proof."   He was a warrior all his days, and was trusted and employed alike by Richard II, and the fourth, fifth and sixth Henrys.

Nor was the strain of nobleness and worth exhausted by his death.   His son Richard died before him, but filled his part in life well and truly.   Among his duties, that of being M.P. for Sussex in 1423 was one.   Whether from humility or sense of unworthiness, he directed his body to be buried outside the north door of the church, and over it the present beautiful porch was probably erected, being more elaborate, and of slightly later date than the rest of the fabric.   The slab—the inscription on which the feet of the faithful have erased—appears to have been afterwards cut in two and carried inside to mend the floor—the invention of some needy churchwarden, on the principle of robbing Peter to pay Paul !   Among the things bequeathed by Richard was " a piece of the Holy Cross."   His daughter Eleanor had special delivery

POYNINGS POST OFFICE IN 1897.
(*By A. S. C.*)

of the fine inheritance granted her, and carried all into the North-umberland family of the Percys, one of whose titles " Poynings " now forms.   Her husband, Sir Henry Percy, bequeathed Poynings to his youngest son Jocelyne, on condition that " he shall be of loving and lowly disposition towards his eldest brother Henry, and give him his allegiance, and that I charge him to do and be, upon my blessing, as he will answer before God."

Of the Great Sir Henry Poynings, K.G., Lord Deputy of Ireland, collateral to the inheritance, Lloyd, in his *State Worthies*, says— " It is the unhappiness of some monarchies that they have not men answerable to their employments ;  but it was the unhappiness of this that it had not employments suitable to its men."

Much more might be written of the Poynings family, but enough has been said to show that though the fine church exists to tell of their greatness and to beautify the place from whence they take their name, yet for those who read the history of their country aright, it is not only natural beauty and architectural grandeur that glorify a spot, but the record of noble lives nobly spent in the service of their King in years gone by.

Of the house only an ivy-covered fragment now remains. It stood just north-east of the church. There is an engraving extant showing portions of it.

*En passant*, the hill-side rising above this old fragment of Poynings

EDBURTON CHURCH.
(*By A. S. C.*)

House was, and perhaps still is, the habitat of one of the most beautiful of English moths, the " forester." Those who seek for schemes of colour, cannot do better than learn a lesson from this specimen of Nature's perfect artistry. The fore wings are of a delicate, yet glossy green, and the hind wings of a dull, smoky tint, both colours almost transparent. Then, as if to add the necessary high light, the body is of a beautiful metallic green ! It embodies what we may call unconscious art. It is meet that such beauty should not be hidden. Unlike most of his kind, the forester is a lover of the sun—a daylight moth. They are very local in their habits, and will swarm about a patch of common sorrel and there only.

Poynings has few interesting old houses. The old Post Office

is perhaps the best of them, and its interest is rather of the
eighteenth century than of an earlier date ; of the day when houses
were built and appointed in a homely rather than an artistic or
appropriate fashion.    I use the word in its humble sense.    Rooms
were low pitched, small and not too pretty.    Ornamental details
were rigorously excluded, and most things done something after
the style of a doll's house, rather than for the daily use of " grown-
ups."    Witness the tiny shop window—and even this is altered
since the sketch was made.

You leave Poynings by the western road, and at the entrance

Edburton Church
Sussex

INTERIOR OF EDBURTON CHURCH.
(*By the late Joseph Diplock.*)

of Fulking there is a half-timbered house, which makes a good
sketch, with the downs for background.    Clapper's Lane, known
to but few, winds a green way north of this house for several miles,
and where the stream crosses the path there is a spot which
would be difficult to get a sketcher by without a rope or some
equally persuasive argument !

The *Shepherd and Dog* Inn stands at the western end of the
hamlet, by one of the sharpest turns that Sussex roads, noted for
sudden crinks, can show.    It is a picturesque spot, for at the
bend the stream which comes from under the hill not a hundred
yards away, gushes into the ditch, close by a quaint little pump-
house erected to the memory of John Ruskin.    Here is the sheep

wash, and when that is in progress, there is subject enough for any artist.

Edburton, the parish church for Fulking, lies still farther on. It will probably be somewhat of a surprise to those who happen to know how near it is to Poynings, and have not thought it worth a visit. The latter church lies so directly under the eyes below the Dyke, that the more retiring and older building is seldom seen. Edburton Church stands embosomed in trees about a mile west of Fulking, and although it cannot be said to vie with Poynings in originality and beauty, still it is by no means to be despised therefor.

It is large and full of interest for the antiquarian. The restoration, with scarcely an exception, has been lovingly carried out. The simple seating has distinct merit, both as to design and mouldings, and anything which had age to recommend it has been retained, and wisely, too. It is a well-known fact that everything made prior to the beginning of the reign of shoddy and veneer was, in the main, well proportioned and artistic in design and ornament. That is why it is nearly always safe to copy old models.

Edburton possesses one of the only three cast-lead fonts in our county, and perhaps the oldest of them. It is late Norman, and has panels of floriated design at the base, with a similar encircling pattern above, surmounted by an arcade of trefoiled arches. There are only twenty-nine of these fonts in all England, and therefore they are of great interest. Simple in form of course they are, and usually stand on a stone or wooden base. The lead is about an inch thick, and shows signs of the pattern being a repetition of the same segment of wooden mould impressed in the sand or clay that received the molten metal. The one at Piecombe is somewhat similar, but more ornate ; and that at Parham is a unique specimen of the Decorated period, being ornamented with shields and bands of inscriptions in beautiful Lombardic capitals.

One of the bells is amongst the oldest in Sussex, and bears two shields and an octagonal medallion. One of the shields has the crossed keys and a dolphin, a laver, a wheatsheaf, and a bell in the four quarters.

The history of Edburton, Adburton, or Abberton—as it is differently styled in old records—is of the quiet kind, suited to its situation. Once only does the tide of spiritual war seem to have reached it, when Michael Jermyn, the Rector, would not " conform " in 1655, and was ejected after thirty years' ministry, Nicholas Shepheard being installed in his place by the Lord Protector, Oliver Cromwell.

Edburton is connected with the Metropolitan of England, the advowson belonging to Canterbury. There are traces of no less than three altars, one of which was founded in the north transept by William de Northo in 1319, in honour of St. Katherine.

This modest list exhausts the historical interest, and apart from an antiquarian excitement which fluttered for a brief space over some Roman remains, chiefly notable for their scantiness, Edburton may be compared with the violet in its retiring nature. Like that simple floweret, it must be sought to be found, if one may descend to a truism so evident, yet justifiable. The charms of scenery are not always realised at a glance. Where these are so instantly in evidence, there is usually little more to discover ; and where only an occasional visit is made, it is enough for the time being— the eye is satisfied and asks for no more just then. But if it is often dwelt upon, one gets to wonder whether it is quite so fair as it seemed at first, and then the less striking locality has its day of quiet examination, and begins to improve on acquaintance. Sunrise, sunset, and the different moods of weather help to make a beautiful panorama worth seeing ; but it is only one view, and tires the eye after awhile ; whereas the quieter beauties of winding road or stream, of hedgerow or copse-corner, will bring the artist up with " a round turn " where least expected.

So it is with the scenery in and about Edburton. There is nothing of the startling order to attract one, but there are lots of subjects to linger over ; bits of colour, groups of trees, and fine hills both near and far. A little north-east of where my first view is taken, the village makes a foreground group of roofs not to be despised in colour or in line, and beyond it the grey old church with ruddy tiles fills the right of the picture to entire satisfaction ; while the cornfield fronting all ripples in wavelets of yellowing green in August, to a delightful belt of trees at the foot of the nearest hill ; and far-away Chanctonbury hangs like a grey cloud to the summit of its Down.

This is the view you will see as you cross the upland field to the steep ascent. By the time you reach the top you will have had enough of climbing and be glad to rest on the grass and take in fresh breath and the wider wealden view, before catching the train at the Dyke Station.

\*          \*          \*          \*          \*

There is another delightful walk to be taken from the station eastward down the furrowed turf by the side of the Dyke to Saddlescombe. Up the great coombe, eastward, lies a broad green causeway bank which might have been levelled to allow a troop of Roman soldiery to march up abreast. It slopes up to the top, growing narrower as you reach the ridge. From here you can see, still due east, a barn on the opposite hill, and above it a steep track bordered by bushes on each side, which leads straight up to Wolstonbury Hill. You have got to reach that barn! The valley between you and it is one of the steepest and most wooded of all the Downs eastward of where you stand. If you can find it, there is a path down through the wood by a little artificial pool, or a scramble down as best you may through the trees. Crossing the London Road, you have the corresponding climb, partly across the plough-land to the barn, and on to Wolstonbury. From here the views are many and charming.

Looking eastward you see Clayton Church, below the mills. Make for that down the long slope by the left of the rifle range, and along the " Cinder Path "—or by the London Road—to Hassocks.

# CHAPTER V

## FROM THE DYKE TO SOUTHWICK AND KINGSTON
### (5 MILES)

#### WITH ILLUSTRATIONS BY A. S. C.

AS you gain the grass after leaving the Dyke Station, if you look westward beyond the range of the Ladies' Golf Links, you will see, near the north ridge, a double line of furze at the edge of the cultivation. This furze flanks a cart track which will bring you to a dead stop of plough or crop. It is not, however, very wide, and treading " delicately " you can cross it, and reach the coombe at almost its top end. Descending into its hollow and following its windings, passing by and through many shallow flint-pits, you will reach Mile Oak, where there are waterworks. Look back and see the two fine hollows that lie to the north. It is the drainage of this immense area that the pumps intercept. The valley continues on to Portslade, but your path curves round to the right and brings you at last to the top of the hill whence you can see Southwick, Kingston, Shoreham, and a beautiful view as far as the Isle of Wight, on a clear day.

The track leads you right down past a farm and chalk pit to Kingston Lane, which soon is flanked by fine elm trees. If the subject of the picture here should be recognised as an old friend, seen before in the form of a photograph, I agree with that impression. I, too, have seen it before as a photograph, and before it was a photograph also! The answer to the riddle is to be found in the fact that I had long known of it as a beautiful view, and when T'other saw it and placed his camera in position and all was ready, his remark was a grunt of satisfaction more eloquent than words. But these followed, " Oh, that it had a figure or two ! " Just then the children coming home from school appeared down the lane, and in less than a minute I had seized the idea and the children, and school was again the order of the day.

The result was unusually successful, for it cannot be denied that many of the groups found in photographs have an air of unreality inseparable from conscious subjects. Children are less awkward, and consequently more natural. Certainly, " Springtime

63

Springtime and Sunshine at Southwick.

(By A. S. C.)

and Sunshine at Southwick" came as near pictorial representation as most fortunate photos cleverly caught—in all but the
sunshine! Alas, it was a grey day. Pretty and successful as
it turned out, the sun could not be commanded, nor the padlock
on the centre gate unloosed ; and the roadway was " ower straight "
across the bottom of the picture. However much artistic skill
and thought may be brought to bear on it, it would not be right
if a mechanical process like photography should usurp the higher
functions of Art, so there was nothing for it but to invent the
sunshine, open the gate, and curve the road. Here is the result.

This is a distant view of Southwick Church. Kingston Church
is to be found lower down the lane, on turning a little to the
westward.

Few features of the spirit of research which animates the seekers
after knowledge in our day have attracted more ridicule of the
playful kind than the attempts to give the derivations of names
and terms ; and one rather rejoices when learning is found tripping.
Why it should be so must be sought in the perversity of human
nature, which finds more pleasure in laughing at a wise man than
at a fool. Is it malice, or shall we bring the spirit of the philosopher
to bear on it, and say that folly is not worth laughing at ? Anyhow, the wise man has his triumphs now and again. Reason, or
popular acceptance, had long ago settled that " Kingston Bowsey,"
i.e. By-Sea, was so called because of its position near the realm
of Father Neptune. But the pendent title hails from land and not
from sea. It is of Norman origin, and was the appellation of the
family of Beaucey, Bucy, or Buici. " Chingestune," or Kingston,
was so common a name in the days of Saxon kinglets that it
became necessary to tack on a surname. Hence " Bucy."

Kingston is still a Royal dwelling ; but it is a Princess who holds
sway now. Her name is Peace, acknowledged and acclaimed by
all—at a distance ! Mankind is grateful for her blessings, in a
general way, but does not hanker after a too particular knowledge
of her country seats. Never fear that Demos will overrun the
grassy mounds of God's acre in Kingston-Bucy! Once in this
present year of grace a day fell out when quite a little knot of
friends—simple folk enough, on simple pleasures bent—met, in
companies of two or three, in the little sanctuary. None knew of
the others' coming, and wonder seasoned every greeting, as well
it might in so secluded a spot. But this was the Princess' doings !
She it was who sent her winged messengers to whisper into their
ears of the peace and quietude which " inhabit there," and led
them to seek her rural throne, to bring back gifts of " ease for heart
and mind."

Until you know it better—or worse—how many a country

E

INTERIOR OF KINGSTON CHURCH.

(*By A. S. C.*)

village seems the very abode of harmony. So, alas, has it been with Kingston and its neighbour Southwick. Domesday faithfully reflects the uncertainty which hangs over the boundaries between these two parishes. Its description is involved, and two churches are credited to Kingston. Little wonder, when they are so close as Southwick is to its neighbour. And where such a record as Domesday is in doubt, litigation follows, as a matter of course. It has been a " fruitful source," say the historians.

Historically, there are no stirring themes to enlarge upon. Soon after the Conquest, Robert Beaucy claimed the " right of wreck "— a doubtful *right*—" on the shore of the Rape of Bramber," but the court held that it belonged to William de Braose. In these days the benefice of Southwick was granted by Henry II to the Knights Templars ; from them it passed to the Knights of St. John of Jerusalem, and is now " in the gift of the King." So says Dallaway, who also girds at the fabric of Kingston Church, " as having little to boast of architectural beauty or curiosity."

What exalted notions some writers have of architecture, and of what a village fane *should* be ! To the man who does not carry his head too high, there is much to be pleased with in Kingston Church. The first satisfactory impression comes from looking on an " unrestored " fabric. Not that the pleasure arises from its condition in this respect, but because it will, in these wiser days of renovation, have a better chance than has befallen so many of our rehabilitated, metamorphosed and unfortunate temples in Sussex. I would like to translate—not banish—the square pews which block the chancel, to the west end of the nave, and replace them with some of the fine old poppy-head seats as choir stalls. These date from Henry VII or earlier, and are richly carved. The quaint, old, linen-patterned oak two-decker pulpit might be shifted into the corner just outside the tower arch, and the screen replaced in what was probably its original position under the arch. These comparatively slight alterations would go far towards making it a model sanctuary, especially if the fine old roof were cleared of lath and plaster, and the whitewash removed from arches and piers ; but never a chisel or scraper should touch the stonework, " an I had my will." The windows, except for an old coat of arms, are without stained glass. There is still, therefore, an opening for good taste to have sway.

The seating and the screen were given by the Lewknores, and bear their arms—*azure, three chevrons argent*. This family was very numerous and influential in Sussex. Records of them are many. Hamsey contains a Lewknore tomb almost identical with this one in Kingston chancel. Among armorial bearings, there are several slabs carved with *a chevron ermine between three black-amores' heads*, showing that our trading and colonising influences made a mark even in this out-of-the-way spot.

The style of the church is mainly Early English, and of a better type than many. The tower is central and is vaulted within, the capitals of its pillars being of Sussex marble. A commission on bells, 1686, reported the one bell as " cracked." A later commission, in 1724, mentions " two other bells lost time out of mind." Not things easily disposed of, one would think. The first inquiry caused searchings of heart in Kingston-Bucy, and a desire to amend their ways and the bell at the same time, for we find Wm. Hull, Bellfounder of South Malling, Lewes, bequeathing, in his will of 1687, " all the metal which is rightly mine," to his son. The other metal at his foundry at that time was probably the bell now hanging in Kingston tower, for it bears date 1687, and the initials of the founder, W. H., as well as the name of the Churchwarden, Wm. Blaker.

The north aisle was roofless and ruinous at Bishop Bower's visitation, 1724, and his report of its " having been claimed by nobody for a hundred years, we humbly conceive it may be pulled down, and its material applied to the use of the Church " seems to have again awakened the zeal of its wardens, or owners, for it forms part of the present edifice as the sketch shows. Perhaps the " considerable family," to whom it was supposed to belong, bestirred themselves rather than lose it. The Rectory is an old house, and has a fine, panelled hall with staircase. If I mistake not, the garden gate is flanked by two of the bases of minarets from the Royal Pavilion at Brighton serving as gateposts—a quaint addition to a country parsonage ! The dedication of the Church (St. Julian) was, until recently, unknown.

One more incident is worthy of notice here. A proof of age of John Lillebonne, taken at Crawley in 1363, states that Richard de Redemelde, parson of the Church of Kingston, near Novel Shoreham, " was one of his sponsors." Of the witnesses, " Roger de Brodebrigge *recollects the day because Agnes his wife died on the following Sunday, and the day of her death is enrolled in the Missal of Slinfold Church*" ; Walter Randekyn, " *because he married his wife Amicia the Sunday after*" ; Wm. Granfelde, " *because a great quarrel between him and the father, John Lillebonne, was made up on that day*" ; and John Clympyngge, " *because he went a pilgrimage to St. James on that day*"—a record of joy and sorrow, in which the good prevails, and at least one victory for Peace in Kingston-Bucy.

\*       \*       \*       \*       \*

I know of no spot where the rural and the marine, the picturesque and the ugly are to be seen so close together, and yet so sharply divided, as at Kingston. The division is caused by the high embankment of the railway. One experiences a sensation of quite the panorama type on emerging from the railway arch at the bottom of Kingston Lane. It is to "suffer a sea change" indeed, this transition from country sights and sounds to harbour life and movement, and—if the tide be low down and the sun high up—to "a very ancient and fishlike smell." South of the line, too, the houses are of that dowdy, not to say squalid type, which seem inseparably connected with harbour or shipping localities. But

SOUTHWICK FORGE AND CHURCH, 1897.
(*By A. S. C.*)

this applies more to Southwick, which is rapidly losing its character as a village, and is becoming nondescript—neither town, country, nor seaside. Yet it is one of the few coast villages with a genuine Village Green. It has its school, its forge, its inn, and—until recently—its pond. Its frequenters a few years ago were the children and the sheep, the ducks and the quoit players, the geese and the cricketers, and the superannuated donkey who outlived them all, as pensioners are wont to do!

But all this is altered now, for Southwick has an Urban Council! Things are looking up—or down, according to one's point of view. Streets of houses, where once was field and farm, and a population far more than trebled ; but most of the charm of the place has departed with the invasion of the speculative builder. Still, an hour may be quietly enjoyed in it and its rural surroundings. Southwick Street has lost little of its attraction as yet. It has several quaint old houses, and a country air about it, that commends it at once to the visitor. Then, running parallel with it a hundred yards away, is the Green.

He who would " write up " village greens will find the material for his subject very scarce. Still, if facts of interest are conspicuous by their absence, the greens themselves are by no means rare in Sussex, and are most interesting facts to the youth of the villages happy enough to possess one—to say nothing of the articulate joy, sundry geese, ducks and chickens express in their various quaint ways, when they survey the wide domain. It may even boast a nobler denizen in the person of a musical " moke " ; but perhaps you wouldn't call *his* a joyful note, however articulate.

In whatever way village greens came to be, whether by gift of lord or commoner, or by the needs of localities for some neutral ground to temporarily camp, graze cattle, or hold fairs upon, is scarcely necessary to ask. There they are, where they are, and no village " should be without one," if I had my will. On second thoughts, I should be considerably aged now, to have had a voice in the settlement of the matter originally, so I pass on to speak of greens in general and one in particular.

Of course, we all know their common characteristics. Whether we shut our eyes or not, the vision of the not too tidy, not too level greensward, fringed with houses of all sorts and sizes, some abutting and some retiring—will rise before us. And then there is the white road ! Sometimes it runs right through the middle as if to cut the green into two inconveniently narrow and useless little strips. One seems to see in this the inability of our village forefathers to gaze any farther " through a brick wall " than we can, or assuredly they would have foreseen cricket and football, and made preparations accordingly. Or, mayhap, the exact position of the road was in dispute. The good folk who lived on one side of the green would see both the road and the inhabitants on the other " further first," than suffer the dust of the highway to approach too closely. If the mutual aversion to, or possession of the road, determined its position, it is undoubtedly a fact that it spoils many a village green for present-day sport. Long life to it, say I.

If any one desires an object-lesson on the desirability of instituting free and open spaces for playing fields, let him visit the particular Village Green which lies at our doors at Southwick. On most evenings it is busy enough, but on Saturday afternoons it is alive with a happier, busier throng, sometimes men, oftener opposing teams of the smallest of small boys, with the largest apparent experience of the game and of cricket or football terms. Owing to slight inequalities of service, and of a dividing longitudinal road (now being relegated to the western side, I believe) the Green is not all that it might be, except in an artistic sense. But the pre-dilections of art, which loves hummocks, inequalities and untidiness, must bow to the greatest good of the greatest number, and take pleasure in helping to produce one of the most delightful pictures one can behold—" Southwick Green on a Saturday " !

Since writing the above, the origin of these open spaces has been suggested to me, and the idea is so natural that it may be accepted at once, viz., that they were used to drive cattle into at night when " every man's hand " in one village or locality was " against his neighbour " in another ; when cattle lifting was both popular and remunerative, and the biggest thief was the best known and respected owing to his great possessions and his contempt for any law but that of the sword. It appears that these conditions obtain among communities of primitive habits even now. The pastoral villages in Morocco are built round similar spaces, and these are used as shelters from enemies of both biped and quadruped build.

In some cases the greens have been given by lords of the manor, or have been acquired by common rights belonging to the sur-rounding dwellers. Sometimes the natural features of the land have tended to keep a space unoccupied, and both these proba-bilities have doubtless preserved to Southwick its present play-ground. There is a popular belief that it was given by King Charles the Second, who embarked from Shoreham Harbour in his flight from Worcester—the harbour's mouth being opposite South-wick. Prosy facts, however, point to the ownership of these " common fields," as they are described in 1595, by Lord Howard of Effingham, who granted certain rights of grazing, etc., to the householders, but retained those over the soil, until the manor privileges and possessions were bought by " Dog Smith," an eccentric old London merchant. Many tales are told about him, mostly extraordinary and mostly untrue. Whatever his eccentricities may have been, both Sussex and Surrey have cause to bless his plebian name. He gave many thousands of pounds to various towns during his life, and left many more at his death to further the welfare of the poor ; to apprentice boys and girls, and help poverty generally in many a village in both counties. Whether Southwick benefited in any particular sense from his generosity, I do not know ; but the Green has been kept free for the use of its people, and has become a positive blessing to the boys.

The other circumstance which helped to keep it vacant, was the presence of an intermittent, shallow water or stream, reedy and

SOUTHWICK FARM IN WINTER, 1891.
(By A. S. C.)

flagged, supplied by the drainage of the Downs above in wet seasons. Until recently there were remains of this runnel still traversing the upper part. What a picture it would have made then! It is a good subject now, in parts, but the charms of reflection and water add tenfold to any view. Few of us quite know the possibilities of Southwick and Kingston in an artistic sense. It hasn't any exceptional gifts of colour to commend it, although colour is not absent, especially about the harbour ; but after long acquaintance with them I still find material for a sketch, and there is always something pleasant in finding new qualities in old friends.

Unhappily, the additions to Southwick are mostly of the shoddy, modern type, especially above the Green. Elsewhere, some of the houses are more picturesque, or will be when Time and Nature have softened them down, or covered them with greenery. This, however, can hardly happen to one terrible erection in Church Lane.

One sees the Church with mixed feelings. The tower and spire may be called beautiful, and there is much in the chancel to admire or interest ; but the nave is neither old nor young. If it were either there might be hope for it. It was rebuilt when church architecture was not so much unknown, as not understood, and the result is rather painful to behold.

The farm which stood south of the church has made way for a street or two of mean houses. When the sketch was made it was a pleasant spot.

History has not gone out of its way to make Southwick famous, but there are a few gleams to enlighten the past. Thus, in 1225, the good " Simon Comes (Simon le Comte), moved by Divine Grace, in the presence of Geoffrey, Bishop of Ely, Everard, Chaplain of the Abbess of Barking, the Monk Humphrey and others, bequeathed the church and a third part of the lands and of the sheaves of tithes of Southwick, with the assent of William, the parson of S. Julian, Kyngeston, to the Knights Templars." In their hands it remained, until the suppression of the order by the combined jealousies of the other great monastic houses, aided by the venal Pope of the day, who did not scruple to command torture to be applied to the knights to wrest confession of sinful practices from them. The list of these accusations contains such childish imputations that the wonder is any inquisitor or man of common sense should have been found willing to credit them, or treat them seriously. With this dark page of our history has Southwick been connected. Who but the bookworm would give it a thought as he gazes at the happy children at play upon its Village Green.

# CHAPTER VI

## SHOREHAM AND ITS HARBOUR

ILLUSTRATIONS BY THE LATE LOUIS MEADEN, FRED DAVEY, THE LATE FRED EARP, A. E. PAYNE, BROOK HARRISON, AND A. S. C.

PROBABLY the last place any persons but painters —folk of singular tastes and cranks at best—would be sent for an afternoon's enjoyment, is to Shoreham Harbour and its demesnes. Still I would recommend them to become better acquainted with the region which lies on the shore west of our town. I know the first objection that will be made. It takes the usual form of strong terms : " Why! what on earth is there to see ? " I answer, " Go and look ! "

Mind, you incredulous and gainsaying person, whoever you may be, I am not unaware of the feeling which raises your eyelids and puckers your brow when the suggestion is made. I remember the first visit to Bosham (before whose name every artist makes an involuntary obeisance), which is noted for its rapid transformations from light to dark, from sparkling water to a drab waste of odorous or malodorous mud, and back again to life and movement, alternately repelling and delighting the beholder.

I do not say that Shoreham has quite the peculiar attraction of Bosham, but it has other virtues in compensation. Except just west of Shoreham Town, there are no very wide tracts of mud, and so it is more likely to please than the western port. But its charms are none the less evident, or why is there a constant erection going on of more or less dainty structures called by the ugliest of names— " bungalows "—on the ridge of beach which stretches in a mighty sweep from Lancing to the fort at the harbour's mouth ?

Take my advice, unwillingly if you like, and go prejudiced and sulky across the Norfolk Bridge. If the mood continues long, it is chronic, and therefore hopeless. But if not, take a look Brighton-wards as you leave the causeway to reach the beach. That is one view beloved of artists. From the ridge of shingle look up the valley towards Bramber and see if it is not worth going for that view alone. It matters little whether the tide be in or out. Lancing

Shoreham Harbour from Norfolk Bridge.

(*By the late Louis Meaden.*)

College and Old Shoreham Church stand like sentinels asleep at a gate which is always open, and beyond lies the " blue goodness of the Weald," with the reaches of the river stretching towards it.

If it be a day of clouds and sun, the view of Brighton beyond the shipping of the Basin, backed by the hills and the shining cliffs, at the end of the great crescent of yellow shingle will make you an artist in desire if not in reality.

But this is not all. If you like flowers, go and see if the wilderness cannot blossom for *you*. To look for rose-bushes and stately lilies on a sea-strand is to expect an unreasonable thing. But don't think the beach-stones have it all their arid way. You will find that many a delicate floweret triumphs— I use the word advisedly— " in its day and generation " on the stony shingle. A short-lived triumph, perhaps, but none the less a victory. Let the sun glare

SHOREHAM FROM THE HARBOUR.
(*By Fred Davey.*)

never so fiercely on the parched beach, there are yet little hollows where flotsam and jetsam of driftwood and kindred things have decayed, and where the rain and sea-birds have fertilised the soil— such as it is—and the seed brought by birds and breezes have struck root, grown, blossomed and faded in a few days. But not perished. Struck root—and what roots they are ! How many years of stress and struggle they represent ! Gnarled, but deep-delving, as if the stunted growth above ground were compensated by the eagerness of the central root to reach the moisture. The leaves and flowers spread over square yards of stones, and when you lift up the trailing tendrils, you will find one knotted, snake-like root, typical of the wisdom which impels the plant not to waste its strength in many aims, but to put all its effort into the central source of life. A parable from Nature, truly.

But one thing I cannot, from very ignorance, do—tell you all the flowers that grow on this marge of the sea. Yellow sea poppies and nightshade, bachelor's buttons, sea lavender, and such-like simple, every-day growths, with here and there a rarer plant, such as samphire, to attract attention.   But the chief characteristic of these beach plants are the myriad of blossoms they bear.   They positively flash out into bloom, come with a rush, and as quickly turn to seed, as if they knew the ultimate triumph of vegetation over the arid shingle depended on these and these alone.

There is another long stretch of beach on the east of the harbour-mouth, where these flower-growths can be seen undisturbed by the neighbourhood of the encroaching bungalows.   Here flourishes exceedingly that feathery plant, the tamarisk.   It has moments of beauty in the flush of summer, but looks dishevelled and untidy most of the year.   Its affection for sea-breezes is but ill requited by the ruder winds of ocean, but it grows in spite of them.   A

The Basin, looking West.
(*By A. E. Payne.*)

large tract east of the Gas Works is a veritable paradise for children, to whom flowers appeal by beauty and colour and not by rarity.

To reach these last two spots there is a wooden bridge near the Lock at Southwick, and the road by the *Adur Hotel* at the east end of the Basin.   The two sketches here given prove that the harbour affords ample opportunity for the artist who can use his eyes. These localities lie, however, nearer Brighton.

As you return across the Norfolk Bridge, go to New Shoreham Church.   There is not much else to see *in* Shoreham.   The High Street has a quiet interest, and there is a fragment of an old friary, now used as a workshop.   Also, one of the inns has the figure-head of the *Royal George* lost in Portsmouth Harbour, as a sign ; but the glory of Shoreham is its church.

With Boxgrove, Winchelsea, Steyning and Rye in mind, of all Sussex Parish Churches I think it is the noblest.   Of the others, Boxgrove and Winchelsea, like this, have also lost their naves.

It is, of course, the fine tower which gives it its distinction. It is dedicated to St. Mary de Haura, and Swinburne writes thus beautifully of it—

" Strong as time, and as faith sublime—clothed round with shadows of hopes
      and fears,
   Nights and morrows, and joys and sorrows, alive with passion of prayers
      and tears,—
   Stands the shrine that has seen decline eight hundred waxing and waning
      years."

" Tower set square to the storms of air, and change of season that glooms
      and glows,
   Wall and roof of it tempest-proof, and equal ever to suns and shows,
   Bright with riches of radiant niches and pillars smooth as a straight stem
      grows."

" Stately stands it, the work of hands unknown . . ."

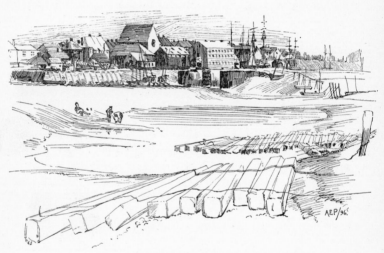

THE LOCK, SOUTHWICK.
(By A. E. Payne.)

It was nobler once. The extent of the nave can be clearly seen, and it does not require a great stretch of the imagination to picture it to the mind's eye. Its restoration has long been desired, and it is to be hoped that the means may be forthcoming. The result would probably be better than if undertaken twenty years ago. The present nave is of one bay only, but that is sufficient to indicate the majestic nature of the whole. The western door is of Norman detail, but pointed arch, probably made up from the fragments of the old west door. Three of the tower arches are of great height and boldness, but the chancel arch is the original which opened on to the eastern apse. This apse and its fellows north and south probably gave place to the present beautiful Transition chancel.

A nice problem thus awaits the restorers when the nave shall have been rebuilt. Shall this chancel arch be raised ? If vista and fitness be studied, yes ! If archæology merely, no ! I think the former should prevail, especially as it is only a question of raising. The arch itself is absolutely in keeping with the rest.

Of the beauty of the chancel there can be no two opinions, and the variety is as charming. The pillars on one side are round and octagonal, and have tied shafts on the other. The carving of capitals and arches is most unusual and beautiful. It has been pointed out that these show French influence. This is not to be wondered at, as it was given by Wm. de Braose, Lord of Bramber, to the Abbey of Salmur.

The vaulting springs from the floor on the south, and from quaint corbels on the north ; while the north arches are foliated, the opposite are plain. One of the most interesting features is the arcading along the wall of each aisle, of simple round-headed Norman work. The triforium arches are nearly all different, and the whole effect is fine ; but—the nave should be rebuilt ! Strange to say, the want of it is more apparent within than without.

Shoreham is known to have been of far greater importance than now. The fickle sea, or the uncertain river, have between them played shuttlecock with her fame as a port. The mouth of the harbour is said to have been at any point between Lancing and Hove. Under such unstable conditions it is not remarkable that her prosperity should lapse. In the third Edward's reign Shoreham contributed no less than twenty-six ships to the Royal Navy. King John landed here on his accession ; but the most notable item in her history was the sailing of Charles II in Captain Tattersell's ship for France after his escape at the Battle of Worcester. I purpose telling the story for those who do not know it.

In the working out of the great drama of " The Making of England," it is fit that the county on whose soil the enslavement of England was begun in the Battle of Hastings, and which bore the birth-throes of her Parliamentary liberties and freedom in the Battle of Lewes, should be the scene of the closing act in the flight of Charles, with whose withdrawal those liberties became consolidated and her Parliament supreme. Years have come and gone since then, and Time has healed the deep wounds she bore. The rights and wrongs which stirred her sons to thirst for their brothers' blood are only remembered when read of in books ; and although " the King has come into his own again," we are all Parliamentarians now. " Other men laboured : ye are entered into their labours," and what a work it was ! What horrors, sufferings and miseries it entailed on those " other men " and those dear to them !

New Shoreham Church
(By the late Fred Earp.)

Looking back on those days, and carefully sifting the evidence, it may be said that Sussex as a whole—her yeomen and farmers—was " for Parliament " ; her gentry " for the King " ; but party feeling did not run so high as in some counties. The temperament of her people is against haste and impulse, and the relations of gentry, yeomen and labourers had much of the " family " about them, derived from agricultural life and isolation—isolation caused by her " miry ways." Doubtless it was such-like considerations which determined the route of Charles through our county.

(Here I would like to record the feeling that has always obtained since the Norman Conquest, that Sussex is a danger spot where invasion is concerned. It was at Pevensey the Romans landed. At least, it is as much favoured by historians as Deal in Kent ; and the construction of the Martello towers during the Napoleonic scare points the same moral. The following letter of Sir Francis Drake to Walsingham, 1587, is not generally known :—

" I assure your honour the like preparation was never heard of nor known as the King of Spain hath and daily maketh to invade England. . . . Prepare England strongly and most by sea. Stop him now and stop him ever. *Look well to the coasts of Sussex.*")

What were the incidents of Charles's journey ? Here comes in the novelist. Such a theme could not fail to attract fiction where fact was wanting ; and what fascinating fiction *Ovingdean Grange* is ! We are none the worse for a little romancing in these matter-of-fact days ; but for " a plaine tale," there is incident enough in what Charles's Sussex guide, Col. Gunter, has left on record. This loyal servant of the King had but just returned from London to his house at Racton. It was late evening, and his wife informed him there was a Devon gentleman awaiting his return. This was Lord Wilmot, afterwards the libertine Earl of Rochester. " The King is neare, and in great distresse ; can you help us to a boate ? " was his message. Emsworth was originally intended for the point of embarkation, and arrangements were decided upon in council. When Lord Wilmot had been lighted to his bed, the good Colonel had another difficulty to settle ere *he* retired to rest. Mrs. Gunter's curiosity had been excited, and upon his evading her questions the lady " broke out into a very great passion of weeping." And one cannot but feel sympathy for the good woman ; what trouble might not come upon the house in those troublous days of plots and counter-plots ? It ended in her being taken into the secret, with the best result : " its success did not a little depend of her concurrence." Next day Emsworth was tried, and no boat could be found. Lord Wilmot returned to the King in hiding near Salisbury. A long, wet ride on a dismal night for the Colonel, and another interview with Wilmot, and back again to Racton.

F

A few hours' sleep, and a ride to Chichester, where, through Francis Mansel, a French merchant, it was arranged to find a boat for the King at Brighton.  More hard riding for poor Gunter, and at last he and his brother " mete the King at Hambleton, in Hampshire."

They took greyhounds with them " as a blinde," as if for coursing. That night they slept at Tom Symones', his brother-in-law, " a loyal and hearty gent, but too great a lover of the bottle," who, until he was assured by Gunter, was inclined to quarrel with the " round-headed rogue "—for Charles was " cropped " and clothed as a serving-man in sad-coloured attire.  It ended in his drinking beer with the " rogue," and in Charles, with ready wit, reproving him for a profane oath.  This visit was not forgotten by the King, as a punch-bowl with the Royal Arms engraved upon it was, after the Restoration, presented to Master Symones in memory thereof.

At daybreak the fugitive King, riding behind as a servitor, left Hambleton and began his perilous journey—for perilous it un-doubtedly was.  Short shrift in all probability would have been given by the fanatical soldiery of Cromwell to either the monarch or his faithful friends.

Whether the party followed the Downs or the by-roads to the north is matter for conjecture.  The roads were bad and infested by Parliamentarian troops ;  and the Downs, though free, were not wooded, and riders could be seen for miles.  The popular belief that the Downs were chosen may be wrong ;  but from them danger could be descried at a distance, and the by-roads of the Weald were in the nature of a trap.  Moreover, the presence of the leash of greyhounds seems to point to the hills as the route.  They would be put on the track of any hare to give reality to the " blinde."

If anything could divert the poor King's sad thoughts, it would be the lovely prospects before him.  It is said that at Glatton Hill, he pulled up and surveyed the glorious scene from the Isle of Wight in the south to Leith Hill in the north, with the varied and beautiful country between, and the exclamation burst from his lips, " *This* is a country worth fighting for ! "  Whether by hill or vale, they came at last to Houghton Forest, and suddenly Geo. Gunter reined in his steed, exclaiming in an undertone, " We are undone—here's Captain Morley, the Governor of Arundel Castle."

" Never mind," quietly replied the King, " move on."  Then follows the dangerous interview, so well described in *Ovingdean Grange*.  Did ever men breathe freely, these must have been they, when the Roundhead troops let them pass on !

At Houghton, the fugitives stopped at the alehouse to discuss the " neat's tongue," and then rode on, either to Amberley—where tradition has it the King slept—or towards Brighton.  Rising Amberley Mount, the King's horse casts a shoe.  A smithy is found either at Burpham or Lee Farm.   There is a local tradition of the shrewd blacksmith, to which Ainsworth does full justice.   Over the hills between here and Bramber they go.   It must have required all their nerve to pass through Bramber.   Only the night before had Colonel Herbert Morley's troops quartered themselves in the village to guard the way of Beeding Bridge against the fugitives ;   " but luckily or by very special Providence, the soldiers were then just come from the Bridge into the town for refreshment. We came upon them unawares, and were seen before we suspected anything.   My Lord Wilmot was ready to turn back, when I stept in and said, ' if we do, we are undone.   Let us go on boldly, and we shall not be suspected.'   ' He saith well,' saith the King, and so passed through.   Farther on, a new terror pursued us—the same soldiers, riding after us as fast as they could.   Whereupon the King gave me a ' hem.'   I slacked rein, and by that time the soldiers had come, who rudely passed by us, being in a narrow lane, so that we could scarcely keep our saddles for them."

From here Gunter rides ahead and reaches the George Inn, in West Street, Brighton, to prepare the host and provide the supper. In short time came the King and Lord Wilmot, sorely tried, if it is true, as Gunter indicates, that the whole sixty miles from Hambleton had been covered since daybreak.

Supper over, up comes mine host ;   he runs to the King and catching his hands, says :   " It shall not be said that I have not kissed the best man's hand in England."   While Gunter bargains with Captain Tattersell (who had sat by the King at supper), the King retires to rest ;   only to be roused by the anxious Gunter with word that the wind has become suddenly fair, and that he has persuaded Tattersell to sail at once.   The " persuasion " took the form of ten pounds, cash !   They go aboard " at two of the morning."   At eight o'clock the sails are hoisted and fill, and watched by the faithful Gunter, the little craft with its royal passenger slowly forges seaward.   It was past noon ere it was out of sight.

So Charles left his kingdom, not an hour too soon for his safety. Gunter's diary adds :   " I was not gone out of the towne of Brighthelmstone two houres, but the soldiers came thither to search for a tall black man, 6 foot 4 inches high ! "

The Happy Entry was the name of Tattersell's ship.   " The Happy Exit " would have been more in keeping with the event. The vessel was of Shoreham.

Here I am able to record what is little known—the name of the man who carried the King through the surf to the land (in France ?). A small fact, maybe, but interesting to Brighton folk, at least. He was, of all men, a Quaker, one Richard Carver.   In the Letters of early Friends there are " paseges consarning richard carver that

carried the King of his backe." After the Restoration, Carver
besought the King to release his fellow Quakers to the number of
110, who had lain in prison about six years. The King took the
list, and said, there were many of them, and they would probably
be " in again in a month's time, the country gentlemen complain-
ing to him that they were so troubled with Quakers." So he said,
he would " release him *six*."

One side-light more and the story is told. The Merry Monarch
was forgetful—to put it lightly. Gunter died before the Restoration. A petition from his widow to the King, in 1662, on behalf

" RED LION," OLD SHOREHAM.
(*By Brook Harrison.*)

of her son, or some other provision for herself, ends with these
words, " as often promised " !

\*        \*        \*        \*        \*

There are two direct ways to Old Shoreham—the broad but not
too interesting high road, and a by-way which begins sombrely by
burrowing under the Swiss Gardens, but emerges in a charming
path across the fields, having a pleasant view of Buckingham to
the north-east. Passing some very old elms in a field, you come
to all that remains of Old Shoreham. It was probably of greater
importance in early days, but the erratic ocean in making new
mouths for its harbour, robbed it of its prosperity ; and a few
cottages, its beautiful church and inn—the " Red Lion "—are all
that remain.

In olden days inns and hostelries were of more legitimate use
than many are to-day—mere drinking shops. They frequently

partook of the nature of a monastery refectory, where poor way-farers could find charitable sustenance and those of fuller purse more delicate fare.   The exact connection inns, such as the "Star" at Alfriston and the Old Flushing Inn at Rye (on the walls of which semi-religious frescoes have been recently found), had with the Church is not plain ; but enough is known to point to many such houses being used by pilgrims on their way to famous shrines, like that of St. Thomas à Becket at Canterbury.   This probably accounts for the names of those taken from sacred subjects, like the "Cross" or the "Lamb."

Mark Antony Lower divides inn signs into seven categories : those originating in Religion, Heraldry, Distinguished Persons, Emblematical, Trades, Sports and Pastimes, and Miscellaneous.

"The Cross" as a sign requires no explaining.   Religious sym-bolism is apparent at once, and Chichester with its "Golden Cross," Rotherfield with a "Red Cross," and Cuckfield with a "Green Cross," tell their own tale.   Sometimes the name of a saint is added, like "Mark Cross" and "St. John's Cross," Mountfield.

These appellations probably come from the presence of wayside shrines in old days, at the intersection of roads.   Peace of mind would naturally lead to thought for the inner man, and refreshment would be welcome after fasting and travel.   Shrines such as Stone Cross in Laughton ;  High Cross in Framfield ;  and Wych Cross in East Grinstead—sacred to the name of St. Richard de la Wych of Chichester—would be the bourn of many a pious pilgrim, and even in very early days, the house-of-call was probably at no great distance from the shrine itself.   Such houses as these would probably have had a semi-religious origin, and many possibly have been kept by some lay-brother in the interest of his monastery. The "Star" at Alfriston is close by the Market Cross, so-called.

"These wayside crucifixes were also called *Crouches*, from the Latin *Crux*," says Lower—such as the Crouch at Seaford, etc.

"The Lamb, everywhere a common sign, was formerly the 'Holy Lamb,' bearing a cross and banner."   At the Lamb Inn, at Eastbourne, the cellar is of Early English architecture with a high vaulted roof.   This is undoubtedly one of the oldest inns in the county.   While on this subject, I may refer also to the "Seven Stars" (another old title) in Ship Street, Brighton.   When it was rebuilt, I obtained the central oaken pillar turned on an old pole-lathe, with capital and base like a Norman pillar.   It upheld the great beam of the flooring above the cellar, and stood for some days in the rain, which softened the thick coatings of whitewash, and disclosed the original mediæval paint with which it had been adorned.

The "Maiden's Head" at Uckfield may have reference to the

Virgin, and at Burwash there is a " St. Katherine and her Wheel." Indifference to its religious origin, or the habit of curtailing a name " for short," has brought the Saint into a subordinate position. Her wheel is first thought of, and even that is apparently a secondary consideration, the house being known as the " Burwash Wheel "— a localisation which does not add dignity to St. Katherine's story.

The Star and Half-moon, otherwise the Crescent, are probably older than any signs, or they may have had their origin in the Crusades.   The two " Stars " most famous are those at Alfriston and Lewes.   The record of the first is of quiet, humdrum coming and going ; but the other has the page of its history lurid with the burning of the Protestant Martyrs at the stake before its door.

From this episode it is pleasant to pass to the Heraldic Signs. Sussex has its full share of these, and their origin is obvious.   The great House of Lancaster had large possessions in East Sussex, as the Howards had in the West.   So the Swan and the White Ante-lope or Hart, being supporters of the Lancaster coat-of-arms, and the White Horse and White Lion those of the Howards, appear on many signs in both parts of the county.   The earlier ancestors of the Howards—the Mowbrays—had the same supporters.

Then the family names of great houses, such as Pelham, Sheffield, etc., are found to designate many hostelries.   The Dorset Arms is commonly known as " The Cats," which is considered by the rural mind as a good enough name for the spotted leopards of that escutcheon.   The  " Three Pelicans "—the  arms  of Pelham— was once a sign in Lewes.   Then the Pelham " Buckle," the Curteis " Bull's Head," the Gage " Ram," the " Red Lion " of the Thomas' Arms, and the " Ash Tree " of Ashburnham, " The Tiger," the crest of the Michelbornes at Lindfield (*temp*. Edward IV), " The Griffin " at Fletching, " The Spread Eagle " of the Montagues, and the " Turk's Head " of the Darrells of Scotney—all these, together with the " Black Boy " and the " Boar " are heraldic.

Some signs are of a punning or " rebus " nature.   Thus at Warbleton, a battle-axe stuck in a barrel of foaming ale—" War-Bill in Tun "—is in the somewhat far-fetched humour of its day. " The Crow and Gate " at Crowborough Gate, and the " Runt in Tun "—a young cow enthroned in a beer-barrel—formerly at Runtington.   Lower says, " The Bull's Head rejoices in its proper sphere at Goring ! "   Other and more obvious signs are the " King's Head," etc., but the " Royal Oak " has a special significance in this county.   This Royal sign alludes, of course, to the escape of Charles II at the Battle of Worcester, and his hiding in the oak at Boscobel.   This sign became a favourite for Sussex inns about a century since, when Mr. Charles Pendrell, a lineal descendant of one of the brothers Pendrell, who preserved the King's life, settled at Alfriston, in enjoyment of his hereditary pension of a hundred marks and right of universal free-warren, conferred by the Merry Monarch on his preservers.

Signs denoting inns such as the " Barley Mow" and " Leather Bottell " ; " The Plough," " The Wheatsheaf," " The Ship," etc., are of agricultural or maritime origin. The " Gun " has a special interest, being derived from the Sussex ironworks ; while the " Greyhound " and such signs are eloquent of hunting ; and the " Green Man," near the Broyle, refers to the forester. " The Eight Bells " has also a hand-shaking connection with the Church.

The only difficult sign to explain is the subject of our sketch— " The Sussex Pad." A pad is a small horse or cob. Mark Antony Lower asks, " But why *Sussex* Pad ? " I expect the answer will

" THE SUSSEX PAD," LANCING (destroyed by fire in October, 1905).
*(By Brook Harrison.)*

not be forthcoming at this late day, unless it is found to refer to some once famous but now forgotten trotter. Some say it means a wayfarers' resting-place, preserved to us in the word " foot-pad." The only thing known with certainty about the house itself is its use as a smugglers' rendezvous when that trade was flourishing. Bands of sixty or more would come by arrangement at night with horses and light carts, thread the marshy flats to the shore by Lancing, off which the vessel and its contraband cargo lay. All would lend a hand in landing and loading the cargo, and before morning the whole would be safe in inn cellars, such as the unusually capacious ones at the " Pad," or distributed in smaller quantities in mills, farmers' houses, or in thickets. Many a shepherd's or yokel's " bovine stare " of apparent stupidity has concealed behind its vacancy the knowledge which a Revenue

Old Shoreham Church and Bridge.

(*By A. S. C.*)

Officer would have given his ears to obtain ; and many a haunted house contained spirits other than it was credited with possessing.

I repeat for those who may not have heard it, the story of the kegs of brandy whose noses were showing above the surface of the mill-pond while the Revenue Officers were searching the mill ; and how the miller and his wife kept them employed while an urgent message was being sent to the upper mill to release the water there, that it might drown these tell-tale witnesses. This story is told of various mills, I believe, but it was given me by two different people (the miller being one) as a fact relating to Poynings Water Mills, and it seems very likely true of that spot, as there is close at hand (or was, till fire consumed it) an upper mill and mill-pond. Another amusing smuggling story is told of the eastern-most parish in Sussex—East Guldeford—the parishioners receiving notice that the parson was " indisposed," and there would be no service in church. The fact was that a hard-pressed band of " free-traders " had induced the worthy man late on the previous evening to allow them to hide their kegs in the sacred building. The word " indisposed " never had a truer meaning—in one sense at least. Our so-called Free-Trade—or system of Coastguards— has made the trade that claimed to be free less necessary but certainly risky.

\*          \*          \*          \*          \*

For the antiquary few churches in Sussex have greater charm than Old Shoreham. Within or without, it is good to look upon. The south-western view is the one generally given, but that from the opposite point of the compass is equally interesting. Although it misses the Norman doorway it gives you the unusual tower stairway, which is yet not a turret, as in so many later styles. Our view is from the slope of the down and gives the bridge as well. It has been pointed out that the towers of New Shoreham and Southwick churches, also, have points of similarity, which suggests that one architect designed all three. We should have cause to be grateful to the unknown craftsman were only Old Shoreham Church remaining. We owe a heavier debt for three such gems.

Within, the four tower arches are notable examples of the zigzag and cable mouldings, and the latter is the ornament of the old oak beam just above the nave arch. There can scarcely be an older specimen of wood-carving in the county than this beam. The small zigzag window in the south transept—the church is cruciform— is one of two in Sussex, the other being at Clymping. It pierces the upper face of one of the flat buttresses which are so characteristic of the Norman style.

# CHAPTER VII

## LANCING OVER STEEPDOWN TO BRAMBER (6 Miles).

With Illustrations by Miss E. Neve and Douglas S. Andrews.

LANCING North and South are quite distinct from each other. The latter is the quiet little seaside resort beloved of invalids and avoided by the tripper. The houses straggle, in hybrid fashion, towards the station, with one pretty little Georgian house in " South Place," and after a group of suburban villas, end in more rural sort at the farm close by the path which runs through orchards and gardens to North Lancing, where the older village clusters round the moss-grown red-roofed church standing amid some fine elms. There are many such elms in the neighbourhood. There is a quaint, tottery old cottage facing you as you regain the high-road, and the way to the hills lies to the right of it.

The church itself is interesting and in the main is Norman, the porch and west door being of that period. In the chancel is an Easter sepulchre bearing a large incised cross. The records give particulars of several of the ceremonies connected with this church. Processions were as great a feature in English mediæval times as in modern France to-day. That they were undoubtedly picturesque, and that our rural life has lost much interest by their discontinuance, will not be questioned by those who witness the *Fête de Dieu* in Brittany. Special mention is made of that " round the corn of the village on the Eve of St. Mark," to celebrate the gathering of the harvest, presumably—a fitter celebration than many Harvest Homes, in all likelihood. Then on Rogation Day, a special procession came from Cocham Chapel in Sompting " to the church at Launsynge." As there were constant feuds between the spiritual owners of Sompting Church and the temporal powers of Cocham Chapel, this was possibly one way of showing that Lancing held first affection in the heart of the chapel-of-ease.

Whatever truth there may be in the conjecture that this fertile parish of Lancing took its name from Wlencing, one of the sons of Ella, the founder of the South Saxon Kingdom, matters but little, for Lancing under some other name was there before him, and not unimportant either.   On the downs above by Lancing Clump a Roman Prætorian had his dwelling on the ramparted road which connected Cissbury with the Applesham Wells by Lancing College, long before the Saxon inroad, and probably centuries of British occupation marked the fertile fields between the downs and the sea ere the Roman located himself there.

It is one of the charms of written history that it is not too accurate.   It still leaves a good deal to the imagination, and to surmise.   One thing, however, is certain, that whoever he was who first pitched his tent on the Down at Lancing, he had in mind the good a fine prospect gives, and probably grunted with the satisfaction of pure pleasure each time the sunrise met his gaze.   For what a beautiful view it is, every inch of it, as far as the limit which

LANCING CHURCH.
(*By Douglas S. Andrews.*)

Beachy Head forms !   How sweetly the hill slopes to the wood in the foreground !   How deep the green of the trees, the blue of the sea, and how sunny the cliffs far away with their fringe of golden shingle.

Whether the Briton first loved the spot, and called it by the equivalent for " home " in his rugged tongue, who shall say ?   But as to the Roman, here, without doubt, he dwelt.   The remains of tessellated pavement and the relics and coins of Rome were here unearthed to bear witness of his " knowing a good thing " when he saw it. It had another advantage besides the view. It was nearer the water-wells than Cissbury. " So he built him a house and planted a vineyard." Thus the archæologist, who points to the present-day name of a piece of land by Cissbury called " The Vineyard," as a proof that the Roman brought the grape with him from sunny Italy. Less imaginative people say that this assumption is too problematical and fanciful. But the archæologist is an obstinate man to tackle. He notes triumphantly that the southern slope of Cissbury is exactly the spot for its growth, and that there is no other spot in Sussex called by such a name. Let truth prevail! although Pilate's query has much force in cases where the evidence is lost in mist of years. But of the Roman villa itself there were sufficient remains found to put it beyond doubt.

There is little doubt, either, that the fertile fields below were not neglected. But after the Roman came the Saxon, and what he thought of it, or how he fought for it is a closed book so far as history goes. It is only when the Norman came that conjecture gives place to fact. Domesday, in its dry and curt fashion, with its somewhat sordid aims, counts its acres and the worth of them, its inhabitants and cattle, and Lancing is enrolled on the pages of history.

\*    \*    \*    \*

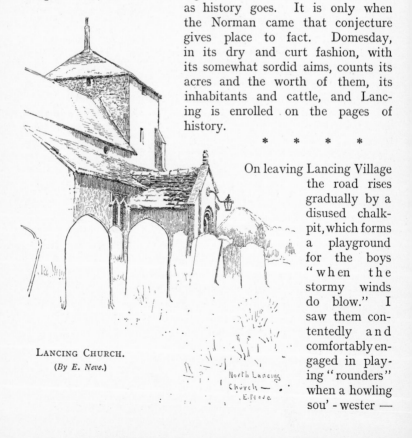

LANCING CHURCH.
(*By E. Neve.*)

On leaving Lancing Village the road rises gradually by a disused chalk-pit, which forms a playground for the boys " when the stormy winds do blow." I saw them contentedly and comfortably engaged in playing " rounders " when a howling sou' - wester —

almost strong enough to blow one into the pit—was careering above their heads.

Beyond, the hill rises gradually to Lancing Clump, one of the few coppices which crown the summits, and forms, with Chanctonbury Ring, landmarks from afar. Looking from Brighton, it is often mistaken for the more celebrated eminence. The Roman villa was situated just north-east of the wood. From the Clump run two old ways—to Cissbury and Chanctonbury across the south and north slopes of Steepdown. The former is the more interesting, as it seems to have been protected by a bank where it passes exposed positions. This is supposed to have been used by the Romans to fetch water from the fine spring of Ladywell at Applesham. These old tracks have a deep interest for the lover of the Downs as well as for the antiquarian. It is conceivable that centuries of traffic may have sunk the road below the level, but where was the traffic to come from ? I think the dictum of the antiquarian must be accepted, that the bank was thrown up for a purpose—to conceal the movement of troops from point to point. They are not deep depressions now. Too many centuries have come and gone not to have lowered the bank and filled up the track. There is, however, quite enough remaining to stir the imagination, and bring to the mind's eye the troop of helmeted soldiers passing along, or escorting immense water vessels drawn by sturdy horses, for the use of the great Camp on Cissbury.

Undoubtedly it is the human interest the Downs evince in these old marks of traffic, cultivation and signs of dwelling which gives them an attraction denied to merely natural features, however great their beauty. This, and the mental contrast raised by the utter solitude now, and the coming and going then.

The other " way " leads straight on to the far-off North Ridge, with a branch cut into the hillside from the west to ascend Steepdown. The hill itself somewhat belies its name on the east side, but on the south and west is steep enough. It is different from most hills, being covered with juniper bushes, which from a distance give it a scrubby look, something akin to the week-old growth of an unshaven chin. This is the first acquaintance you make with the juniper bush. It flourishes freely here and westward, but " nowhere east of the Adur." (This, however, is one of the legends which will not bear investigation. I myself have found it " east of the Adur," but very sparsely.) In the shelter of the coombes it grows tall, like young cypress bushes, and at dusk or through the mist resembles a regiment climbing the slope.

You will see at a glance from the western side of Steepdown the great expanse of hill and vale called " No Man's Land "— probably because of its solitariness. It is bounded on one side by

Chanctonbury and the North Ridge, and falls away in long lines until brought up by Cissbury's sudden ascent.

If you wish for solitude, here, as on Plumpton Plain, you can indulge in it to your heart's content. You are unlikely to meet anyone but the shepherd the livelong day, and it is only by such an experience that the subtler influences of the scenery can be felt and realised. Paradoxical as it may seem, all loneliness is not the same. The feelings inspired by wild coast scenery, wilder mountain gorges, monotonous marsh lands and desolate moors, are not alike. Although solitude may be the abiding presence in all, it is accentuated or softened by the prevailing characteristics of the scene. The sense of peace is not conveyed by the roar of the surf, or the savagery of the mountain gorge. Nor is the feeling of impotent insignificance engendered by moorland or down. Analysis of these impressions is difficult, and perhaps they differ in individuals. Possibly no two impressions could be expressed in similar words. But that these downs exercise a special influence of their own is undeniable. It is one of their charms, not seen but felt ; and only those who seek shall find. It is this that differentiates the true downland man from the dweller in wood or weald. The latter cannot understand the former's enthusiasm. In short, such scenery as this " is caviare to the general."

Leaving Steepdown by a sudden drop at its north end, the track becomes a broad, grassy way with cultivations on the right for more than a mile. Across the crops a lonely, weather-beaten farm caps the summit. Tennyson's tower that stood four-square to every wind that blew, could not be more defiantly placed. With its red roofs, varied pile and wide surroundings, it is no mean picture ; but to-day your path lies ahead in the direction of a barn flanked by trees, standing at the head of a great coombe. Before you reach it the plough-land ends, and a cart track, turning sharply to the right, points down the long slope towards Bramber, which is in full view.

You will find the descent very pleasant underfoot. It is only when you reach the bottom that you realise the size of the coombe. If you happen not to have turned before to gaze up the great hollow, you will immediately experience a strong touch of that influence I have endeavoured to describe. Strange to say, the sense of loneliness is incomparably greater in this bounded view than in the vast distances of " No Man's Land."

The track passes another farmstead, and is cut through a low hill to ease the gradient, thereby making a subject for a sketch, especially as cattle and sheep are rarely absent. Then low, battered trees begin to fringe the banks and you are brought at last to Maudlin Farm, which has a bracketed canopy to its door, a fine

Horsham-stone roof, and an evergreen oak for background.  Water collects by the roadside after winter rains, and from the corner of a barn opposite the gate a pleasant picture presents itself, well worth sketching.  It was only after three visits that I succeeded in finding this view, of which I make you a free gift.

The lane from here drops rapidly and delightfully to Bramber Station, and brings your journey to an end.

# CHAPTER VIII

## SOMPTING TO CISSBURY (8 MILES).

### ILLUSTRATIONS BY WALTER PUTTICK AND E. M. DAY.

PERHAPS I ought to say from Lancing Station. The road immediately to your left brings you, after several right-angled turns, to a stile leading across a field to Cocham hamlet. Thence through a lane and fields north-west till you issue on the Sompting road.

The sudden turns to be found on the wide strip of land lying between the Downs and the sea all the way to Chichester are characteristic of very ancient occupation. This always was, and is still perhaps, the richest land in Sussex. There is more corn grown between here and our Cathedral Town than anywhere in the county—and long may it so continue! Only those who have seen the corn-lands turned into pasture, know what the landscape misses in colour, as well as in interest. "The joy of harvest" is a very real pleasure, not only to the farmer!

These sudden kinks and corners show how little of the highway or main-road traversed these ancient holdings. A cart track from farm to farm was probably the only communication, dignified by long use with the name of "byway." And a very appropriate name too! It does go "by" almost every field it comes to, but seldom strikes across one. The result is a rectangular progress to which the peregrinations of a pawn on a chess-board are direct-ness itself. To reach Littlehampton from Worthing sea-front would seem a short run along the coast; but when after many turnings and twistings the unaccustomed traveller finds himself at Angmering, far north of the railway line, he credits the motor 'bus with being more than usually erratic—and hopes for the best.

If record speaks truly, Sussex roads in old days bore that appella-tion by courtesy only, such quagmires and sloughs did duty for them. Lower quotes an old rhyme describing "Sowseks full of dyrt and myre"; and it is currently stated among country-folk that the length of leg for which Sussex youths and maidens are celebrated is an "adaptation to environment"; an outcome of centuries of " leg-pulling from the clay," as it was rendered to me by a Wealden man.

It is our habit to credit the Romans with the great work of road-making in Britain, and in so far as the great trunk highways are concerned theirs is the glory. Perhaps these were the only roads worthy the name. The British track-ways were neither raised, paved, nor straight, but wound along the tops and slopes of every hill which lay in their course. They do not lead to Roman towns except when placed on the site of British strong-holds. They are, however, bordered by tumuli, like Roman roads.

It seldom strikes us what an im-passable tract our Weald must have been in those days. Many centuries of drainage and cultivation have brought the lowlands to what we now know them; but

SOMPTING CHURCH.
(*By Walter Puttick.*)

swamp and morass must have occupied every stream-course, and an impenetrable forest the higher grounds. By a recent return the Sussex woodlands are numbered by several hundred thousand acres *now*, although almost destroyed by the ironworks of two hundred years ago. What a dense growth they must have pre-sented in the first half of the Roman occupation we gather from this fact, that from Regnum (Chichester) the only road to London lay through Clausentum (Bittern, near Southampton), Winchester

G

and Silchester. Later, the Stane Street (of which more anon) from Chichester through Pulborough to Dorking, etc.—was made by them. It is still, in great part, used as a public road, and is even called by its original name at Ockley.

Neither does it occur to us that the Downs, which seem so sparsely populated now, so solitary, and bear so apparently primeval an air, were with the coast-line by far the most civilised tracts in Sussex. No doubt the Romans marched by preference over the Downs, and that the chain of earthworks were used for the reception and shelter of their troops. It took them many years to subjugate the Wealden tribes, and then they made but little use of the Weald, save to pierce it with roads to London from Pevensey and Seaford.

An Itinerary was made for one of the Emperors Antoninus and his generals, which gives the great roads in Britain, the stations on them, and the distances between. It is written on a parchment roll, but owing to later interpolations is much confused. Many of its problems and difficulties were, however, solved and previous conjectures confirmed, by the discovery of a MS. of sites in Britain by a monk, Richard of Cirencester, with an Itinerary added, probably copied from some genuine Roman document of the latest age, because many stations, towns and roads hitherto unknown are mentioned. It was unearthed in 1724 by Gram, the Librarian to the King of Denmark, and Mr. Bertram, a professor in the University of Copenhagen. One proof of its antiquity is the placing of the north part of our island, to the east. "Strabo and Ptolemy did the same, and even Mercator and Ortelius."

Our turnpikes now require little praise. They bear witness to their own excellence. Many of those about and north of Battle have for years past been metalled from the heaps of slag refuse cast out from the old furnaces and iron-works. It makes a perfect road, but is being rapidly used up.

\*     \*     \*     \*     \*

If one may so designate the main road on which it lies, Sompting is a village of one street, reminding one of many French villages, not in similarity of dwellings, but in the prevalence of high walls, making it somewhat unalluring. A certain luscious and alien fruit—the fig, to wit—is responsible for these. They protect the trees from the cold winds—for Sompting and West Tarring have been famous for their fig gardens ever since St. Thomas à Becket, or St. Richard of Chichester, introduced these trees into England. The figs they bear are well known at Covent Garden and, apparently, in their native country also, for when ripe, the beccafico comes all the way from abroad to these gardens, and to no other place in England.

This is the pretty story told of the fig gardens of Sussex, and when we know how unfailingly the swallow departs with the autumn and returns with the spring, there is nothing improbable in the visits of the beccafico.

And here a quaint thought occurs to me. If the fig is responsible for the high walls, is the " bearded barley "—whose attitude, even when wealth has crowned its head, is still one of lowly obeisance— innocently answerable for the presence of no less than three inns in little Sompting? A proportion reminding one of Falstaff's " intolerable deal of sack to one halfpennyworth of bread."

SOMPTING CHURCH : VIEW FROM THE EAST.
(*By E. M. Day.*)

If, owing to its mural environments, Sompting is not too attractive, nevertheless its history and church make up for what it lacks in looks.

If mere age be honourable, Sompting Church can boast an origin as primitive as the oldest sacred edifice in England, and can in addition claim an element of originality in form quite unique in our island. The lozenge-shaped spire is found abroad, but nowhere in Britain, and whatever the rest of the church may be, is undoubtedly of Saxon workmanship. There are many other features of interest which demand a visit, among them the adaptation of floor-levels to the hill-side—the south transept being several feet below the nave. The body of the church is Norman and Transition, although the windows are mostly of the latest date of Gothic—Perpendicular. Two old sculptures of Saxon work, a quaint corbel, an Easter sepulchre, a triangular piscina, and other features, are worth study ; but the Saxon tower is of the most absorbing interest. The arch from the tower into the nave is " like an ill-roasted egg, all of one side " and of very rude workmanship. The long and short work is very apparent on the angles outside, and in the centre of each wall a pilaster runs up the tower and is interrupted by double lights with triangular heads and rude capitals. It is one of the remarkable buildings in Sussex.

Its history is less known than itself. Small and out of the way as Sompting is, it has engaged the attention of Kings, Dukes, Empresses, Popes, Bishops, Abbots, Templars and Lawyers, and has been a bone of contention lasting through many generations.

There is an altar-tomb in the chancel without inscription, which has been identified by the armorial bearings as that of Richard Burre. His Will describes him as " ffarmer of the Parsonage of Sompting called the Temple, which I hold of the House of St. Jonys " ; " that my chaplen syng for my sowle by the space of xi yers "—intervals of rest and refreshment are, of course, understood—" and an obbit to be spente in priests, clerks, ringers, and pouer people xiii–iv d." If Lower be correct, the great London Company of Fishmongers were represented in the person of the worthy " ffarmer "—according to the shields on his tomb. Dick married a lady of high degree, and so obtained recognition in heraldry.

The aforesaid extract shows that the church belonged to the Knights Templars, a society encouraged by the Church until her jealousy was aroused by its power and riches, and then as ruthlessly suppressed with every kind of accusation and cruelty. One seems to see in this the present attitude of the Church of Rome towards Freemasons. Devotion to the cause of charity is as nothing in the eyes of Rome unless she can rule the roost, or call the tune. In 1154, however, the Templars were on the crest of the wave, and Sompting Church was given " to God, the Blessed Mary, and the Brethren of the Temple of Solomon." The Knights are referred to as " Brother Henry English," etc., and in shrewd forethought as to the future, the transfer begins, " Inasmuch as it has been the custom of old to transmit by letters what was wished to reach posterity with assured truth—lest at any time his gift should be withdrawn or disturbed by the vexatiousness of wicked men." Bishop Hilary of Chichester confirmed the gift, and reported to the Archbishop of Canterbury " that he considered it his duty to assist and give comfort to the poor committed to him by God, and especially to religious Brethren, etc." The high ones of the earth witnessed the grant in the persons of Duke Henry of Normandy and the Empress Maud, his mother.

In such manner were the Knights Templars referred to and instituted, and it seems impossible for language to be more explicit as to the aims of the Brethren. But when Rome wanted to be rid of them, no accusation was too absurd.

To return to Sompting. The life interest of the two ministering priests were expressly reserved. The Templars undertook " to build a mill and two fair houses for the use of the Vicar and pay him two marcs a year." Other bequests and transferences were made, and the opposition of Payen, the clerk of Findune, was bought off for " 20s. paid in Sompting Church every Michælmas."

Thirty years later the clergy of Steyning, behind whom was the Abbot of Fescamp, claimed right of burials and tythe of parishioners. One can fancy the discovery of these " rights " by the clerical claimants, and the joy thereof, and the fierce refusal of the " men in possession " to recognise such a claim. Thus came Sompting under the eye of Rome. Pope Julius II deputed Waleran, Bishop of Rochester, 1183–4, to hear both sides and judge between them. The Templars came off best, and the Abbot of Fescamp renounced all rights in Sompting.

Later, one of the new Templars, Philip de Bernehus, in confirming a gift of an acre, impressed the wax " with his teeth instead of a seal." Among other gifts by the same family was the chapel of St. Peter at Cocham, in Sompting, of which there are slight remains. The gift was disputed, and again a Papal decision was invoked from Honorius.

A very characteristic quarrel, showing the Englishman's love of his " rights," arose over the services of this chapel. As often happens, the mother-church claimed most attention, and William de Bernehus, in order to get his chapel properly served, probably finding remonstrance unavailing, kept back the dues, and locked the doors on the chaplain, as the Templar priest was called. William, in answer to accusation, said he had the Bishop on his side, and his argument seems to have been—" Do it well, or not at all " ; the chaplain's—" If you want it done well, pay for it." The result, as usual, was compromise. The Templars promised to hold regular service, and William paid up and gave four acres for the better support of the chapel. The two Priors who arbitrated say, " We lovers of peace confirm this agreement."

Once again did Cocham Chapel assert itself in the person of William. " Adam of the Temple," Vicar of Sompting, refused to hear confessions at the chapel, requiring parishioners to come to the mother-church, whereas Cocham claimed all church rites except sepulture. Adam thought that William wanted too much for his money, what with frequent processions, etc. ; and in the end these had to make way for the more spiritual exercises. Certain processions were, however, retained for Cocham ; such as that on Palm Sunday ; on the Eve of St. Mark round the corn of the village, a kind of Harvest-Home ; and round the fountain with chrism and oil—a blessing of the waters.

In after years the Church had its revenge for the "stiffnecked-ness" of William and his successor, Nicholas. A later heir, with less backbone, "moved by conscientious qualms," paid up before the Bishop at Henfield "all that his father had unlawfully held back, and Nicholas, his father, did penance." Adam, with an eye to his dues, and on his appeal (I suppose), got a further grant of land "to help pay for the services in Cocham Chapel."

When, in 1308, the Sheriff of Sussex, in virtue of the King's writ, laid hands on the property and on Sompting Church, 59 broad acres were its appanage, valued at £51. Of this the church, reckoned at £17 only, came into the hands of the Hospitallers by whom it was annexed. A good picking for the Sheriff or his master !

\*         \*         \*         \*         \*

Where the lane above the church turns to the right, there is a wooded bank. Mounting this and going up the line of crops will bring you to a wood, and following the border of this brings you to the edge of the valley across which Steepdown rises, and on the left of it "No Man's Land" stretches right away to Chanctonbury. You will notice the beginnings of a more wooded prospect, which increases as the Downs stretch westward, until at Arundel and beyond they lose their chief characteristic of unbroken greensward.

As you stand you can see the ramparted Roman way on Steep-down coming down the hill towards you on the opposite side of the valley. To your left, the ridge you are on stretches away in a bold sweep to the north-west, and if you follow its brow it will bring you to Cissbury. A good part of the way will be over this very Roman road. There are many pictures in the valley below. An artist friend saw "subjects enough to keep one busy for a month or two, if only one could find food and lodging—especially the former—in the farmhouses yonder." This inability or disin-clination of the rural housewife to cater for strangers may not be characteristic of Sussex only, but is undoubtedly a fact—not excepting the inns !

It is a gradual ascent from Sompting Wood to Cissbury, and you come at last to the entrance of the famous camp. On those un-familiar with them these ancient earthworks make a great im-pression, notwithstanding there is little more than a couple of grass-grown mounds with green hollows or trenches at their feet.

But looking on the immense area they encircle, the veil which hides the unknown past seems to lift, and gives a glimpse of those far days when this was the almost impregnable sheltering place, when danger threatened, for all that the " fugitive, low-browed men " held dear.

These strongholds stretch in a triple line from end to end of the Downs—north, central, and south. Every commanding hill is crowned with single, double or even triple trench and mound. Archæologists see in their shape—round or square—an indication of British or Roman origin ; but the form seems to be influenced by the character of the summit, and with one or two exceptions they are probably prehistoric—each tribe possessing one for a safe habitation against other tribes or wild beasts. Many of them enclose great areas—Cissbury as much as 60 acres.

Cissbury is the monarch among downland strongholds of neolithic man. This solitary summit, wind-swept and sunburned, over which the white clouds sail, to which the sea-mist clings ; silent as the graves of those who dug its mighty trenches, was a veritable " place of arms " long before Britain had a name. Here the very weapons which held it inviolate were fashioned from its flinty bosom, as if it desired to endow its defenders with the means of defence. The pits from which the flint was quarried are there to tell the tale, and large numbers of implements and weapons, finished and unfinished, broken halves and fragments, have been found and are still at times obtained, thrown up by those diligent excavators, the rabbits.

In their anxiety to be precise where all must necessarily be conjectural, too much stress seems to be laid on the origin of some features they present. One learned writer sees a Druidical use for the fifty or more great pits which occupy the western part of the enclosure. Another concludes from the finds and fragments of flint weapons that they were quarries and workshops for these. The excavations carried out by Colonel Lane Fox in 1878 prove that shafts and galleries dug in quest of flint of the particular quality adapted for chipping, existed long before the earthworks were thrown up and the ditches dug—these shafts and galleries ramifying even under them. In one the skeleton of a woman, head downward, was found, as if she had fallen in, or the body thrown in, when the shaft was filled up. Many and interesting were the " finds " in the shape of implements of flint, oyster and snail shells and pottery fragments at different depths.

So much for the antiquarian, speculative and proper. Both admit that these pits *may* have been underground shelters or dwellings. Less learned folk will probably decide for themselves that while all three conclusions may be granted, the last is most reasonable.  Those who know the Downs well, know also how exposed these heights are to every wind that blows.  For women and children shelter was absolutely necessary—and even for men.  These deep depressions, funnel-shaped now, were without doubt carefully excavated pits, roofed with tree-trunks and turfed with grass.  Later excavations by Harrison prove conclusively that they were cave-pits for dwellings.  One had a roof of concrete, and even the fire-place was found, as well as a network of galleries and chambers connecting shaft with shaft.  In short, just as the Briton succeeded neolithic man, and the Roman was followed by the Saxon in possessing Cissbury, so, in all probability, were the flint workings converted into dwellings when the hill-top became a fortified refuge.  And just as on its windy, rugged summit you may see the rabbits scurry into their burrows, so its ancient inhabitants would vanish when hard pressed, or fearful of danger.  But what you may not perhaps realise is the fact that the apparently solid hill-top is honey-combed beneath with an endless maze of galleries connecting cave-pit with shaft, into which the cave-dwellers could disappear as the rabbits do now.

Cissbury's wonderful story had almost ended before our history began.  True, the Roman held it, and its present name is derived from a comparatively recent Saxon King ;  but he was the inheritor of other men's labours, and only added the lustre of his name.  Time so remote that neither tradition nor written word illuminates, can only provide material for speculative ideas ;  but the archæologists, who say that the hoary monoliths of Stonehenge are youthful compared with Cissbury and its fellows, are probably not far wrong.

These great fortresses for shelter against foes and wild beasts, are the embodiment of the proverb " Self-preservation is the first law of nature " ;  while temples for worship such as Stonehenge and the like, argue a comparatively settled state of society.

Crowned with pointed palisades of oak, these slippery slopes were practically impregnable against such weapons as bows and arrows, stone-headed axe and spear.  Assault would have but little chance where the defenders had similar weapons and vantage ground to boot—until the men of the Bronze Age or the Roman appeared before the virgin fortress.  Then it changed hands, but not its use.  It still fulfilled its purpose, much in the same way, only the defenders were men of other times and methods.  Then the rolling centuries saw men multiply and grope, however blindly, after unity, rendering such eyries less necessary ;  saw strange, new powers evolved, against which Cissbury, in all its pride of place, could avail nothing, and it became the desolate, deserted spot it now is.

Yet it is well to reflect that the same " whirligig of Time," of which the poet sings, is bringing back the old order that had changed. It is just such earthworks as these, but more vast and scientifically constructed, that are becoming the ramparts behind which men are best protected against the devastating engines of modern warfare.

As you stand on the southern rampart of Cissbury you see a deep valley below, which opens out towards Worthing. This is the site of the "Vineyard." The western ridge of this valley or its hollow will bring you to Broadwater Green and Village. Too little attention is paid to the fine cruciform church, owing probably to ignorant restoration. The exterior being complete vies with New Shoreham in dignity of style, although here and there cement and brickwork are in evidence. Within it is disappointing; not perhaps in general effect, but in poverty of detail. The nave has little interest, and the chancel in part seems ill at ease with the rest. The tower arches are finely decorated Transition, the western one being almost of horseshoe form. There are fine renaissance tombs to the Lords de la Warr, several brasses, an old altar-stone with five consecration crosses, and good stalls and misereres in the chancel. As a whole, however, the church just fails of being fine, in the sense that Boxgrove or New Shoreham are fine.

# CHAPTER IX

## FINDON TO BURPHAM AND ARUNDEL (9 MILES)

### BY RAIL TO WORTHING AND MOTOR-BUS.

#### WITH ILLUSTRATIONS BY A. JOBSON BROWN AND ARTHUR B. PACKHAM.

I GIVE this excursion because it covers unfrequented ground. The 'bus meets certain trains at Worthing, and will land you at Findon, four miles north. It is a pleasant but rather dusty village, without any special feature except its beautiful situation. The church, although possessing a spire, has to be sought for among the trees by the hillside. It is late Norman and Early English. The nave pillars are Transition, and there is an arch with Norman mouldings and an ornamented circle below it in the south transept. The windows are Decorated, and an unusual feature is a doorway between the two sedilia in the chancel. Its fine old roof, which covers its twin naves, was deemed by Sir Gilbert Scott almost unique. There are traces of mural painting on the north side.

It is an interesting building, and the contents of the belfry alone redeem it from the charge of mediocrity. Besides possessing one of the small " Sanctus " bells, Findon has a fine old bell among its four dedicated to St. Gabriel, and bears the arms of the See of Winchester, perhaps because the foundry was in that See. These Findon bells are a very mixed lot, having relationship with two groups in various Sussex towers. Some of these have a lion's face, a most " fearful wild fowl " indeed. This is the only case of an animal's face being limned on Sussex bells. On the other hand, there is real beauty of design in many of the crowns and crosses figured.

Here I purpose digressing to speak of bells in general and to tell the story of the Sussex Bells in particular.

For all their gift of sonorous sound, and nathless their long tongues, neither the Sussex nor any other bells can tell us when or where they were invented, or by whom. Poets and rhymesters, novelists and story-tellers, are never weary of extolling their music, their message and its meaning ; the joy-bells of marriage or of festival ; the chime for worship or the toll for death. Indeed, they endue them with moods and voices as though they were animate beings, wilfully ignoring the sexton and his fellows in the belfry below, who pull the ropes and are responsible for the moods, at least. True it is, their voices can awaken chords in many hearts ; but they cannot tell their own story, nor can their masters either, except in part.

It is but poor comfort to the inquirer to be told that they came into use in Europe in A.D. 600. We are so desirous of reaching back to the beginnings of everything, that it is annoying to be brought up short by the stone wall of an impenetrable past, and left to conjecture only. It is probable, say the experts, that East and West invented them independently (East, of course, in this connection means China, which had everything before everybody else, and heartily despises our mushroom Western antiquity). What was the original form of the bell is a matter for question. The earliest of large size may possibly have been metal clamped, brazed, hammered and hardened, such as—in a small way—the sheep-gong we are all familiar with on the Downs. This, or something like it, was doubtless the first approach to its present form, and it is partly borne out by the shape of the oldest founded bells, which were taller than those of later and present date, whose proportions are these—the diameter of the mouth exceeding the height by one-fourth. The reverse is the case with the older bells.

As to their invention many plausible guesses have been made. These may be passed over, but one story is interesting. It is told of the army of Clothaire II, that it laid siege to the town of Sens, in Burgundy, early in the seventh century, whereupon the citizens rang their bells, and frightened the besiegers away, who had never heard the sound before. In 623 bells were in use among the Christians in the East. Mahomet is said to have had some thoughts of introducing them as his call to prayers, but was dissuaded by a dream of one of his followers. It is to be regretted that the result of the worthy man's temporary indigestion, a mere dream—" unsubstantial as the caves in combing wave "—should have robbed us of what would doubtless, in Arabic hands, have borne many quaint, distinctive features and ornament.

Bells, therefore, being a Christian institution, led to the erection of church towers to receive them. Think of this, ye who live under the shadow of the church, and who are apt to murmur and " wish the bells further " off, when the ringers are somewhat too insistent in striving for the honour of completing an intricate peal ; think how poor a figure our noblest churches would present without the majestic towers with their tapering spires or pinnacles—and let the bells ring on ! You are suffering from being located too near the holy place. While you grumble at the noise, your distant friends are saying, " Listen to the music of the bells ! "

In Saxon times King Egbert commanded every priest, at the proper hours, to ring the bells of his church, and at the Norman Conquest the art of bell-founding had arrived at considerable perfection. Very large bells must have been made if we judge by the size and strength of the towers built to contain them, and from the institution of the Curfew.

To come to Sussex bells. Imperishable though the material and make of them may seem, there are yet only four bells dated previous to 1570 ; so that many must have disappeared in some way. There are fifty-two undated and uninscribed bells in the county, and some of these may be of early times ; but as the older bells are generally ornamented with the sacred sign, and dedicated to some saint, these are probably of a date when " a bell was a bell," and only a bell : something to give forth sound, and on which ornament or inscription would be wasted.

Although at the Reformation many churches were despoiled of their bells, and many more disappeared, being " embesiled " for their metal, Sussex suffered less than many counties. There are still 106 ancient bells, the earliest dated bell (1369) being at Dunc-ton—a Dutch bell.

Remodelling old peals, that is, recasting three or five large old bells into a lighter peal of six or eight, to adapt them to modern change-ringing, is responsible for the disappearance of many old bells ; but it was often necessary to recast, as the bells wore thin where the clapper struck, making itself a pit, and eventually cracking the bell. Of course, change-ringing wears them out still more rapidly, so that the most ancient bells are generally found in little country villages. Ancient bells have seldom any date or name of founder ; nothing to show when, where, or by whom cast ; but they have very beautiful Gothic or Lombardic lettering in the dedication or invocation to some saint, together with stops of ecclesiastical pattern between the syllables and names, crosses—floriated, plain or formed of fleur-de-lis—shields, crowns, coins, medallions, with now and then the initials of the founders. These and the inscriptions render them objects of great interest, inasmuch as they almost all show that they are the outcome of reverent and religious intentions. The nearest approach to light-heartedness is the inscription on an old bell at Eastdean, near Beachy Head, which bears this legend—" There is not a better bell under the sky." If it has such a good opinion of itself it may be overlooked, which is more than the legend is often likely to be, seeing that it is in Latin and a dark, dusty church tower ! The bell at

East Dean, near Chichester, is less jocund—except, perhaps, in brightness and clearness of tone—being content with the Archangel's greeting, " Hal Mari ful of Gras."

An old bell at Bramber proclaims its antiquity, not so much by what its inscription records as by what is left out ; viz., its founder had not yet acquired a surname.    It tells that " Nicolas made me," and is dedicated to " Jesus of Nazareth, King of the Jews."   " Nicolas," whose name is shrined in the gloom of the tower of Bramber Church, has other sanctuaries.   At Madehurst he adds a homely prayer which shows that he at least was not selfish—" God help Sancte Maria ! "

The bell of Hove Church is of great antiquity, evident from the style of the lettering, bearing simply the initials T. H. and a cross. They probably stand for Thomas Hickham, who cast some bells for Canterbury Cathedral in 1358.   If so, it is as old or older than the Duncton bell.

Kingston, near Lewes, has also three ancient bells, all different. At Ninfield there is a fine old bell, with shields, cross, and medallions between each word, which bears " William Ffounder me fecit," and the inscription in Latin.   This is a notable bell in many ways.

At Tarring Neville the Crucifixion is borne on a medallion ; while Graffham (in addition to a shield of the Royal Arms from Henry V to Elizabeth) has an appeal in which the limitations of the Latin tongue seemed insufficient and the heart speaks in terse language—" Jsu merci ladi help."

West Hoathly bell is about 1554 date, and the casting was paid by John Bryan, who bequeathed vjs. viijd. for the purpose.

Sullington and St. Botolphs are dated, and with others are beautifully ornamented with crowns, shields, busts of Henry VIII, and elaborate stops.

Twineham's second bell has a curious inscription, which tell us " here I am again, rechristened Peter "—reminiscent of clown and pantaloon, but in reality referring to recasting.

At Woolbeding the infrequent examiner is informed that " this new bell is named Margaret."   These extracts seem to show that the ancient founders had pretty much their own choice as to what they put on the bells.   Extra inscriptions meant extra expense, as is shown in an old churchwarden's account—" for making the scripture about the bell xiijs. xiiid."   The dedication would be in the price, but more than this was left to " Master ffounder," who, from obedience to orders, or with the modesty characteristic of his day, forbore to either date or sign his work.

This can scarcely be said of modern founders and their bells. These bear witness to an entire change in the spirit brought to bear on the work.   The purist may doubt whether the new mode is quite consonant with the sacred nature of their use ; whether the doggerel rhymes and inscriptions glorifying the donors are quite in place : while their apologists may plead that the couplets and the wit are eminently suitable, being of the ponderous order, harmless enough, because, in a double sense, they are not easily seen ! Then it is a gain to the archæologists in that they tell their own tale, and as the centuries roll on, the very quaintness of the phrases used will be enhanced and become less objectionable.

The beginning of Elizabeth's reign was the great epoch in the history of bell-founding, as indeed her rule was for greatness in many ways—the change of religion, the Renaissance movement, the introduction of Roman capitals and Arabic numerals. There were three periods of spoliation in the reigns of Henry VIII, Edward VI, and the early years of Elizabeth herself. What can have become of the hundreds of bells in the monastery towers at the Dissolution ? Glastonbury had " in the tower, viij. very great, in the churchyard iij. most huge."

These last would be swung in a massive oak frame. It is said that many were sold and exported, many " embesiled " and broken up for their metal ; but Sussex seems to have escaped the fiercest waves of fanaticism or greed, or how else can we account for so many cases of two or three old bells in one church.

Later in the reign of Elizabeth came a change and a Royal Proclamation forbidding further depredations, and bells were no longer among the things which " noryshe any kinde of superstition," as was said of them in the reign of Edward VI. When this pro-clamation was made, there were probably but two bell-founders left, at Reading and London, and it took another ten years for a revival to set it. Bells of this date are not well cast, nor were the founders flourishing, as petitions extant to the Lord High Treasurer, for payment due by donors of bells, bear witness.

Before the sixteenth century a great movement began, due in part to the modern system of change-ringing, as well as to a reaction in favour of bells. " In all directions we find old bells being re-hung, recast, and new bells added to peals, so that till the civil war there appears to have been a greater demand for bells than at any other period." Bell foundries sprung up in all the neigh-bouring counties, three even in Sussex itself, though of no great importance. The civil war closed most of them, and Puritanism did the rest. Not until 1700 did the second revival commence, and still continues to this our day.

The first Sussex founder was Edmund Giles, of Lewes. Nineteen bells only stand to his credit in as many years, so that his was a small way of business. Still he labels his castings with the words

" bell-founder," as if proud of the distinctive title.   His largest
bell is the fourth of Rotherfield, weighing 15½ cwt.

Roger Tapnell, at West Tarring, is another Sussex founder, and
Thomas Wakefield at Chichester.   These joined hands at the trade.
Records exist by which these worthies warranted bells in accordance
with the usual custom for " a year and a day," which was necessary,
their bells being poorly cast, the letters and words being often
reversed.   Wakefield, however, made some efforts to ornament
his bells.   On three at Stedham and elsewhere a fine fleur-de-lis
occurs.   John Sulham, at Chiddingly, in 1651, was another small
founder with large charges, as the churchwarden's accounts of
Cliffe Church show.   £25 in the current coin was a considerable
sum for the recasting of two bells.   William Hull is the East Sussex
bell-founder, whose record is interesting, seeing that he had learnt
his profession under a great London founder, John Hodson.   It
is an onerous task, that of bell-founding, and requires experience
and knowledge.   These William Hull had, for he was sent by his
master to cast the bells at Hailsham, at a spot called Bell Bank.
He afterwards set up for himself at South Malling.   There are
more than twenty bells of his in the neighbourhood, the biggest
being Catsfield tenor, 16½ cwt.

Among the founders, John Waylett must be mentioned as a regular
itinerant, there being more than forty bells cast by him in their
own and neighbouring parishes.   It may be interesting to know that
in casting bells, the metal is still melted by wood fire—generally
beechwood.   So much for the founders.   Now for the bells.

A commission sent in 1686 to report on the state of the churches
roused the wardens and people to a sense of their responsibilities,
and repairs and recastings became the order of the day.   Of Berwick
bells it is said that—

> " The Parson was poor and so were the people,
>    So they sold the bells to repair the steeple " ;

and a small ship's bell was bought from a wreck on the coast by
way of compensation.

The couplets and inscriptions on the bells of this and later periods
are often amusing.   One at Bolney bears this couplet—

> " Ralph Hair my doner's prais ile sing,
>    And Michael Harmes y$^t$ p$^d$ for my cast——."

Whether the hiatus represents the worthy " doner's " objection to
the faulty scansion of the verse is a matter for conjecture.   He
need not have troubled.   When once hung, very little scanning of
any kind would the gloom of the tower permit !

West Hoathly—" Joseph Carter made me Bettrer," 1581—a
very " downright " Sussex phrase.

Southease—" Johannes Aleyn me fecit."
Midhurst—

> " Our voices shall with joyful sound
> Make hills valleys echo round."

—a slight omission that would puzzle a child to understand how the sound of a bell could " make hills valleys " !

West Dean—careless dating makes the bell cast in 1901—a reversed 6.

BURPHAM CHURCH.
(*By Arthur B. Packham.*)

Patcham bears witness to itinerant casting, having no mark but a dozen scratched crosses.

West Thorney bears only one word, but that one more dedicatory than a dozen, viz., " Jhesus."

We know Rudyard Kipling's love of Sussex. At Racton, one of the bells was cast by Joshua Kipling in 1742. Is the poet of Sussex stock ?

\*          \*          \*          \*          \*

If this long digression has not driven the ostensible purpose of this excursion from Findon to Burpham out of mind, I would say that a mile westward by the road next to the " Gun Inn " will bring you to the low ridge connecting the northern and southern ranges of the Downs. Looking westward still, Burpham lies five miles by wing as the crow flies, and six as *you* go. The chief characteristics of these Downs are their greater loneliness and special form. The first you will soon appreciate ; the latter is shown in isolated hills of fair height with spread bases, as if loftier mounts had been pressed down to fill a larger space.

It is useless to give paths where none exist. Therefore, westward set your face, and take hill and hollow as they come, sometimes across the plough-lands, but mostly on the green. After the fourth descent and third climb you will see Burpham Church tower rising sweetly among its trees some distance off. Reach it in your own way. You will have your reward. It is one of the churches of Sussex that pleases me most, perhaps because of its variety ; but chiefly because, on the whole, it has been tenderly dealt with in restoration. It is pleasant to say a good word for work often carried out with the best intention but little taste. Even here a mistake has been made in substituting the present chancel arch for a simple Saxon one, which was a link with the earliest past, the rest being rich Norman or Transition. The chancel has a vaulted roof, which is rare in small village churches, and with the lancets is wholly satisfactory. The variety of ornament in the nave and transept arches is great, especially in the prominent undercut zigzags. There are other points of interest, but perhaps one of the most pleasing is the original fifteenth century oak benches beautifully carved and of most chaste design. In restoration and additions to these, old timbers out of a neighbouring barn were used.

Burpham stands at a point on the river Arun evidently of importance in the eyes of the Roman invader. The village lies practically under the protection of a great earthwork thrown across the entrance, the river running at the foot of a cliff or escarpment caused by primeval floods or torrents.

Below the church the road drops suddenly to the river-bank. Artists are much in evidence here, as at Amberley and Bury a few miles farther north. The way from here leads along the bank with the Castle of Arundel facing you continually ; and a very beautiful walk it is. It brings you out at the Bridge.

H

# CHAPTER X

## GORING, FERRING, EAST PRESTON AND RUSTINGTON
### (7 MILES)
To Goring Station.

### WITH ILLUSTRATIONS BY A. S. C.

TURNING south the road goes straight towards the sea. Goring lies to the left. You see it across the hedgerows. The church with its spire looks best from a distance, having been rebuilt in perhaps the deadest period of ecclesiastical architecture, some seventy-three years ago. The only ancient relic is a tomb with brasses of 1600. The village is pleasantly set among cornfields, and there are many fine elms about it. The need for shelter from sea winds accounts for the comparatively large number of trees in these levels. Except to the north, where the great Goring Wood covers the entire southern slope of the Downs, there are no plantations, but long lines of trees fringe the fields. You will be struck by the number of evergreen oaks. They are of no great stature, but they form the finest screen. Their characteristics are the thickest of foliage, and branches starting quite near the ground. Indeed, the trunks may be said to be all branches, enabling the fullest protection to be given to the standing corn.

At the " Bull Inn," a path leads to Ferring, and just south of it there is a mile-long avenue leading to Goring Hall from the west. These oaks were planted some sixty years ago, and when every other tree is bare, give a touch of summer opulence to the wintry landscape.

Looking north as you go, Cissbury is prominent to the right, and Highdown Hill immediately before you, crowned with its low entrenchment, and its slopes forming the last resting-place of Saxon kings and warriors, and probably older races still, for weapons and relics associated with the Bronze Age have been found. The graves of these long-forgotten dead form the glory of this prehistoric hill, far more than the tomb with its automatic arrangement of death's heads, erected in his life-time, by which an eccentric miller sought to obtain notoriety. It has disappeared, and probably, in no long time the memory of its owner will die too.

East Ferring Lane is a pleasant hamlet grouped amid trees. Here are the entrance gates to the long avenue. Close by is a fine old farm-house, which would have gladdened the heart of Richard Jefferies, who revelled in describing the delightful want of regularity of floor, roof and gable; the chimney-corners and low-pitched rooms; with most of which I cordially agree—but not all. Perfection is of slow growth, and even the sixteenth century did not hail its coming of age. There is a composite and rather upstart word, yclept—"adaptability," which will thrust itself upon our

RUSTINGTON CHURCH.
(*By A. S. C.*)

notice, warning us not to be too great a slave to sentiment. I, too, love old houses, and spent many youthful days "in the country," but the glamour and delight did not blind me to the fact that comfort is a comparative term even where chimney-corners are concerned; that passages and staircase were often ill-lit, and not even the "adaptability" of youth reconciled me to that other virtue claimed for these old houses, the irregularity of floor— "a step up into one room, and down a step into another." Shade of Jefferies, forgive! but not even love of thee can obliterate the memory of the "croppers" I have come in days gone by; unless, indeed, like Touchstone and his wit, I shall be taught to recognise a virtue "by breaking my shins against it." Sentiment cannot survive such shocks ! To me the most tolerable " dead level " is that of the floor. The wise architect takes unto himself all that is good in these old-time dwellings, and adds the experience the passing years have taught him. This is how the " House Beautiful " is built.

Ferring Village, also embosomed in trees, if not possessing any distinctive features, looks prosperous and well-cared for. The builders of its church seem to have shrunk from braving the winds, and it presents the appearance of what one might call acres of roof to mere strips of wall, with an equally unaspiring bell-cot squatted on its western end. The porch has a pointed doorway blocked up on the north side. One wonders what purpose it served. There is a square-headed priest's door on south side of chancel, also walled up, and a good modern lych-gate stands at the entrance of the churchyard.

The inside is of a piece with the lowly nature of the exterior, and its homely, unpretentious character is common to many a Sussex church. How quaint it may have been only the older inhabitants can testify. It has suffered restoration twice since 1870. In style it is Early English with three Perpendicular windows. Its chief ornament is a fine stoup of the same period, a piscina with a marble shelf, and an Early English font. The nave arcade, like the church, is of modest altitude. Arches seldom " soar " in Sussex churches, and " fretted roofs " are quite the exception. The sacred buildings would seem to reflect the humility of their worshippers, and many of them were probably " home-made." How cold they must have been on winter days, however glowing the vestments of the priest and his acolytes ! Religion was a reality in those times.

At the west end of the village street a path turns north by a very low-thatched hovel, and appears to lead anywhere but to East Preston, judging by the map. It points to Highdown Hill, but a short distance on, a westward track, crossing streams and dykes, brings you " by devious ways " within sight of your goal. " All roads lead to London," the old saying avers. Here they all make for the sea, only field-paths going east and west. In this we may see the attraction the sea has always had for man. Not only does its ceaseless movement charm him, but it is the source of endless mystery and surprises. Who could say what its tides and waves might leave upon the strand ?

To-day, however, the field path claims your wandering feet. It turns south at last and joins the highway ; but a hundred yards on, a stile leads to yet another path, quite beautiful, but following the same long lines of trees, until you see the spire of the church again surrounded by elms, notable for height and shape. Artists would be wise to visit this part of Sussex more often than they do. The views presented by these level lands, bounded by distant hills, not only ask for a special aptitude in delineation, but demand the affection of those who aspire to paint them ; otherwise their failure is assured. This is the native home of that " artist's tree " —the elm. Of this tree, in the neighbourhood of Boxgrove, I saw more fine shapes and colour than anywhere else in Sussex, and even nearer the sea the influence of the south-west winds only seemed to add to their variety of form.

EAST PRESTON CHURCH.
(By A. S. C.)

The near presence of the Downs makes this a delightful walk, especially as the immediate surroundings are so open.

East Preston Church presents the usual medley of styles. An old Norman doorway with carved capitals, but minus pillars, and a very old oak door heavily studded with nails, with simple hinges ending in doubtful fleur-de-lis, adorn the porch—a welcome example of " home-made " ironwork. The nave was probably Norman and the chancel Early English, but Time works many changes, and churchwardens more, so I won't dogmatise, except to say that the tower and spire are certainly late Perpendicular, the detached lancets of the east window of any date from Rufus to Henry VIII, and that there is a little old " quarried " glass.

The road to Rustington (which is almost a suburb of Little-hampton) presents no difficulties. It begins to betray its urban character by more frequent tenements, but gardens and trees help to content you with the near approach to a town, and the church will please you well.

In considering the evolution of architecture, one sees how the tendency to heighten and lighten churches progressed. Built originally as potential fortresses, and actually used as such in times of stress, with tiny, shuttered windows, high up—the attraction the later styles would exert accounts for the alterations and additions such as Rustington exhibits. In the matter of light, what a difference the Early English window must have made ; no doubt, the greater use of glass was largely responsible for the change, but the movement went on until in the hey-day of the Perpendicular style there was often more window than wall ; and the same principle was applied to interior arcades. Here at Rustington, the low, obtuse Transition arches on the south side of nave seem to have been replaced in the north arcade by two elegant, acutely pointed arches without capitals, while the other pillars are massive and have carved capitals. A portion of the stairway to the rood-screen, when this existed, still remains ; but the stonework throughout the church has had too free an acquaintance with the mason's scraper during the restoration.

The chancel is Early English and has a very interesting low-side window by the side of the priest's door, evidently inserted later, with a wooden shutter. There are also two unusual pointed recesses on the east side of the chancel piers, and a squint connecting with the north transept. Here are some fragments of tombs inserted in the wall. One of a knight, his lady and family kneeling in prayer on each side of the figure of Christ ; above them, carved representations of the instruments of flagellation. The other fragment is of good Decorated panelling, with a shield of leopards' heads. Two grotesques on north aisle and tower arch, some good stained glass, and a good modern memorial tablet of hammered copper, complete the list, unless it be the mixture of Early English and Transition in the transept window.

The exterior will please you most, by reason of the delightful Transition tower and the two old porches, especially that over the west door. Note the woodwork, how solid and good—and the original barge-boards ; above all, the silver-grey colour of the weather-beaten oak.

Altogether, Rustington Church, like Bishopstone, is too little known.

# CHAPTER XI

## CLYMPING, TORTINGTON, FORD AND YAPTON
### (7 MILES)
#### From Ford Station.

ILLUSTRATIONS BY LOUIS GINNETT AND ARTHUR B. PACKHAM

SO as not to miss one's opportunities, a few hundred yards north of Ford Station lies Tortington, hidden among the trees. It is tiny, but the interest is great. Built early in the twelfth century, it has late Norman detail of most quaint character. The chancel arch is almost unique in Sussex, being both rich and plain. The lower arch is quite bare, the upper member carved with beak-heads of two kinds—grotesquely human or owl-like, each crested with feathers or leaves. They are curiously like the carvings on Maori granaries. These beak-heads, or cats' heads, so called, remind me most of the octopus in motion, with its lack-lustre eyes full of a dull horror. Symbolism is responsible for most ornament, but there is little doubt that pagan and heathen symbols were continued by craftsmen as ornament, long after their meaning had died out.

The south door is also richly carved with zigzag and leaf ornaments. One oak bench, similar to those in Burpham and Clymping, and a chaste Jacobean pulpit in the same material, are things to be seen, no less than the aisle arches and the black oak roof. The ancient bowl of the font has been erected on a modern base, the whole resembling a chalice ; but however good the symbolism intended—that Baptism leads to the Lord's Supper—it is curiously clumsy in appearance. The bowl has a bunch of semi-classical foliage in double panels formed by two small Norman arches.

It strikes me as an ideal village church—but the village is wanting. In old days there was probably a greater population, and a Priory existed, of which traces can be seen in an old barn some distance north of the church. Early English pillars in cluster and part of the vaulting only remain to tell of former greatness.

In looking at these relics dedicated to holy uses, one is tempted to wish that they were still in full beauty scattered up and down the land, fulfilling their sacred purposes as of old : and if those purposes, as practised in the earliest days, had been strictly adhered to by the Church, many of them might still be standing as hospitals perhaps, as well as religious houses, for local needs.   But in stretching forth to grasp temporal power, she involved herself and her system in almost universal ruin, and had to begin afresh, shorn of nearly all her glory.

So it will probably be again, should the religious orders, once more establishing themselves in England, forsake the path of spiritual progress and charity, and grasp at temporal power.   England will have none of it.   But it is grievous to see so much that has been so beautiful lying waste and ruined.

South of Ford Station lies Ford Church, an almost exact replica of Tortington.   Neither have a tower, and the same builder might have erected both.   A Norman nave and chancel arch and piscina, and a Transition chancel, are the chief architectural features. To the casual observer it would seem always to have been what it is now, a tiny building with one or two cottages neighbouring it, but there was a time when a fine moated mansion of the Bohuns kept it company.   Of this only the uneven surface of a field near by bears witness.   How completely a building can disappear these hummocks testify.   Whether fire was the destructive force is not known.   Certainly the church suffered from it, and remained roofless for many years, until a saying arose that " Ford Church was lost among the stinging nettles."   Archbishop Laud's Injunction stirred the inhabitants to restore it in 1637, when the quaint brick porch was added.   " The spirit moved them " to do likewise in 1865—as the word was understood then.   "It was done ruthlessly enough," ancient seating and doors being swept away, and the font thrown out of the church into a neighbouring farmyard as a bath for ducks.   The oak seating had fleur-de-lis and poppy-heads for finials, and there was a unique ladder of the pigeon-house variety leading to the bell-turret.   It was formed of a rough tree-trunk with stout pegs inserted on each side.

Small as the building is, no less than seven styles of architecture are represented—eminently suggestive " of its varied fortunes." Part is undoubtedly Saxon, added to and enlarged by Norman hands, and altered or embellished by later work.   There is a beautiful Decorated east window, and many interesting things have lately been discovered.   There are crosses cut on the jambs of the south door, and sundials and pilgrims' marks on the south-east quoin of nave externally.   Also an X-shaped star, probably referring to St. Andrew, to whom the church is dedicated, and a round-headed niche in chancel for the reception of some relic of the saints.   An interlaced Celtic ornament on a stone built into the arch of the north doorway seems to link the building with a far-away past. It is of stone of an unusual kind, and was, perhaps, part of the arm of a cross. A complete slab, similarly decorated, was found under the floor at Bexhill Church.

Frescoes of the " Doom," the " Agony " and other subjects covered the walls in earlier days, and where possible these have been uncovered. These paintings date from the early fifteenth century, and certainly represent local art, if little else, so primitive is the execution. Otherwise this " Doom " is of the approved type. There are the usual groups of souls—little naked figures with faces outlined in black and with yellow hair—representing alike the good and bad ; the latter being pitchforked by the usual demons with forked tails and clawed feet into the " Jaws of Hell," a yawning sea-monster of lurid red, belching flames from its mouth.

Whether such drawings inspired awe in the simple minds of those days we cannot tell. They would send the modern boy into fits of laughter, and would be considered better than the comic papers. There is " a delightful touch of local colour " in the figures of men and women's souls rising not only from coffins, but from *boats*—in reference to the passage " and the sea gave up the dead which were in it." The perils of the ocean must have been real enough to Ford fishermen.

Several jars have been found built into the walls, supposed to have been placed there (with a thin layer of plaster over the mouth) to improve the acoustic properties of the building, but they may be early cinerary urns used as material by the builder because they were of a semi-sacred character, or happened to " come to hand " in laying the courses.

One of the parish priests of Ford, John Forbe, deserves to be remembered. The milk of human kindness was not unknown in 1535. In his Will he seems to have forgotten none of his parishioners, good or bad—if only they came to his " buryn." Among the items is this—" To every mayden, marriageable, 10d., and to every mayde of 10 years, 4d."

I have drawn freely on an article by Mr. Philip Mainwaring Johnston in the Sussex Arch. Coll., vol. xliii.—a paper so informing and complete, so descriptive where there would seem to a casual eye to be so little to describe, that it is a model of antiquarian research, and an object lesson in what true restoration consists. Would to Heaven such as he had been Inspector-General of Ancient Monuments with plenary powers to curb the destroyer's rage—as one may without exaggeration dub the restorer and his misplaced zeal.

Ford House, a fine old mansion, lies half a mile west. It has fine panelling and chimney pieces. One room is panelled with cedar wood.

Near by Ford House there is a field-path direct to Yapton Church. It takes you through the same level fields of rich soil, which are characteristic of the whole district south of the Downs right away to the borders of Hampshire. Flat the land undoubtedly is, yet somehow, whether from the bordering of hills or sea, both near at hand, it never seems empty and bare as do the levels in many counties. Maybe the hedges and trees thrive more bountifully in the deep loam, and the hamlets, with here and there a mill, suffice to form limits to what is in reality a very long plain indeed.

YAPTON CHURCH.
(*By Arthur B. Packham.*)

One forgives Yapton Church its "churchwarden's Gothic" and farmhouse dormers to nave and aisle, because it is practically unrestored —and that is a crowning mercy to relate in the twentieth century. A strange admission, perhaps, and one wonders whether the finished work of those who added to or beautified their churches in mediæval days was looked upon with such rueful faces, as greet the efforts of those who set out to improve the fabric in recent years. Whether the fact that they of old had something to add that was the evolution of church architecture, while we have nothing but the copied work of other days to offer, makes the difference, I know not ; or whether the spirit in which changes were made ; the reverent handling of sacred things rather than the hasty, unconsidered alteration, or sweeping removal—whether this accounts for it, who knows ? but certainly the typical " restorer " is in bad odour, and very often with but good reason.

Therefore I rejoice at the unregenerate condition of Yapton Church. Every year that passes will increase its chance of meeting with better treatment than so many Sussex churches have received at the hands of the renovator. Now there is a spirit abroad which thinks not once nor twice, but many times before making sweeping changes ; and brings the methods of old workers to bear, with patience and love of things so sacred, because so old.

Yapton is quaint for other reasons than those of Georgian origin —the dormer windows, to wit. It has a funny, squat tower, separate and decidedly obese, with a simple cap-roof surmounted— I suppose by way of contrast—by a very long wooden cross. It has large Transition double windows under one semicircular head. Its bulk would seem to have tired it, for it inclines to the south at a distinct angle, and generations of solicitude have added buttress to buttress to correct the tendency to fall, until the support is almost as bulky as the tower itself. Our " restorer " of thirty years ago would have underpinned it, and swept the buttress away. I am glad to hear that the tower, and the south aisle which threatened to follow its example, have both been underpinned, but the overgrown buttress, composed of much homely work, has been allowed to remain as a relic of ancient, anxious care.

The grey old fourteenth-century porch is also quite untouched, its hoary timbers being panelled with brick and plaster to keep out the rain. Like so many of our churches, the building is almost purely Transition as to details, and yet one Norman window remains to tell of earlier work.

The double arcade of diminutive nave arches with octagonal pillars (except one round one) have carved capitals of different design of the rudest character, and the aisles are of the most modest pitch, the north wall being destitute of windows. The south wall has two tiny " port-holes," one quatrefoil and one circular, almost level with the ground. They are indeed " low-side windows " with a vengeance ! If intended to give light, they were not very successful—hence the dormers.

The restored chancel is Early English and its arch is of great width, with a " hump " in its spring, and the east window has three divided lancets under one pointed arch evidently replacing three lancets of earlier date. To correct the settlement the west end of the roof is supported by massive oak beams. They are too quaint ever to be removed, I trust.

The font is circular Norman, with a chevron band round the edge, and nine slightly recessed circular-headed panels, with a

Maltese cross in low relief in each one. These, with some old stained glass, and a fourteenth-century bell, are the chief things to see, and one leaves the church better pleased than with many more pretentious fanes.

The curious name, " Yapton," is supposed to be Saxon, but of a far more poetic form—" Eappa's-town." If nearly everything did not deteriorate with time, it might be a matter for wonder why place-names should invariably become vulgarised.

The village itself is small and scattered. The old canal runs by, but is void of water—hay is grown in its verdant hollow. There is a pleasant stretch of road, some two miles or less, to Clymping. During the latter half of this walk the trees get less frequent, and away towards the mouth of Littlehampton Harbour, if the sun is shining, you will see what is not very common on our coast, except at Rye, the ragged edges of the sand-dunes.

Clymping lies south-east of Yapton. There is a thoroughly Saxon ring to the name. One expects to find traces of old times in visiting it, and although there is nothing quite so ancient as its name, yet the tower of its church runs the title very close. In respect of beauty—that is, beauty of the proudly dignified order—there are few churches in Sussex or any other county to compare with it. Not that it is over-large or lofty, but for a certain distinguished bearing or appearance, due perhaps to the solidity and originality of its Transition tower, and to the purity of its Early English, of which style the main part is built.

Our sketch of Clymping, full of sunshine and vigour, only gives the tower and porch, but it is sufficient to indicate the dignity of the whole fabric. This tower is claimed as " a good specimen of the Parochial Fortress "—to be used as such, I presume, by the inhabitants in case of danger, and the extreme thickness of the walls (4½ feet), and the recesses for the ends of the drawbridge, are among the indications of this. It also shows the weather-moulding of the original Saxon church on the inside of the south transept, at the end of which the tower stands. The tower doorway is very beautiful, with zigzag and dog-tooth mouldings, and there is a zigzag lancet above it piercing the buttress, as at Old Shoreham.

A rare feature of the church is presented by the circular windows above the lancets at the east, west and north ends. The east window is a triple arcade, each lancet differing in width, which provides a problem for the curious. Some of the windows have rusty hinges, showing where the shutters were originally hung before glass was obtainable, and in the vestry is a beautiful Early English " Crusader's " chest, such as Pope Innocent III, on the last day of the twelfth century, ordered to be placed in churches for offerings to enable poor knights to go on a crusade to the Holy Land.

There are some of the original seat-ends in the nave, while the porch is of good design. There are also two fine bells, one of 1636 with the legend " Gloria Deo in Excelsis," and the other, 1654.

It is essentially a church to be seen, and although some things which should be there have disappeared in the course of what is called, oddly enough, " restoration," there is still much to be admired. The stonework fortunately was not touched, and still shows the original hatchet work. As late as 1854 there were good, if dilapidated, screens in chancel and chancel aisle. They have been " restored " to the primitive use of their material, i.e. firewood !

CLYMPING CHURCH.
(*By Louis Ginnett.*)

A large and elegant twelfth-century consecration cross inserted in the interior walls has also been " improved " out of existence. It is strange how things highly valued by some minds are deemed worthless by others. There come periods when the indifference of a community may work untold harm to the precious relics of the past.

Of Clymping itself (quaintly spelt " Climplingg " in an old record and " Clepinges " in Domesday) I have not been able to glean much. The manor belonged to the great Earl Godwin, the forceful father of Harold, slain at the Battle of Hastings, and was given to Roger de Montgomerie by the Conqueror, and afterwards granted by the Earl to the Nunnery of Almanesches in Normandy. In a cottage at Bilsham, two miles to the west of the church, there are the remains of ecclesiastical architecture.  This may have been the sisters' home.

A few rays such as these from the dark clouds of bygone years lighten our path towards a knowledge of Clymping history, but not many.  Thus, the Vicar was not unacquainted with the flavour and qualities of the silvery herring—more or less fresh—for " he hath customarily tythe herrings at flue time," called " Christ's share."   Probably this is not an unknown description of gifts to the Church, but it has a touching sound, and doubtless, in this case at least, Christ's poor had their part in His share :  " I will take of Mine, and give it unto you."   Of these gifts to the Church, there were bequeathed by the Will of Margaret Hartlee, in 1524, various items in loving, homely fashion.   First, in pious phrase, " my body to be bured in the Churcherd of Our Lady of Clymping." " To the altar of the said Church," the lowly gift of 4*d*.   " To the Mother Church (Chichester Cathedral), in like manner, 4*d*."   " To the God's Cross of Clymping (the Rood Cross) my wedding ring." " Item to the Rode-light, one quarter of whete ;  item to every light in the body of the Church, one bushell of whete."   (No wonder the use of votive candles increased in those days !)   " Item to the said Church, a cow (!) for an obitt to be kept yerly, with dirge and masse for my soll, whereof the curet to have for hys labor, 6*d*." Here we have the origin of the word " obituary."   In religious houses a register was kept of the obits or obitual days of bene-factors.   Good old " soll," she at least remembered to give !   In these days the virtue of almsgiving is more and more apt to be left for the few who have kindly hearts and a sense of duty.

While speaking of religious houses, it will not be out of the way to refer to one touch of romance in the neighbouring parish of Lyminster.   In the Confessor's days the Abbey there was presided over by Edgwina the Abbess, but " Love, who is lord of all," found entrance into, and overruled her gentle heart, so that the handsome Suane, one of Earl Godwin's sons, enticed her to " break sanctuary " and marry him, which she did ;  but what in these days would be rather smiled at and openly applauded, in those times was a different matter.   He, or both of them, had to fly to Denmark to escape the wrath of the Church.

The Abbey of Seez in Normandy was also interested in Atherston Manor now chiefly " drowned by the sea," and had lands and a chapel at Farm Place, at which a bailiff-monk was stationed to watch over its interests.   It is still called Bailie's Court, and the house is in Littlehampton Parish, while the ancient chapel adjoining is in Clymping.   This, of course, has led to " finesse " in evading Poor Law requirements.   One of its owners made his servants sleep in the old chapel to make them parishioners of the latter parish. In the same way Clymping has been mulcted in the matter of sustenance. The Arun divides the two parishes also, in part. Ships were moored on the Clymping side, and those apprentices whose time was out during the ship's stay had a legal claim on its Poor Rates. 'Hampton had all the benefit of the trade of the port ; poor Clymping not a doit, except the burdens.

Our second sketch is of a cottage at Wick, east of the river, and is chiefly interesting as being a good specimen of domestic architecture. The house is well built of native flints, and the windows have stone quoins and mullions. The heavy thatched

COTTAGE AT WICK.
(*By Louis Ginnett.*)

roof had and has its disadvantages from risk of fire ; but these in rural eyes are more than balanced by its coolness in summer and warmth in winter. There are many examples of these small tenements in Sussex, which tell a tale of quiet life of toil and prosperity in the old days, when comparatively humble cottagers could build, or have built for them, these substantial dwellings. They are, perhaps, not quite up to our modern ideas of loftiness of pitch, but where doors stood generally open and the inglenooks were so wide, there was probably quite as much ventilation as was consistent with comfort, and to avoid being " blown up the chimney."

# CHAPTER XII

WITH ILLUSTRATIONS BY FRED DAVEY AND LESLIE CARTER.

"AMBERLEY God knows" is a name almost as common in the rural mouth of Sussex as Botley "Assizes" in the vulgar tongue of Hampshire; and Amberley folk are also credited with being web-footed. Both title and assertion have their origin in the situation of the village, which stretches along a low escarpment of chalk into the marshes of the Arun at the foot of the most solitary portion of our Downs. It lies off the main roads, and until our Sussex artists "discovered" it, was probably as little known and visited as any place of human habitation could well be. This would seem to point to the derivation of its somewhat irreverent cognomen. Things differ when seen from various standpoints. Good churchmen might see in it an indication that Amberley was in an especial sense under the protection of Heaven, and in proof thereof point to the fact that until recently it has been an episcopal residence ever since there were Bishops of Selsey; while the ungodly might reply with the rude old saw, "the nearer the church, the further from God"—Amberley requiring a note made of the fact that it was at all within the celestial purview.

There is a variant of the phrase, which Mr. Lucas points out—"In winter, if you ask an Amberley man where he dwells, he says, 'Amberley, God help us.' In summer he says, 'Amberley, where *would* you live?'" "Amberley God knows" is, however, the name it is known by and called of Sussex country folk.

Anyhow, for good or evil, Amberley—with or without the suffix—exists, and those who paint and those who love archæology know and love it, though "all the world forget." Fisher-folk are among its maligners now. Once "Amerley Trout" were fat and well liking, and of flavour fine; the Gentle Angler, Izaak Walton, waxing eloquent over them. But the last record calls them "few and of inferior quality." Thus reputations fall in the scale, and the finny tribe is not even exempt when mankind means to "call a spade a spade."

AMBERLEY.

(By Fred Davey.)

I

The village itself bears witness to its secluded situation.   Most
of the houses are thatched and old enough to satisfy the Knights
of the Brush, to whom ramshackledom and "local colour" are so
dear.   That which the housewife calls mildew and dirt, the artist
blesses and reproduces with his choicest tints.   A long street ends
as in our sketch, at the church, beyond which lies the castle, whose
history is akin to itself in unheroic, humdrum simplicity.   Romance
has endeavoured to plume itself within its walls, but with little
result.   Whether it ever echoed to war's alarms and shocks is very

AMBERLEY CASTLE FROM THE WILD BROOKS.
(*By Leslie Carter.*)

doubtful.   A country residence of the Bishops of Chichester originally, it was "embattled" in mediæval times by Bishop Reede.
Bishop Sherborne, in the sixteenth century, built the dwelling-
house inside the walls.   There are "donjons" and cells below the
entrance which is flanked by two round towers.   The whole is an
oblong of massive walls, and from the marsh to the north forms a
fine view notwithstanding that there are few points raised above
the ruined parapet.   The chapel, inside, has a large beech tree
growing in its midst, and the whole of the enclosure is a beautiful
lawn bordered by young trees.

It was either dismantled by Waller's troops, or an equally destructive enemy—Old Time. That Charles II slept one night within
its walls, in his flight through Sussex, is possible, as it was held by
a faithful adherent, and being at the marsh edge, offered an easy
means of escape in case of surprise.

The Church of St. Michael or St. Paul stands just without the
walls, and is older and more interesting. The nave is Norman
and has three windows of the same style, and the chancel arch is
round-headed, and richly carved with zigzag and other mouldings.
The whole building is spacious and lofty. The need for enlargement, or desire for change, led to the chancel, south aisle and tower
being built or rebuilt in the Early English style. The beautiful
south door is fine Decorated, with natural vine and oak leaves in
the sculptured capitals. A brass, with surcoated figure to John
Wantle, 1424, is in south aisle, traces of frescoes near the chancel
arch, and a stand for the hour-glass near pulpit. This latter provision is eloquent of the garrulity of preachers in our fathers' days.
The font is Norman, and there are two square-headed piscinæ.

One incident in the history of Amberley shows the power of the
Church in earlier days, when even the most haughty of nobles
had to bow to her will. One of the young Earls of Arundel had
to do penance, and be publicly absolved by Bishop Gilbert on
Christmas Eve in Houghton Chapel, close by the castle. " Hunting the deer " was the crime committed by the fiery youth. But
the deer were not his, but the Bishop's, and it was called by the
uglier name of poaching, with the above result. By the way, it
was in Houghton Forest, and on his way to Amberley, that Charles
had that narrow escape from being recognised, the fugitives stumbling across Waller himself and his troops. A good subject this
still untreated by our artists.

# CHAPTER XIII

## TO PULBOROUGH BY RAIL

### WITH ILLUSTRATIONS BY A. S. C.

AT Pulborough, apparently, the Romans drove the first wedge of civilisation into the Weald. Dallaway says there are two great military ways, undoubtedly Roman, which are unnoticed in any of the itineraries, and which penetrate in a right line through the forest of Anderida ; the one from Regnum (Chichester) to Novio Magus (near Woodcote, Surrey), and the other from Pevensey to Holwood Hill and through Bromley to London. Probably owing to there being no strong military station or *castramenta*, the otherwise remarkable and direct road from Regnum to London did not enter into the itinerary of Antoninus. It started originally from Bracklesham Bay or the Port of Itchenor, but this portion has not yet been traced. From the east gate of Chichester it runs to Sea Beach and Bury Farms about a mile from Halnaker. As with so many points on the Downs, the Saxon (being the chief stock on which our language is based) gives it the name of Stane Street, probably from the solid metalling. Leaving the present turnpike, it may be found forming the boundary of fields and properties, and is to be distinctly traced in a more or less perfect state going straight north-east through the North Woods to Gumworth Farm. Within these woods Mr. Martin (in vol. xi. of the Sussex Arch. Coll.) says virgin tumuli are to be found concealed and protected by the trees. He mentions two found at Avisford and Westergate, the stone cists of which had brackets in the four angles, on each of which stood a lamp. One could not help being struck with the conviction that the lamps had been left burning when the coffer lid was finally closed, as though (if it were not indeed a part of the ceremony) the piety of the survivors made them averse to leaving the urn and its sacred contents in utter darkness. Mr. Martin thinks that similar finds might be made in these North Woods, knowing as we do that the Romans were addicted to placing their supulchres by the roadside.

The " way " is not always easy to follow on foot, being overgrown with bushes in places ; but is raised above the ordinary level, and there is no difficulty whatever in tracing it. The " metal-ling " is still *in situ* in places just beneath the turf, which has pro-tected it—and still does—from the wear of wind and weather. The road had various forms, being sometimes forty feet wide, with a ditch on each side and a central mound rising ten feet above the general level, and in other places is like an ordinary road.

Controversy has been rife as to the use of this central ridge. Some think that the Downs were covered with brushwood, and that this elevated position enabled the advanced scouts to guard against ambushes—or for drainage.

To any one imbued with reverence for the past, it is deeply interesting to follow this ancient road. I have done so, and can testify to the pleasure and wonderment to which it gives rise. No one can look upon it without receiving impressions not easily defined, or capable of expression. At Bignor Hill it descends and turns off to the right down to the ploughed fields. Here it is lost, until it reaches a coppice called the " Grevatts," where it appears again as a slightly raised causeway. Here a wooden culvert to drain it was dug up in the " fifties." At its mouth a broken vase was found, and it was probably used as a drinking or washing place.

Leaving the wood, the " way " crosses some pasture lands, with an obvious swell towards a mill stream, on both sides of which hewn stones and broken pottery were also found. Crossing the mill stream the way may be traced, " but faintly," and through a remarkable gap in a sand-bank into the fields behind Coldwaltham Church. Near here, some eighty years ago, there was a large find of Roman coins. From here to Hardham Camp it can only be traced by " the line of aridity or comparative barrenness " of the fields, showing that although the plough has levelled its surface, yet the subsoil is still hard and flinty.

The camp at Hardham was probably more like a temporary bar-rack for soldiers on the march, or a resting-place for travellers. The oak palisades which crowned its rampart have been unearthed. There have been many finds in graves here, even to leathern sandals still laced with a thong.

Another road was supposed to " take off " at the camp and go eastward to Wiggonholt, where 1,800 coins of the third and fourth centuries were found, ranged in the manner of rouleaux, probably to pay the soldiery. From the camp across the swampy ground the " way " is lost. The only certain thing is that Pulborough Bridge was either a ford or a wooden bridge that carried it across the river to the great cutting up the rocky hill, to ease the gradient, which bears witness to the skill and patience of the Roman engineers. From here northwards traces of residences and military posts are

OLD PLACE, PULBOROUGH.

frequent ; and although in Italy it seems in keeping with the landscape to come across the resting-places of the mighty dead—great round towers like the Tomb of Metella—such buildings are scarcely conceivable in our rural prospects. Yet at Holm Street Farm, north-east of Pulborough, with signs of a township of Roman buildings near, antiquarians tell us that the foundations of such a tomb exist by the roadside ; built, moreover, of tufa, brought all the way from Italy for the purpose.

At Broomer's Hill pigs of lead with inscriptions of Tiberius Claudius' reign were dug up. At Borough Farm are other remains of buildings, and at Ashfoldean Bridge farther on, another Roman station like Hardham, the boundaries of which, although broken down by the plough, are still to be traced.

\* \* \* \* \*

Pulborough itself has the usual long street and collection of old and modern houses hugging the roadway apparently oblivious of the dust, but there is a part of it separate from the rest on the crown of the hill near the church, which is charming. Here, gathered together, are several picturesque houses ; the original lych-gate and the church with its fine tower. The cottage at the top of the Roman cutting has been a subject for artists for many years.

The Church of Our Lady of the Assumption is both early and late of architecture—Early English chancel with a Perpendicular nave. The difference in styles is accentuated by the nave being of the very latest Perpendicular—almost Tudor. There are several brasses, a Norman font, and piscina and sedilia of different styles ; and the chancel is not of the same orientation as the nave, which is not an unusual thing in this country.

The surroundings, particularly westward, are very beautiful. There is a delightful path to Stopham, about a mile away, where the finest ancient bridge of eight spans in the county crosses the Arun. It is fourteenth century, and both approaches curve to-wards it, taking away the usual right-angled character bridges are wont to exhibit, and thereby adding to its charm. The view from it northward is most attractive, though the bridge itself stands first in artists' affections.

On your way as you leave Pulborough you pass " Old Place." Custom, like certain deep-delving roots, is not easily eradicated. It is one thing to raze a building to the ground and plough its site, and " another pair of shoes " to wipe out the name of it from the minds of those who knew it in its pristine condition, and hand down the title—if not the memory—to their children's children. It must strike one as strange in rural districts to hear odd points

of mother earth, where naught but tree or grass flourishes, called
by some name which can only have had a definite origin.   It would
be easy to give instances, but it is quite unnecessary.   We may
be grateful that this bias of custom in men's minds—which are
often nimble enough in forgetting services rendered—has preserved
for us the site of many an ancient pile and spot rendered famous
in history.

In the case of our illustration here, custom has, however, suffered
defeat, but has revenged itself by fastening a name to it which

OLD PLACE, PULBOROUGH.
(*By A. S. C.*)

accentuates the antiquity of the spot.   " Old Place " probably
had an earlier and less hoary cognomen.   Some say it was a friary,
and like enough they are right.   The buildings that remain have
an ecclesiastical air, but all Gothic architecture conduces to this,
and the immense barn, which may have been the refectory, may
also have only stored the corn and other fruits of harvest for a
wealthy yeoman.   The gateway which led into a spacious courtyard is now blocked up, but on two sides the original doorways and
windows of carved stone-work remain, over which the heavily
timbered refectory or storehouse is situated.

Friary or not, the fishpond, which usually accompanied such buildings, and the carp are there—the fish, as usual, being of great size and of fabulous age ; almost older than the pond, if that were possible ! We now count the carp a poor thing, and muddy withal, and wonder how the good men of old—to use a schoolboy's phrase— "stood it." One, given to pleasantry, says they were strong men in those days and could stand anything ! Another opines that there was more wine used in the cooking than any native flavour with a proper sense of self-respect could abide, and therefore there was none left to carp—except the diner ! A third gives salt the credit of exorcising the foul spirit from the pond bottom and also

NEW PLACE, PULBOROUGH.
(*By A. S. C.*)

of creating the thirst by which a not less objectionable spirit at times gained the upper hand !

All these, however, are libels. The Gentle Angler had a good word to say on its behalf, and a grand recipe for divesting it of its "muddy vesture." Clean pebbles, cleaner water, cleansing salt, many washings and purifications many times repeated—these, if my memory serves me, were the preparation when carp was plentiful—*and everything else lacking* !

East of the church, not very far from "Old Place," up on the hill, is "New Place," which is newer than the old place but far too old to be a new place itself. Which things are a paradox ; and Custom, not the writer, is to blame for the riddle. "New Place" also is but a shadow of former things, but is well worth a visit.  The gateway is the principal attraction, and is beautifully proportioned.  It bears on its escutcheon the initials I. A. 1569. This refers to the Apsleys, a family of great antiquity.  Equally interesting to the archæologist is the fine old barn close by.  It was undoubtedly built in the time of Edward I, and has lancet windows and stone quoins.  There is something in this old structure which involuntarily raises a feeling of respect for the memory of those who could build their humblest outbuildings so well, and with such regard for the needs of their descendants.  In these days of shoddy and slovenly work, such an example of thoroughness ought to teach its silent lesson to those who think at all.

Inside the house there is not a very great deal of the original work remaining.  One thing will impress you—the chimney-corner in the kitchen, probably part of the original hall.  It has an arch reaching from side to side of the room, and space enough on the hearth to accommodate a cord of oak logs.  Of course, there is a tradition that Queen Bess visited here, but as a historical fact it lacks confirmation.

As you leave, there is a path to the right through one or two beautiful meadows, tree-engirt and undulating, ending in a shady lane which brings you out on to the Storrington road at the entrance to Pulborough.  This is the dusty street spoken of, and it ends at the ascent to the station.

Domesday says that "Uluric (rather a forbidding sort of name) held Poleberge of the Confessor."

# CHAPTER XIV

## THREE DAYS IN WEST SUSSEX (ABOUT 30 MILES)

ILLUSTRATIONS BY LESLIE CARTER, DOUGLAS S. ANDREWS,
FRANK BAKER AND THE LATE JOSEPH DIPLOCK.

ONE is sometimes asked, " Where shall we take a walk which shall not be all high road, with something more than rural views to look at, and—not *too* far, please ? " In these days of long rides and short walks, it would not be easy, in every county in England, to give an answer. But in our favoured county, with its delightfully varied scenery, studded with villages from end to end, with old castles and camps, churches and homesteads, water-mills and wind-mills, pastoral rivers, brooks, woods and downs, it is easier to give itineraries than to find people to foot them.

The modern invention of " week-ends," or the longer period afforded by the Bank Holiday vacations, allow of three days, at least, being available. What would our inquirers say to thirty miles, more or less, spread over these three days, partly by river-side, road, downs, or field-paths, passing *en route* two castles, twenty old villages, with twenty older churches, beautiful views for those who have eyes to see, and all within ten or twelve miles daily ? He who is too poor a walker to cover such distances may stay at home. He who can do this not exhausting requirement, would have ample time to sketch or take photos on the way.

In case any of my readers are on the search for such a walk, I propose to give a rough sketch for them to fill in personally. They must take rail to Arundel, the starting-point. A glance at the map will show village following village in a north and north-westerly direction, at the foot of the Downs as far as South Harting. These villages are : Burpham, South and North Stoke, Houghton, Bury, Bignor, Sutton, Barlavington, Duncton, Burton, Woolavington, Graffham, Heyshott, Cocking, Bepton, Didling, Treyford, Elsted and South Harting. The list is a goodly one, in all conscience, but the distances between each are short, scarcely averaging more than a mile, many being field-paths. From South Harting to Rogate Station, from whence home by rail again.

Lest expectations be raised beyond fulfilment, I will say at once that, with perhaps the exception of Burpham and South Harting Churches, none of them are of great beauty or size ; but each will be found to possess some point of interest, perhaps of regret that the restorer's hand has rested too heavily on them in the sixties and thereabout. Be that as it may, there will be enough collectively amply to repay the trouble taken. My object here will be to add information that the eyes would only see in books of reference.

An hour or two may be spent—and well spent—in viewing Arundel ; but as this book deals with the less obvious features of

BURY, FROM THE WILD BROOKS.
(*By Leslie Carter.*)

Sussex scenery, I will pass on and follow the lovely path by the river to Burpham. I have dealt with Burpham more particularly elsewhere ; but if seen for the first time, the first thing to attract attention will be the great earthen wall which almost hides the village from sight. Its origin is not quite clear. " Probably Roman " is the usual phrase employed when these great mounds are wondered at. Whatever the source, the vallum is there and repays examination. It is seen at once how well it protected the village from attack in olden days, but who the enemy would be is, of course, difficult to determine.

Looking at or from Burpham is equally charming. Seldom is a village so delightfully situated, even in Sussex.

Having spoken of Roman occupation, it may be of interest to glance at the Saxon, in respect of proper names. It is well to remember that most of these are surnames to-day. Domesday gives many of our forefathers' appellations, some beautiful, some

THE ARUN AT NORTH STOKE.
(*By Douglas S. Andrews.*)

less attractive, and many quite unfamiliar, which seems strange, seeing how much more of Saxon we are than of any other of our alien peoples. The usual phrase of the famous book is that " Lewin" —or another—" holds of William." These are some " Sud " Saxon names which were owned by dwellers in Burpham and its vicinity : Lewin—a present-day Sussex name—Ulnod, Brixi, Gida, Frawin,

Corbelin, Roselin and Ernucion. The last has something of the Roman about it, and may have been a survival from that far-off day.

Before leaving "Berchelia" (Domesday for Burpham) don't fail to see the interior of the church (see page 113), with its deeply-carved Norman arches.

The river may cause retracing of steps, but South Stoke Church is also partly Norman and should be visited. It is dedicated to St. Leonard. The tower has a corbel table ornamented with the heads of animals and birds. The main part is Early English, and there is an old altar-slab with five consecration crosses.

The loops of the river are interesting but a little inconvenient. There is a footpath only between the two villages of North and South Stoke. Not far from here two British dug-out canoes were found embedded in the silt, and one of these is at Lewes Castle. The Church of North Stoke is very interesting. It is mainly Early English and Decorated. The large aumbry, and an unusual double niche in south transept—the church being cruciform—a bowl-shaped font, and traces of old stained glass in the east window, will attract attention. The chancel arch is of hard chalk, and is Early English and very curious. The tracery of early Decorated windows should be noted, as well as the " low-side " window.

Houghton is the next in order, and the bridge is perhaps of greater interest than the Early English church, which always receives scant attention from the guide-books, the one item noted being the brass to Thomas Cheyne, 1486.

The bridge, although rebuilt, is a fine structure of five arches, and through Houghton Forest, and over the original structure, King Charles came in his flight from Worcester. In the Forest he had his lucky escape from Morley's troops ; and he discussed " a neat's tongue " at the ale-house near by.

Talking of kings, Saxon coins have been found at South Stoke, of Harold's coining, so evidently fresh from the mint that they must have been lost by some of Harold's Saxons on their way to or flight from the Battle of Hastings. At South Stoke also was a " Swannery," and the duty of the water bailiff was not only to attend to the fish (in old days Arun trout were one of the " four good things of Sussex "), but to " know the swan's nests and seiges " lest any sudden rising of the river should " cold the eggs ; " to report of any firing of guns, whereby the swans and fowls be " frayed " out of their haunts, and " many times killed." This does not mean that swans, like cats, had nine lives. The passage of time alters the sense of words. " Swan-upping day "—to take up swans for marking—became " Swan-hopping day," which has no discoverable sense to the " unlarned." This marking or " nicking " of cygnets has led to another error. There is a hostelry in London called " The Swan with Two Necks," and it is duly figured on the sign-board. But if for " necks " we read " nicks " we see that it has reference to the marking of the King's swans, which were distinguished by two notches. Also, " if any wild swan be caught, it ought to be marked with my Lord of Arundel's marke " —as easy way of adding to property. Among the customs of old days on the Arun, the meshes used in the fishing nets were fixed by a " pin " or measure " sometime kept at Arundel Castle."

Our story, like our walk, being of the casual order, I here remark on the high antiquity of Houghton. It was given by Wilfrid to

HOUGHTON BRIDGE.
(*By Frank Baker.*)

Ceadwalla, the South Saxon King, and we may suppose the site of the bridge to be as old, for " there has always been a bridge here "—which quotation should be a sufficient proof of age !

From Houghton the way brings you to Bury. Like Bosham and Amberley, it is seldom absent from the walls of Burlington House and other London Galleries, nor is it to be wondered at, for the river takes a graceful curve here and the village lies at the bend of the bow, just where, from an artist's point of view, it ought to be. Looked at from east, south, or north, it forms a beautiful picture, and what more is needed ? The grey shingled spire is, of course, the chief object in the view, but the roofs and the fine shapes of the elms are scarcely less attractive, to say nothing of the " gracious line " of the stream.

Historically, Bury gives us a glimpse of the good old times and customs, which we agree to call " good," mentally reserving the comparative term for our own days, and—let us hope—the superlative for those yet to come. Thus the tenants and dwellers at Bury in olden days had many privileges of the " back-handed " order. They were " bound to carry the lorde's corne, cheese and bacon to Shoreham, or any other place adjoining the sea, when appointed to do so." To carry his hay, and work certain days at bedripp (harvesting), a privilege to be had without paying—or being paid, apparently ! Also, " never one of the said tenants, except Raulfe, of Westburton " (lucky dog !), " may marry himself,

NEAR HOUGHTON.
(*By the late Joseph Diplock.*)

his son or daughter without his lord's leave : or sell horse or calf before he have showed the same unto his lord, who may retaine the same ' at a reasonable price ' ! " Oh, the delights of living in Merrie England when Might was Lord and King ! Then the hogs might feed on the beech-mast in Farnfold Wood—for a consideration, of course ; and " of every house where issueth smoake the lorde is to have one henn, called a wood-henn, at the Feast of our Lord, and five eggs at Easter."

Could such a state of things obtain for a time now, I fear there would be one house in Bury—the lorde's—" issuing smoake," and that not by the chimneys only ! One other little pleasure had the tenants of Bury to " round off " their blissful state. They built the lorde's " lot-barne," " he finding timber and a master carpenter," which shows that he was one degree better than Pharaoh of old, liberty making one short step in the course of a couple of thousand years !

By the way, the before-mentioned fine-sounding Saxon name, Ernucion, hails from Bury.

The beauty with which the church dowers the landscape must make amends for the poverty of its interior. "It shows a little Transition work in the nave-pillars and the tower. Note (1) stoup outside south door ; (2) Perpendicular font ; (3) Perpendicular old oak screen ; (4) traces of frescoes "—and the tale is told.

Quite a stretch separates Bury from Bignor, along several miles of pleasant but samely road. So my advice is, add a mile to the walk and many pleasures to the eyes, by " taking to the hills," and dropping down again at Bignor. The first thing you will note is the comparatively wooded character of the Downs west of the Arun. No longer does the line of one bare hill curve to meet another equally naked, which in turn slopes to a third, and so on until lost in the grey-blue distance. Here are large tracts of woodland, not quite forest, but thick shaws ending in fine beech-woods about Slindon and Goodwood ; and across this shaded expanse, the darker lines and groups of elm trees in the levels, with the spires of Bognor and Chichester in the distance ; and beyond—as you have the sun ahead—the molten silver of the sea and its inlets at Bosham and Langston, right away to the Isle of Wight.

If you are wise you will take field-glasses with you, and see how much of the view will render up its landmarks of tower and spire, too far for unaided eyes to discern    But not only south-west and west does beauty lie. North-west rise Blackdown, Hindhead, and the Hogsback, with the dark pinewoods at the foot of the Downs for foreground, and Petworth spire in the middle distance ; and east across the Arun valley the hills to Chanctonbury and beyond, while to the left of them are seen the steeples of Cowfold Monastery and Horsham Church.

Westward, you will note, too, that the grass, except on the higher summits, begins to lose its lawn-like, close-cropped char-acter, and grows more luxuriantly as the hills get more inland, due to shelter from the sea winds. Here, also, the north ridge is more broken. There are more " ups and downs," and no such stretches as from Ditchling Beacon, or from Chantry Down to Amberley.

These views from Bury Hill to Bignor Hill are well worth the climb, and in addition you get a sight of the Stane Street, that wonderful road which runs from Chichester to London, and is still used for long distances in Sussex and Surrey. Here on the top

K

of Bignor Hill you can stand upon its venerable platform—for it is raised above the surface of the down—and can see it point, as Mr. Hilaire Belloc puts it, like a beam, to Chichester spire ; but as a beam widens out, and this contracts, I would rather liken it to the giant spear of Bevis lying along the ground. Although overgrown in places, the road can be followed quite easily, and in many parts the flint metalling is still *in situ*. Turning north-east you can see it descend Bignor Hill and lose itself in the Weald. It can be traced in places between here and Pulborough, but with difficulty. At Pulborough it again reappears, and is now used as the highway for the greater part of the way to the Sussex border and beyond to Dorking.

As you stand and look down on Bignor village you can distinguish to the eastward of it some thatched roofs clustered among the fields and a fringe of trees. This is the site of the Roman villa discovered in 1811 by the plough, in a field called the Berry. It was carefully excavated, and there is no reasonable doubt that it was the residence of the *Propraetor*, or of the legate or governor of the province of the Regni, which was brought under the rule of Rome by Vespasian in the reign of Claudius. It says as much for the Pax Romana as for the Pax Britannica in these days, that a villa reproducing the character and decoration of a Pompeian palace, could be erected on the margin of the Wealden forest with no apparent defensive works other than those provided by the vigilant eyes of the sentinel soldiery. The villa may be described as having been a series of rooms on three sides of an open court-yard, with a colonnade or ambulatory at their doors, the roof of which would probably be supported on Doric pillars. In some half-dozen of these rooms coloured Mosaic pavements were found, more or less complete, and as one of them, when entire, was probably 44 feet by 17, it may be assumed that the villa was of great importance. It covers a space of 650 feet by 350 feet ! Some thirty-six rooms are known to have existed, nearly all of which were paved, some with coarser red or yellow *tesserae*, some with tiles or bricks, but the chief apartments with designs in red, yellow, white and blue. The Seasons, the Goddess Venus, Medusa's head and a charming design of Cupids, habited as gladiators, are among the the chief subjects ; but they should be seen to be thoroughly appreciated.

To the least imaginative of men the sight of these evidences of Roman occupation in its domestic, rather than its military aspect, cannot fail to be deeply interesting. Perhaps I was younger and more impressionable when first I saw the place ; but I must confess that after wonder had subsided, the feeling that succeeded was one of awe. I say it deliberately. It inspired in me a greater sense of reverence than the interior of a cathedral is wont to do.    In a great church the shadows of the mighty dead, grey and ghostly, rise up and pass before the mind's eye.    Here the forms which throng these pictured floors, or stoop to play with the fish in the marble cistern, are, or seem to be, more human and less visionary. They do not appear as cold abstractions, far removed in aim and thought, but as homelier shades born of firelight fancies, not indeed living, nor yet quite spectral.    For it is the magic of the home atmosphere which lingers about these old remains.    Here, besides the classic hypocaust and furnace for warming the rooms, are open fire-places and hearths, so dear to the Englishman—probably the first to be found in a Roman building.    It is pleasant to think that the need of the bright fire to cheer the greyness of the British climate, was felt and welcomed by the austere Roman.    It is a proof of their adaptability to surroundings, a characteristic which is also one of our own traits.

As you descend the hill to visit this famous villa, for assuredly no one would pass it by, there is, or was, somewhere on the hill-side (but most probably on the sandstone strata below) a " molaria " —a quarry for millstones.    This word is only used twice in Domesday, and its exact meaning would have been difficult to define, had not Domesday itself satisfactorily explained it on the second occasion !    It is worth remarking that wherever a watermill is mentioned in Domesday, in most cases it still exists.    This is owing to the fact that tenants were obliged, willy-nilly, to bring their corn to the local mill, and also accounts for their great value, and in no small measure for the independence of the sturdy millers.

Bignor (or in old records, Bygnevre) Church has an early Norman or Saxon chancel arch of unusually large stones, and an equally early font.    There are not wanting those who attribute these to a Roman origin.   The truth is, the border line between the Roman relics and the Saxon imitation of them is so distant in point of time, that there is little data to go upon in determining their exact source.

Our sketch (see next page) gives one of the oldest cottages. Ancient as it is, the materials of which it is in part built—Roman bricks and tiles—go back to a very remote past.

The next village is Sutton, beautifully situated on a knoll under Glatton Hill, from which two springs arise.    From here the richer nature of the woodlands will be apparent to you.    On your left the Downs have turned north and invaded the Weald more suddenly than is their wont, so that chalk and sandy soils are cheek by jowl, with the result that pine-woods flourish almost at their feet. This tract from Burton Park to Midhurst and beyond is by many thought to be the " beauty spot " of Sussex.    Certainly it would be hard to beat.

Sutton Church in the guide-books is described as " of little interest." Verily, the restorer's hand has rested heavily on the chancel. The Transition pillars in the nave are of good design. The west tower is also fine. The font is of Decorated work with eight shafts with beautiful capitals. The east window, though restored, is a worthy ornament to the church. Some old glass remains and Roman pottery have been found beneath the floor.

In the records, there is a story of two monks of Hardham fighting for the deer in Burton Park ; a proof that feasts were as essential as fasts in the life monastic.

COTTAGE AT BIGNOR.
(*By the late Joseph Diplock.*)

This must have been a populous part, for villages follow thick and fast. Barlavington, in old phrase Berleventone, has a tiny church of Transition and Early English, which pleases. It has a quaint old oak door, a squint and a blocked-up arcade.

Duncton lies about a mile away and Burton not far to the north of it. The former has lost its old church, the present one having been built in 1866. The older fabric stood apart until 1876, when it was pulled down. The only ancient things remaining are the sixteenth-century church plate, and the bell. This is the oldest dated bell, perhaps, in England—1389. It is very long in shape. Later bells are proportioned by rule as to height and breadth. The earlier ones were much taller.

Duncton Down (837 feet) lies much to the south-west, and being covered with an extensive copse, does not repay a visit. Little can be seen from it, notwithstanding it claims to be the highest point in the range of South Downs.

Burton Church lies within the borders of the park, amid beautiful surroundings. It is small, but has a Perpendicular screen with rood-loft and remains of painting on it. There are monuments to the Gorings, and a fine brass to Elizabeth Goring, 1558, with arms of the Goring, Pelham, and other families quartered on a tabard over her dress. There is also a frescoed figure in the splay of one of the nave windows.

Your peregrination will be of the return order if you have taken in Burton. You pass again through Duncton on your way to Wool-Lavington. The scenery is so beautiful that you will welcome a second view.

Few places in our county can vie in interest with Wool-Lavington. To the sight-seer merely it is one of the most beautiful spots on earth ; to those who revere the memory of Samuel Wilberforce, the little churchyard will have a charm greater even than natural beauty to attract the pilgrim, for here the saintly Bishop lies beside his beloved wife. In the little Early English church there is a brass to his memory and his pastoral staff has been fixed close to the altar.

Graffham village lies at no great distance. Its church was restored in memory of Wilberforce, and is a handsome structure. The nave piers are Transition, but the rest is Early English. The east window of fine lancets is noteworthy, and the font is Norman. There are a number of Norman and Saxon fonts in Sussex churches, and in some cases, as here, no other trace of that style in the church itself, which points to the total rebuilding of the original structure. Here, at Graffham, the ultimate style had its progress through the intermediate Transition.

A considerable distance separates Graffham from Heyshott— some two and a half miles. In this parish was born the great Free Trade apostle, Cobden, whose economic theories, once fiercely combated, then accepted unreservedly, and now again called in question, have dominated English fiscal policy for so many years. He lies buried at West Lavington, near Midhurst, but was born in a farm-house here. His last years were spent at Durford House, and on Cocking Causeway a pillar is erected to him.

The church, like so many in the district, is Early English, but has some Perpendicular windows, and a curious font, the caps of the angle pillars forming part of the bowl. The nave pillars are worth more than a casual look.

From here your path is a spacious zigzag to take in the villages which lie between here and South Harting. Cocking comes first, and is pleasantly situated under the shadow of the Downs. Its church is good, and repays examination. Norman of an early type, and Decorated are its main styles—the simple and the splendid. When there is such a juxtaposition, there is generally much to see. A fine canopied wall-tomb used as an Easter sepulchre, niches and piscinæ, and an ancient painting of the angel and shepherds, are among the things to be noted.

There is little need to call attention to the character of the scenery. If nothing is said, it is only because it will commend itself without comment.

Bepton follows with a small Early English Church, containing a fine canopied tomb. If it had other features of interest, " restoration " has destroyed them.

Didling lies again under the hills. A more solitary spot cannot well be imagined. The church is of Early English style, and some old oak benches and the altar-rails call for attention. The church was struck by lightning in 1878.

On high ground also lies Treyford and Elsted, the two remaining villages which intervene between Didling and South Harting. *Both* churches are in ruins. The sight grates upon one's sense of loyalty to the piety of our forefathers. The two villages apparently have agreed to build one fane to serve them, and it stands midway with a handsome spire of stone to adorn the landscape. The deserted churches were of Norman and Early English architecture, Elsted possessing an early chancel arch and corresponding nave arcade, with a good Perpendicular window.

Treyford Manor House is an old brick building, pleasant to look upon.

South Harting, our objective, lies some distance farther on. The church's green spire of copper—an unusual feature in Sussex, where the silver-grey of the oak shingles is paramount—attracts attention long before you reach it, and the picture is not spoiled on a closer view. The whole village is good to look upon, and fitly ends our pilgrimage. It is charmingly situated just beneath Harting Down, and is not unknown to artists. Anthony Trollope lived here and Pope's friend, John Caryl, entertained the poet at Lady-Holt, one of the two fine parks.

The church is cruciform and curious. It has several styles, none of which seem to fit the other. The nave arches are unequal, as if enlarged westward, and increased in height. Pillars without capitals raise a mental protest, yet other Sussex churches have them, and in France they are very frequent. Here they are octagonal, and the arch springs from a dainty trefoil canopy, making amends for what always appears, to English eyes, unfinished and bare.

Another peculiarity is evident. For strength, the tower arches have been renewed in a later style than the original Early English, and the dog-toothed chancel arch appears above the other. To guard against a renewal of weakness, the octagon of the pillars projects beyond the mouldings of the arch, in all the four.

The fine roof is Elizabethan—a far cry from the Early English of the fabric. The floor of the chancel is a step lower than the nave. Good arcading in south transept has been mutilated to make room for a Renaissance tomb of 1586, with a kneeling figure in an ugly niche, and two more ugly recumbent effigies perched up on their elbows.

The font is Early English, with too ornate additions to its base, and there are several good Kempe windows, and some others— not good ! The windows are a strange medley of lancets—Decorated and Perpendicular. There was evidently an altar on the rood-screen, when it existed, as there is a piscina above the spring of the south transept arch. In the ruined south chancel aisle are two fine mutilated tombs with recumbent Elizabethan figures, covered by a wooden pent-house.

Altogether, the church is remarkable for its rather *gauche* additions.

Cardinal Pole was rector here in Henry VII's reign.

The view of Harting from the Down should not be missed. It is very beautiful. To see it is worth the climb.

# CHAPTER XV

## THE LITTLE ROTHER (About 14 Miles)

### BY RAIL TO MIDHURST

#### With Illustrations by Arthur B. Packham and Douglas S. Andrews.

NONE of the Sussex rivers have great commercial value, and as the years go by they revert to almost primitive quietness and solitude. The once-used towing-path is either grass-grown or eaten away by the slow scour of the water in the bends, and most of the locks are in ruins. It is not all sadness, these signs of departed utilitarian ways. Rather does it create a great and abiding joy. Other glories have taken their place. Unchecked, the waving reeds and water-plants encroach in sheltered spots. The yellow iris and yellower kingcups flash out in their season ; and the odour of meadowsweet is far preferable to the smell of the barge chimney. No longer the overhanging bushes have their tender shoots torn off by the trail-rope, and their branches held out to meet those on the other bank—and form a shade Endymion would love—ruthlessly chopped off to keep the passage clear for coal.

Now once more might Keats wander in the upper reaches of the Ouse, the Arun, or Western Rother, and people them with nymphs and naiads, fauns and satyrs. Then if he left, as was his wont, the sober paths of fact, and indulged in flights of fancy to his heart's content, who would forbid him, or wish to bring his poetry into prosier channels ? His soul was steeped too deeply in classic imaginings to keep its outpourings within the narrow limits of time and sense. Only to such gifted natures is the power given to describe the things seen from within, rather than those the eyes rest upon. Those whose souls re-echo only the failing notes of Apollo's lyre, heard afar off, are gifted too ; but if they be wise, their word-spinning should be as Nature prompts, each in his own speech, not the affectation of some style, more or less " elegant," and more—than less—wearisome !

" By thy wild banks, by frequent torrents worn," is the opening of a sonnet, " To the River Arun," by Charlotte Smith, " the

Sussex Poetess." The remainder is in the stilted phraseology of its day, and deals with " the mournful muse " and " rustic waves " and " tide " of the sleeping Arun in quite the then approved style. In the sense that it is natural and rural, its banks may be called " wild," just as we speak of a " wild-garden " where Nature works her own sweet will ; but how little of the charm of the stream does the sonnet embody. It tells of oak and beech, of first-born violets, hazel trees, low murmurs, and—of course—the earliest nightingale ; but so do a thousand poems of the time in just so

IPING BRIDGE.
(*By Arthur B. Packham.*)

many similar words. Not a touch of real music from vibrating heart-strings afire with love for meadow, stream, and shade ; only elegant phraseology which could hit off the characteristics of either mountain torrent or purling stream with charming disregard for what Carlyle called " the veracities." Read any one of these old-time effusions, and then read Tennyson's " Brook " ! Fancy the winding Arun or Rother having a " torrent " or a " tide " in its upper reaches ! True, it has its rise and fall. If " rustic waves " mean ripples, it certainly has these. Floods of tears when February comes may scarp a hollow in its grassy banks, and quiet murmuring among the sedges may tell you it flows ever sea-wards ; but the only " wild " things about its banks are the flowers.

Perhaps the stilted fashion of the gardens of those days, with yew hedges trimmed to any form but Nature's, would give an added meaning to a word. Hence, our creeping Arun's " wild " banks. It matters little. Call them what you will, beauty is still there to enjoy. If you strike its course at Midhurst, and face its flow, " e l e - gant" phrases will soon fade from the mem-ory. Nature's language is of t h e simplest Anglo-Saxon, and a b h o r s long w o r d s and polished periods.

WOOL LANE, MIDHURST.
(*By Douglas S. Andrews.*)

One disad-vantage of the falling back of our river to sylvan s o l i - tude, is that riverside paths a r e a p t t o v a n i s h, o r else to be disputed b y t h e riparian owners. I am told that from Midhurst Mill the left bank can be follow-ed to Wool-beeding Bridge, by dint of perseverance and pushing through coppices, and running the risk of prosecution for trespass ; but much of the high road to the bridge is so beautiful that I recom-mend it, especially as Easebourne can be seen on the way. It is not a village of old timbered houses and quaint corners, but is rendered charming by the wealth of rambler roses, clematis, jasmine, and other equally odorous climbers embowering the porches and adorning the walls. There is a grace about the place which one is wont to associate with feminine influences, and who can say that it is not due to the old-time example of the nuns whose ruined house lies in the park just south of the church ? The priory was founded by Sir John Bohun about 1250, and so far as is known prospered until 1441, when a visitation disclosed such irregularities, due to the worldliness and love of display of the prioress (whose fur trimmings were worth 100 shillings), that two administrators were appointed. Whether the gay lady found the soft side of these two worthies can only be conjectured. In any case their supposed economies, and the sale of the afore-said furs to reduce the debt of £40 availed little, the liabilities nine years later having risen to £66. This lady seems to have been the chief cause of trouble, the sisters themselves being stinted to provide her extravagances of dress and living ;

" Thus bad begins, but worse remains behind."

The canker seems to have spread, and in 1478 the sisters also were involved in more serious backslidings. Thenceforward the rule was either too strict or too lax, until in 1535 the King ordered it to be closed, and the few ladies then resident " rejoined the world to spread at their pleasure the mutual recriminations " indulged in at the visitations of the Bishop.

The south wall of the church formed one side of the nunnery cloisters, the chancel aisle being used as the convent chapel. The door communicating seems to have wrought much harm, and it was ordered to be kept locked. Even this failed, and, too late, Sir David Owen, whose effigy in armour lies under a canopy in the north aisle, built an oaken gallery entered from the " dorter," or dormitory only, so that " nobody might see them."

The refectory still stands, with gaunt mullionless windows on the west and south, and a blocked-up entrance in the north wall. Here Queen Elizabeth " and her lordes " were most bountifully feasted, after the suppression, by Lord Montague. Another build-ing with an oblique arched doorway, and evidence of other arches, formed part of the conventual pile.

The convent bells, one dedicated to St. Anna, and both orna-mented with various devices of lions' heads, etc., still hang in the church tower, which had a spire when Grimm sketched it. The church itself has been largely rebuilt. The nuns' gallery, or " quere," disappeared long ago. Very little, therefore, is ancient except the tower and two arches—one corbelled—in the nave. These and the font are Transitional. Its chief feature is the tomb to Sir Anthony Brown, first Viscount Montague, which was brought from Midhurst Church. It is surmounted by the kneeling figure of the knight, and his two wives lie beneath on a wide altar-tomb.

Other figures and shields bearing blazons surround it. It is partly coloured, and a very rusty helmet lies at the foot. I see no reason why such relics should not be kept bright, instead of mouldering into holes, and finally falling to pieces. I suppose it to be the knight's casque, but there is nothing to indicate it.

Another large altar-tomb to the sixth Viscount, 1767, and the effigy in full armour of Henry the Seventh's uncle, Sir David Owen, as before mentioned, lies in the north aisle.

The road westward, fringed with fine trees, grows more beautiful as you approach Woolbeding, being cut through the rock. The banks on either side are rich with ferns and moss, and the decorative greenery which always accompanies these uneven surfaces, due to the scantier opportunities afforded by the crevices only. What a place for primroses in spring, and later, how the foxglove seems to delight in such banks, where its ascending plumes are seen to the best advantage! The road is a fit approach to an equally beautiful valley.

" Woolbeeding " is Saxon, and so is its church. The chancel is modern, but quite tastefully added to the very ancient nave. The oak sedilia and panelling throughout are good, and a Jacobean altar-railing has pilasters of a most refined type. On the altar-steps there is a fine Oriental rug of very intricate design and harmonious colouring. How often the work of Eastern looms is found in our churches. They never seem out of place to me, although the art that inspired them is " far as the poles asunder " from the Gothic. Nor does the use they are put to in our sanctuaries add to their lustre. Rather does the exquisite art and weaving, the loving patience expended in their production, fit them for the holy office. They do honour to the church they adorn.

The screen outside the chancel arch is unusual, making a more spacious sanctuary. There is probably room and to spare in the nave for all the inhabitants of the little village. The carving in the roof is good and the seating is simple and admirable. The carving on the lectern is also beautiful, but very fragile.

There are portions of old stained glass in two of the windows, with Renaissance figures. This was brought from Mottisford Priory, in Hants. Judas can be seen leading the soldiers to Gethsemane, with a view of the walls of Jerusalem. The comforting angel is also figured, but the whole is composed of fragments. The sleeping Apostles can be discerned in the south window. My impression is that much of the one belongs to the other. An expert might make much more of the fragments. The east window is an early Kempe, and is very good.

The pilaster-strips on the outer walls proclaim the Saxon origin of the nave.

The churchyard, with its avenue of yew trees and well-kept turf, suggests, as indeed it should, calm and repose.

Adjoining are the beautiful gardens surrounding Woolbeeding House, much of which is old. The bronze Neptune of the fountain came from the quadrangle of Cowdray. This was the home of our " poetess."

A broad and shady road brings you to the bridge. It is old and worthy, like many another, both above and below. One of its four spans is silted up, and therefore makes it a more attractive sketch.

STEDHAM FROM THE RIVER-BANK.
(By *Arthur B. Packham*.)

Although " the Arun, which doth name the beauteous Arundel," as Drayton says, is the best known title for the river, the local name for the stream that rises in Hampshire, a few miles beyond the border, and falls into the Arun at Stopham Mill, is the Rother—or Little Rother. It flows through the most beautiful part of Sussex, and receives other streams of smaller volume all the way. Enough interest lies upon and near its course to make it almost as historically attractive as it is to the sight.

Near Selborne, the home of Gilbert White, whose delightful writings have a perennial charm, it leaves the " caves of earth " and begins its lovely course. Many of the facts given in White's *Selborne* were noted on its banks. Three branches leave the parent fountain, but not for long. At Lyss they meet like children who have been separated at play, and hand in hand pass near Petersfield Heath. Thence a sudden turn brings them to the Sussex border, where the Nursted stream awaits them, and together they flow on under Dureford Bridge towards the east.

Your route, however, is westerly from Midhurst. At Wool-beeding Bridge the right bank can be struck, and few views will meet your eye more charming than this narrow, winding mead enclosed on one side by a crescent bank of the most umbrageous foliage of the loftiest trees, with the shallow river fringed with willows and bushes on the other.  It is just the scenery that inspired the earlier painters before the love of clear sunlight, air, and distance asserted their sway upon artists.  This view is typical of a thousand canvasses, with classical group or figure, to be seen in any picture gallery of our older mansions.

This sylvan scene ends at the stepping-stones leading over to the modern Roller Mill, whose presence in such surroundings will give you something of a shock.  Engineering science and the rage for time-saving has indeed brought milling to a " fine " art—if white, overground flour, robbed of half of its nourishment, is beneficial to the community.

STEDHAM CHURCH.
(*By Arthur B. Packham.*)

Stedham Bridge, close by, is a fine structure of six spans and would make a good view, only that the mill-dam below " drowns " the arches by keeping the water above the spring at the curve.

Stedham is one of the oldest villages, as its purely Saxon name reveals, on the river. There is little, alas, of the old church to linger over.  Churches, in their material fabric, cannot, like Rother stream, " go on for ever."  Mortar will crumble and stone decay, and Stedham Church has little of its Saxon walls left.  The new lancets and east window are filled with good glass in memory of those who fell in South Africa.

Many interesting relics were found in pulling down, among them mural paintings of uncommon merit and colouring.  St. Christopher, St. George and the Dragon were among the subjects ; but although a long article is printed concerning them in the Sussex Arch. Coll., that, I take it, is all that is preserved.  These " continual sermons for those who could more easily be taught by the eye than by the ear " were numerous in Sussex churches, and the pity of it is their ruthless destruction at the hands of the " restorer."

There were brasses, too, as the matrices in the slabs prove, but they also are lost. Stedham was Earl Godwin's, and the tenant who held it is mentioned in Domesday. Her name was Eddiva. Later, part of the revenues of Stedham—" one knight's fee "—went to support a " God's House " (hospital) in Portsmouth.

Next beyond Stedham is Iping. Wayfarers in the region watered by Western Rother are often obliged to cross it, and although grateful in a way for " the bridge that carries them over," give little heed to its appearance, age, or design. Yet many of them are several hundreds of years old, and quaint withal. Our sketch of Iping Bridge shows what beauty may nestle about their ancient masonry and surroundings. Of nothing else is the saying so true, that " their value is only realised when they are gone." A broken bridge is a calamity for the whole region round about, and its disappearance or rebuilding is no less a loss in an artistic sense. Many a lovely picture has been painted with such a bridge as Iping for its theme, and only old work seems to

STEDHAM BRIDGE.
(*By Arthur B. Packham.*)

be in complete harmony with art. New bridges seem so very new and uninteresting.

As for beauty, our river has enough and to spare. It may not, perhaps, have quite the charm which appertains to the Arun proper at Stopham Bridge—the most delightful structure in the way of a bridge in all Sussex—for the middle reaches of all rivers are usually the most lovely, due to the breadth of the stream. But there are smaller bends in the upper reaches, and more surprises, if less breadth of view. The water has more life, more light and shadow where it runs more swiftly. Further down the lilies grow in quiet pools, just bending their long stems to the current ;

but here the ripples take their place, and only in the back waters are lilies to be found. As the beauty is less, so are the beds of reeds and iris in extent, but the upper waters run through woods and smaller meadows, and there is more variety where there is less range.

Iping has no antiquity to welcome you within its church, which was rebuilt in 1840. It is erected on the foundations of a Norman church, of which style it may be presumed the older building was. Among these foundations, fragments of Roman vases and urns were found, which opens up the interesting problem of whether the site was a Roman cemetery. Land once consecrated to the dead has often received consideration from later faiths. It is, or should be, holy ground. Yet the bones of the mighty dead have not always been allowed to rest in peace. A poorer revenge, indeed, can scarcely be conceived, unless it be, to unearth and scatter to the four cardinal winds of heaven the ashes in a Roman urn. This last outrage would seem to be too

CHITHURST CHURCH.
(*By Arthur B. Packham.*)

petty, or forgetfulness had dulled the edge of religious animosity, maybe. In any case, Iping is not the only Sussex church connected with Roman remains. Arlington, near Hailsham, preserves an urn found in restoration.

Chithurst, with a tiny church close to the river, lies next. It has a chancel arch of Saxon workmanship and a Norman window, a lancet, a squint, and an old altar-slab with crosses. An alms-dish, with quaint figures of Adam and Eve, is treasured. A small priory existed near the church. It is now a farm-house, some of the windows of which belonged to the religious house, whose holy men lie interred in the churchyard.

Following the windings of the stream through delightful meadows, you are brought to Trotton Bridge. The bridge has special features of interest in the ribs beneath the arches. It was rebuilt—together with the fine church—by Thomas, Lord Camoys, in the fifteenth century. It still spans the unresting stream in quaint beauty, and may a long period of usefulness lie before it. May the tide of water and of life pass beneath and over it for many a long day, ere its sturdy, vaulted ribs make way for ugly iron girders.

Why Time, which usually beautifies most things as they grow old, should in almost all cases vulgarise names, is hard to say. Perhaps it is because man has a hand in it ; but so it is. Our own town of Brighthelmstone, if more quickly designated, lost a third of its title, and most of the beauty of it, when the second syllable was dropped. Domesday has " Traitune." Trotton is the depth of commonplace after this. " What's in a name," its inhabitants might urge, " if it has distinction in other ways ? " " Did it not belong to Githa, the mother of King Harold ? Has it not passed through several descents of the knightly house of Camoys, one of whom (the husband of Shake-

OLD HOUSE, CHITHURST.
(*By Arthur B. Packham.*)

speare's ' Gentle Kate,' whose first spouse was Hotspur) led the left wing of the English Army at Agincourt ? Is not its church possessed of many ancient and curious tombs and brasses, well worth a visit ? And last, but not least, as regards Trotton—however dead the rest of Sussex may be to the fact—was not the poet Otway born here ? " The " poet " Otway indeed ! In his own county it is, alas, necessary to label him, lest he be undistinguishable from the " common herd " bearing the like South Saxon name.

If our stream had nothing else to grace or mark its banks, the birthplace of one of the first of Sussex poets, and not the least among the chief of England's playwrights, should give it a rare distinction. But it remains true of Sussex, as of other counties, that one of her most brilliant sons is unknown to all but a few, and by these not too well acquainted.

L

If the last lines could catch the eyes of ninety-nine out of every hundred of Sussex folk dwelling in the Weald or on the Downs in this year of grace, I wonder how many would know to whom reference is made. If, in addition, they were told that next to Shakespeare in dramatic poetry stands a Sussex poet, the characteristic gravity of gaze, for which South Saxons are noted, might widen and deepen, but that is all. Centuries of an agricultural bent have endowed them with that "bovine stare," and the eyes have grown to greater importance at the expense of the ears and the general intelligence. When the strange news has slowly sunk through these unaccustomed channels, the mouth will broaden into a grin of incredulity, but the eyes show no sign, and when the smile has faded away, so has the desire to know more of the Sussex man who stands next to Shakespeare in depicting the power of human passions! Even the Bard of Avon is only known to many of them by name and fame—their own poet by neither the one nor the other!

TROTTON CHURCH.
(*By Arthur B. Packham.*)

Having "delivered" myself, I pass, like our stream, to "fresh woods and pastures new." I would like to tell the whole story of "Gentle Kate" and her lover - husband Hotspur, both territorially connected with Sussex; but it is too long. That her name was really Elizabeth shows that Shakespeare was well aware, for all his question, that there is a good deal in a name. It may absolutely ruin the best of poetry—an ugly or unmusical name. (No better instance can be quoted than that of Tell's invocation, where the "yes, Emma," simply kills the sentiment—such as it is, the whole speech inclining towards rant.)

Gentle Kate seems to have been equally happy in her second choice. Lord Camoys was another brave, and in some respects, a better soldier than Hotspur, being less impulsive. In Trotton Church a fine brass depicts him holding the hand of Gentle Kate, and their infant son at their feet. This attitude may be the usual one in old brasses, but there is little doubt that it represented the bond between them.

Only Rogate lies between Trotton and the border, and it is fully a mile from the river. If you decide to take it in, you will see a handsome, enlarged church, rather over-restored. The pillars and arches of the nave are Norman or Transition. The timbered roof of tower, the sedilia, aumbries and piscina, are worthy of notice, a stoup with a coloured star at the back, an old crusader's chest, seventeenth-century candelabra and memorial tablets to the De Fyning and Paget families. There is a shingled spire.

These and the village are worth the walk from the river. Here let me confess that I have not traversed those portions of the banks that lie between Rogate Bridge and the border. Nightfall and bridge were reached together, so I am unable to say if the two miles between here and the site of Dureford Abbey are practicable, or whether there is a path. It is sure to be charming scenery.

The history of Dureford Abbey is fully given in the Sussex Arch. Collections, and is well worth reading for the insight it gives into the formation and life of the smaller monasteries.

The only remains are mere fragments of arches, and a tomb with a raised cross, roughly built into the garden wall of an old moated farm-house, which is the site of the vanished abbey. So completely has it disappeared, that it seems impossible to believe that only the fish-ponds and these few carved stones and tiles are its sole remains ; and yet it flourished for four hundred years !

Its founder was Henry Hosee, or Hussey, in 1150. First, it seemed much as it is now—" If you wish to leave a name behind you, build a church." The mediæval equivalent was—" found a monastery." There was little hesitation in following this advice, because in the founder's mind the interpretation probably suggested itself that perpetual prayers by professional monks were more likely to be acceptable than his own perfunctory devotions. Anyway, these foundations for White, Black and Grey friars were laid like mushroom-spawn in rich soil. They sprung up in all directions. Sussex had others besides Dureford, and the chief trouble with all of them was lack of means.

The records describe the perpetual struggle with poverty, and the various means taken to raise funds. Looking back, it may be said that had the Church been as faithful, unselfish and careful for the souls of her children, as those children had been for her temporal needs, Dureford Abbey might, in altered rule, perhaps, still rise in beautiful old age on the banks of the Western Rother. But it is not so. A sterner decree than even " Ichabod " has gone out against it, and were " the doleful creatures, dragons and dancing satyrs " spoken of by Isaiah at present existent in Sussex, they would have to find other deserted houses than Dureford, of which " not one stone remains standing on another."

Grimm in 1782 sketched the remains which had been built into a farm-house, which has since disappeared. The few pieces of stone preserved seem to show that it was of Early English architecture.

It is impossible to leave Dureford Abbey history without a reference to the upholding of the authority of the law of England over any foreign jurisdiction, whether civil or religious. Dureford, owning Premonstre in France as its parent, paid tribute money to that Order and its Abbot. Any such payment to aliens became illegal by the Statute of Carlisle, 1307. Premonstre requisitioned the English Houses in 1310 for their annual remittances, but the Abbots, fearing the wrath of the King, excused themselves. This alone points to the wholesome influence the civil law had upon religious bodies in England at this early period. Even the threat of excommunication which succeeded had no effect, in view of the express command of the King forbidding such payments. Excommunication duly followed, and also an appeal to the Pope. If there was an occasion in which that dignitary might have been expected to uphold vested interests and foreign control, this would appear to be that occasion. But the doggedness of the English character was fully appreciated at Rome, or it may have been considered an opportunity of curbing the power of these great Orders. The result was the non-suiting and censure of the Abbot of Premonstre for imposing taxes contrary to the laws of the Order and for the burdensome character of his visitations, " when countless monies had been received and extorted by him." So the solemn rite of bell, book and candle had to be cancelled and absolution given. After this, Premonstre took very little personal interest in the English branches of their Order, deputing one of the English Abbots to act for them.

With this we must bid farewell to the Western Rother, and making our way to the station at Rogate, take train for home. I am aware that many beautiful spots, such as Midhurst and Cowdray, have been omitted ; but this is intentional, the object of these papers being to call attention to the lesser known features of our county.

The whole river is delightful. We dwellers by the sea and under the Downs scarcely know the beauties of the Western Rother, and the north side of the same hills about Harting and Elsted.

BOXGROVE PRIORY CHURCH.

(*By Douglas S. Andrews.*)

# CHAPTER XVI

## OVING, TANGMERE AND BOXGROVE (6 MILES)

### BY RAIL TO DRAYTON STATION.

### WITH ILLUSTRATIONS BY DOUGLAS S. ANDREWS AND ARTHUR B. PACKHAM.

THESE papers, while giving accurate information as to the routes, require the reader to second such " with the forward child, understanding," as Touchstone says, and will be not less plain with the aid of a good map. There are convenient pocket " Ordnance Maps " dividing our county into sections, and these I would strongly advise those who seek for pleasure in seeing Sussex to obtain. Not only do they point the way, but often indicate places worth seeing just off the track. Not that this particular walk requires a map. The most casual wayfarer could follow this information. A footpath points directly to Oving steeple just outside the station gates, but it saves its character by winding slightly. It goes through meadow and cornfield, with fine trees bordering the fields and the Downs in blue woodiness far to the north, Halnaker Mill being prominent on its bare hill, and Tangmere Church lifts its tiny spire among the trees to the left. A number of brooks run through these " long level lands," no less than three, bridged by stile and plank, being crossed on the way.

Oving has an importance and dignity all its own, in that it has been considered a sort of half-way house to the Bishopric, and other dignities of Chichester. Moreover, one of its vicars, deprived for loyalty in 1660, afterwards became Bishop of Peterborough and Norwich.

There is an old saying that it is good to " live under a crozier," and the very uneventful history of Oving would seem to bear out the truth of the proverb ; for if it can only point to its connexion with the Church, and a past of sacerdotal tranquillity, there is at least nothing against it. Nay, let it not be forgotten that Shopwike Egle, a very ancient manor within its borders, was part of the Honour of the Eagle (de Aquila) of Pevensey Castle, and William Mortein, son of King Stephen, was Lord of the Eagle. This manor

was given by Henry I to Reginald Hareng, a veteran soldier who
had been wounded in the King's service.

There are many items of interest in the history of Oving : one,
of the list of precentors, or " chanters," as they are quaintly called,
the first of whom was, in 1220, Karlo, which name is still among
us, but as a favourite name for the " friend of man." Then, just
as Hove should be called Hoove, the proper pronunciation of Oving
is Ooving. The Ecclesiastical Commissioners are now the Lords
of the Manor and of the emoluments of the " Chanter." In the
old days part of the income went to the chantry of St. Pantaleon,
Martyr, A.D. 302 (of Nicomedia, and physician to the Emperor
Galerius Maximianus). One of the Deans of Chichester in 1332
founded a Chantry in the Chapel of St. Faith, at the Cathedral,

THE MANOR HOUSE, OVING.
(*By Arthur B. Packham.*)

for the repose of the soul of a vicar of Oving ; but whether the
endowment failed or faith waxed cold, in 1441 the Chantry priest
did not celebrate, and trees grew in the Chantry. A bequest of
Thomas Sandam of two bushels of barley each to the rood and
*beam* lights, the latter a term often met with in old records, enables
us to locate its position. It was hung from the beam, and is expressly stated to be " in the quire before the Blessed Sacrament of
the altar." Many an antiquarian puzzle has been cleared up by a
search among musty will parchments.

Oving has also provided a loyal member of Parliament in
1695–1713, William Elson. He sent " two dozens of wine " that
the lady visitors of the Lady Mayoress of Chichester might drink
Her Majesty's health (Queen Anne) on Coronation Day, and £25
to make " the conduit run with wine," a custom " more honoured

in the breach than in the observance," I suspect, and at best but a bestial observance, a remanet of the *good* old times.

Oving had two other prebendal estates in Colworth and Woodhorn. Drayton Priory, founded in 1149 as a cell to the Abbey of l'Essaie in Normandy, was appropriated and given by Edward III to Boxgrove. But gifts from royal hands were of an evanescent character. It was "seized by the Crown and sold" in 1535, one of its subsequent owners rejoicing in the alliterative appellation of "Bet Boniface." The Duke of Richmond is now its owner.

The two fields near the church were called Bell-rope Fields, the rent being applied to the purchase of bell-ropes; but the

OVING CHURCH.
(*By Arthur P. Packham.*)

churchwardens let it lapse at the beginning of the last century. The cruciform church was built in 1220, and is a fine example of Early English throughout, except for one or two good Decorated windows. It evidently replaced an earlier building, the foundations of which were recently uncovered, and of which fragments of zigzag moulding are inserted in the north transept wall. The nave is of ample width, as if a double arcade of Norman arches had been removed. Two lancets high up in what would seem to have been the aisles on each side of the tower, point to the same supposition; but the somewhat drastic refacing of the outer walls has obliterated traces of what might have been Norman windows.

It was "restored" in 1840, and as usual in restorations of that date, a clean sweep was made of anything ancient, rendering it

eminently respectable.   Certainly, by an account given, it was
badly in need of repair.   One of the good things then done was the
ejection of an enormous gallery erected in 1787, of which erection
an entry is triumphantly recorded in the Parish Registers, that it
was by subscription of vicar and inhabitants " for the conveniency
of the singers ' setting ' together."   When it was perpetrated, it
must have brooded like an inky cloud over the worshippers for a
hundred years, until a wiser generation " bundled it out neck and
crop "—as Sussex folk say when they mean to be emphatic.

One of the vicars, Thomas Carr, tided over the troublous times
of the Commonwealth.   Whether he was of easy disposition, or
had friends in high places, is not recorded.   Certainly he " experi-
enced the Established Church as Episcopalian, then Presbyterian,
and Episcopalian again.   He saw the Book of Common Prayer
abolished, and the Presbyterian Directory enforced by penalities,
and he lived to see the former restored."   In those days it was
probably no disadvantage to be vicar of a drowsy rural parish.

The dedication of the church was lost in the mist of indifference
which settled over the spiritual life of England in the seventeenth
century.   The windows being all in threes had suggested that it
was originally raised to the name of the Holy Trinity ;  but it is
now known to be to St. Andrew.

There is some good stained glass ;  that filling the Decorated
east window being quite beautiful—designed, I opine, by Burne-
Jones or a disciple of his.   The subject is Faith, Hope and Charity,
with figured square quarries below, and laurel or bay branches
above ;  the quatrefoils being filled with a floral pattern.   The
two outer figures have silvery-blue over figured garments of gold
and white, while Hope has the colour reversed—blue garments
with white robe.   Each has a halo of light ruby or cerise, of great
beauty of colour.

The triple lancets in south transept are by Kempe, of angels
with censers and scrolls about a Madonna and Child, with figured
purple-blue setting.   The effect of the whole is most satisfying.

The other windows are various—" poor to middling," as country
folk say.

Under the communion table is an altar-stone with five consecration crosses, and the north door is worthy of note.   The font is
thirteenth-century.

One little act of kindness by one of the ancient " Chanter " vicars
deserves special mention.   Roger de Clare gave his faithful servant
a piece of land in Oving " for him and his heirs for ever," and in
return exacted only "the rendering of a garland of roses for the church
on the Feast of the Nativity of St. John the Baptist."   It is not
unlikely that in this extract the dedication of the church is revealed.

A few hundred yards north of Oving the road turns westward, and a stile under a lofty elm leads to a path across the fields to Tangmere. Its position so near the former and to Boxgrove gives one food for thought as to the reality of the religion of our forefathers. They were not content to let others provide them with spiritual necessities. Each little community must have its little church, of which tiny sort Tangmere is an example. The proximity of the Cathedral town would stimulate zeal. Churches are " as plentiful as blackberries " in this neighbourhood.

The nave is Norman, with small, round-headed windows high up, as if for defence. Lancets have been introduced with the Early English chancel, while the chancel arch is Transition springing from corbels. Two long lancets, wide apart, as at West Wittering, pierce the eastern wall, and a round-headed niche for a saint's statue, with cusps, is recessed beside the chancel arch on the north side.

The font is very primitive, a sloping bowl in the shape of a flower-pot on a circular base.

The very rude and strange carving, forming the head-stone to one of the tiny Norman windows, may be the handing of the head of St. John the Baptist to Salome ; but is beyond all things archaic in workmanship, the figures having enormous heads. Two projections between them may be meant to represent the sun and moon. This sculptured stone may be Saxon. I have seen no mention of it except in one instance. Our archæologists might be able to determine the subject.

Few churches have old silver chalice and paten. These at Tangmere are Elizabethan in design and dated 1693. In the churchyard is a notable yew-tree.

A mile further north, through the same fruitful fields bordered by elms, which, if not " immemorial " are of surpassing beauty, you come to one of the few famous churches of Sussex—Boxgrove Priory. It is only a fragment of its former self, but archæology is to be congratulated on the existence of this " fragment." As you approach it, a sense of the mediæval gradually possesses your mind. In these material days it may be rash to attribute this impression to that invisible aura or emanation which may well proceed from such sacred and venerable walls. We may put all such explanations aside as superstitious and out of date, but the feeling is there : it may be a common experience to all who come across fine old churches and abbeys asleep in the sun, and dreaming away the hours as old age is wont to do, unconsciously investing itself with a sense of detachment from the world.

With old religious buildings it is impossible to escape this influence, and the reverence it begets. Its effect may be greater—I

think it is—where other buildings are not immediately in evidence.
It is so at Boxgrove. From the south its massive bulk is mainly
visible, embosomed in stately elms. If the sun is shining, its
ancient walls put on such sober brightness among the dark trees
as might illumine the robe of a grey friar sunning himself in its

BOXGROVE PRIORY CHURCH.
(*By Douglas S. Andrews.*)

priory orchard. If you see it thus, and have, beating within your
breast, the heart of a pilgrim on his way to visit the shrine of
Boxgrove for the first time, you need not fear that you will be
wanting in reverence on a nearer view. The sacred influence
has already enveloped you, and you enter its door, expectant
of a blessing from its holy associations, although no voice from
the high altar may utter it in sound.

One wishes that the enthusiasm which inspired our forefathers to tramp long miles over dangerous roads, to kneel before the shrines of St. Mary and St. Blaise in Boxgrove Church, could still inspire all Sussex folk in these degenerate days to do likewise, or, at least, to go and see for themselves. Then would the dry-as-dust descriptions, which make the very name of guide-book anathema, be unnecessary. Then would the sight of noble arch and column, chantry-tomb and mullioned window, bring exaltation to the spirit, and the stately interior would rise in majesty before the mind's eye whenever the memory recalled the day of visitation. But times have changed, and those who cannot "go a pilgrimage" must be content with the reiteration of archæological terms and description more or less unintelligible !

I would rather tell its story, as it might have appeared to one of those pious pilgrims allowed to follow the devotions of the Prior and his brethren, from behind the beautiful oaken grille of the wooden gallery filling the arch of the north transept. A wall across the nave just west of the central tower divided the edifice in two, of which the western half is in ruins.

There is still discussion as to which portion constituted the Priory church, as distinct from the parish church. Perhaps the evidence is in favour of the present building being the Priors' church. As in many great conventual buildings, the original parish church would appear to have been enlarged at both ends, as the Priory grew in wealth and importance. This is seen in the invasion of the windows of the upper story of the Norman tower, by the higher roof of the Transitional clerestory.

From the vantage-post of a front seat in the aforesaid gallery, our pilgrim could see most of the interior, including the high altar. What would he gaze upon while watching for the procession of the brethren of the Priory ? A building of which it has been well said that "in these beautiful churches the ancient Romanesque style breathed its last sigh."* The structure that met his eyes was the latest word in that art which had many glorious phases yet to come, of which he could but dimly imagine the transcending beauty. Yet this was beautiful enough. The evolution from the heavier Norman was sufficiently marked to make these still substantial round-headed arches, enclosing a panel of two pointed ones, look light by comparison ; and this would be vividly heightened by the great lancets of the east window, soaring from above the altar right up into the vaulting of the chancel. Although but the beginnings of that Early English style which found its perfection on a later day at Salisbury, it was, no doubt, very fair to look upon. The beautiful chantry and other tombs would not be there, but

* *English Cathedrals.* By F. Bond.

the fine vaulted roof was—and was not only of the latest form, but still remains unique in England to-day.   The cold stone walls of these later times would glow with colour or needlework, when our pilgrim and his successors beheld the gorgeous vestments and banners of the procession enter the porch, and all the panoply and ceremonial of the Church unfold before their eyes.

For you, a latter-day pilgrim, all these solemnities have vanished, and with them much of the glamour they threw over the building has departed too.   You must get your exaltation of spirit by the processes of the imagination, and, at least, only the reverence and the worthier features of those " solemn assemblies " will rise before you.   How much that was unworthy, mean and unspiritual, worldly and tyrannical in the power wielded by the Church in those days, history, and the culmination of events at the Dissolution shows. There is a significant " Injunction " extant, " given to the Prior and Convent of Boxgrave " in 1518 by Robert, Bishop of Chichester, which would seem to be an endeavour—but too late—to ward off the impending catastrophe by reforms.   That all was not as it should have been, one feels in reading between the lines of this document.   It is one long indictment of wrongdoing.   " My Lord Prior " is taken sternly to task, and the enumeration of reforms desirable leave no doubt that life in the Priory was best designated by the word " loose."

That the first injunction should enjoin " the filling up " the roll of his brother monks, followed by an order to enter and audit all expenditure, points to what was one of the most effective accusations brought against the great religious houses.   The income of Boxgrove was considerable.   Neglect had, however, reduced the value of the buildings to £125 at the Dissolution.

Neglect of rules, failure to train and supervise novices, admission of unfit persons, luxury, gluttony, hunting, cock-fighting and hawking, general worldliness, and worse, the admission of women into the kitchen, hall and pantry, and other interior places of the priory—all these point to a state of things justifying, in a large measure, the drastic methods employed at the Dissolution.

One complaint brought against the Prior shows that the " hunting parson " is a direct descendant of that worthy prelate.   His holiness is thus admonished :  " Also, because you, my Lord Prior, are noted for an archer even outside the Priory with laymen, and because you wear out the time, which ought to be your leisure for contemplation, and wholesome reading, in vain forbidden sport, and in unlawful matches," etc.—an emphatic indictment, with a touch of unconscious poetry in the phrase, " wear out the time."

The culmination comes when " it is ascertained that the honour

of the Order, its rules, constitution, ceremonies and other observances *have long since passed away into disuse among you*, not without
your great peril, my Lord Prior, we therefore enjoin you," etc.

As it is the custom, now that time has dulled the edge of controversy, to hold that the Dissolution was not justified, it is significant that this " Injunction " was addressed also to the Priors
of Tortyngton, of Hardham, of Shulbrede, of Michelham and
Hastings !

After this, it is scarcely to be wondered at that a petition to
Thomas Cromwell from Sir Thomas West, ninth Lord De-la-Warr,
of Halnaker House, hard by, whose splendid tomb is one of the
glories of the church, was of no avail. The ridicule aimed at the
modern mother-in-law finds no echo in those far-off days. He
pleads that his " auneystorys and his wyffy's mother " lie buried
there. Also that he had built " a power chapell to be buried yn "—
an intention never fulfilled. Whether the suppression of Boxgrove Priory destroyed its attraction in his eyes, or the surrender
of Halnaker in 1540 to King Hal severed the link which bound
him to the old home, certain it is, that only his wife rests in the
beautiful " chapell " he prepared. He himself reposes beneath
a fine Renaissance tomb in Broadwater Church.

It would be interesting to know the reason for this separation.
Perhaps the priest at Broadwater was able to wean his mind from
old associations in those last years. Even in death these puissant
lords brought profit in the shape of masses said for the repose of
their souls, as well as renown to the fabric. One can almost hear
the good divine urging that two churches would benefit by the
mortal remains of husband and wife lying apart.

Yet another reason is prompted by the fact that at Halnaker
the rooms to the right were called " my lord's side " ; those to the
left " my lady's side." This suggests a rift in the marital lute
which even Death found unrepaired.

      \*       \*       \*       \*       \*

As a visit to Boxgrove has been pleaded for, it only remains to
call attention to special features in the church ; the clustered
columns near the altar, similar to those in Chichester Choir ; the
slender marble shafting throughout, and the remains of fresco
decoration on the vaulting ; the glorious arcade of Transitional
work *inside* the tower ; the beautiful oaken galleries and Norman
arches of the Chapter House and the ruins of the nave.

The two galleries in the transepts are rare adjuncts, very different
to the structures raised in early Georgian days, when all the floor
of our churches was plotted out and filled by high square pews for
the " quality," the less important were exalted—against their wills !

Where the chantry is built, one of the beautiful grouped pillars had to be sacrificed, and the double pointed arch made into one.

Plain Norman arches lead from transepts into aisles, and in both places altar-tombs and canopies mark the resting-places of some of " earth's great ones " ; whose greatness, however, has not survived the disappearance of carved or painted inscriptions. One of the Countesses of Derby is proclaimed as " our benefactress " by a brass cross in the south aisle, which also has some old tiling. Anent these latter, it may be pointed out that most of the encaustic tiling was the work of monks in mediæval days.

On the exterior a dog-toothed moulding runs round the dripstones of all three eastern lancets and forms a kind of double stringcourse across the east wall.

Of stained glass, the east window, although a mass of geometrical scrolls of many colours, with nine panels of the Nativity, Crucifixion, etc., is so obviously copied from similar old windows in our cathedrals, that the effect from the nave is at least bearable. With one or two exceptions this may be said of most of the other windows, but they will not bear close examination. The noble church dignifies *them*. They do not greatly adorn the church.

Of the Priory proper, the Refectory is in a ruinous state, and was so in Queen Elizabeth's days. A " Survaye " mentions the "scyte of the late Pryorie walled round about w$^{th}$ brick and stone, w$^{th}$ divers ruynous houses, among them being a Brewhouse, a Barne, one Dove House, and a Kyll to dry Malte, a well but no Cestrall—cistern."

So much for the archæologist. The artist should pray that the sun may deign to shine when he pays his visit to Boxgrove. There are unexpected contrasts of light and shade in the ruined nave and Chapter House arcade, not to speak of those shadows cast by flying buttresses across the rugged walls and roofs. To minds that are not merely methodical, these old walls are a delight, being composed of derelict materials of every kind used in making repairs, forming a charming patchwork possessing every artistic virtue save that of pattern !

Our walk is at an end, unless you decide to go on to Halnaker, and beyond to the ruined mansion of Sir Thomas West. I fear that Boxgrove will have spoiled your appetite for the somewhat heavy gateway and empty shell which alone remain to tell of its former glory. However, if the jewel is of little beauty, the rural setting is delightful, and should make amends for the addition of three miles, more or less, to your walk.

Your day will have provided much food for reflection as you make your way back to Drayton station.

# CHAPTER XVII

## BOSHAM

### BY RAIL TO BOSHAM

### With Illustrations by Fred Davey, H. Schroder and W. H. Bond.

BOSHAM is undoubtedly one of the most interesting spots in Sussex, and, in some respects, in England too—for a variety of reasons. It is to be seen by the casual eye in a quarter of an hour, but the artist lingers in and about it for months ; and the antiquarian seldom tires of visiting it. The pictures it has furnished or inspired would fill a goodly gallery, and its popularity does not wane. It has a touch of Venice in its colour, and, with the estuary on both sides of it, more than a touch of Holland in its situation. The waters rise at flood-tide to the sills of the cottage doors, and sink at ebb to a mere rivulet in a wide waste of mud and silt. Exposed to the full force of the sea winds, and shone upon from rise to set of sun, it is bleached and tanned, reddened and stained, and everything has a sea flavour about it. The tide even laves the wheel of our mill—the more modern wheel inside the walls. This quaint wooden one is now, alas, decayed and gone, only the shaft remaining. The mill itself, or its site, doubtless formed one of the " 11 Mills," mentioned in Domesday as belonging to Bosham. It is novel to see the boats float at the doors of the houses, and the household linen fluttering in the wind and sunlight, over the sparkling ripples of the creek, for the clothes-posts are set in the margin of its bed. The good folk themselves seem to smack of the place. Bosham is well known among *genre* painters. Until recently, shipbuilding went on in a way which is delightfully characteristic of this old-world nook, with a launch every dozen years or so. It greatly added to its charm as a haunt for painter-folk, but excepting occasional repairs to small craft, I fear the industry has passed away for ever.

Of the various places in Sussex in which the Roman occupation of Britain is distinctly traceable, Bosham is undoubtedly one, and in many respects a notable example. Owing to its creek or harbour, sheltered and landlocked, it probably became useful to them at a very early period of their conquest. It is traditionally claimed, but with no historic evidence, that Vespasian had an entrenched camp here, and that " Old Park " was its site, earthen mounds having formerly existed on its borders, although long since levelled by the plough. Fiction is ever more voluble than fact, and the Roman general was located in a " villa " at " Stone Wall," where, it is said, there were seventy feet of masonry until a few years ago, beside an oblong pool which apparently supplied the residence with water. I visited the pool in this year of grace (1908) but there was such a luxuriant growth of nettles, rushes and water plants, that the only remaining portion of the stonework, if it ever existed, was invisible.

The legend, however, has its use. It brings vividly to mind the antiquity of Bosham as a Roman port or habitation, for Vespasian quitted Britain at the beginning of the Siege of Jerusalem ! Of the Roman occupation itself there is better evidence. The discovery of a Roman building in 1832 at Broadbridge, a small hamlet in the parish, with the foundations of many rooms, a circular bath, and an atrium or hall, settles the question " for good and all." These foundations were dug out, and coins of Antoninus embedded in the mortar seem to give the date of its erection. A life-size marble head, of Roman workmanship (now in the British Museum) was dug up close by, which is pronounced by experts to be the portrait head of a member of the Claudian family.

In all villages there is found some intelligent inhabitant whose age enables him to call to mind things otherwise forgotten. This is especially the case with Bosham. Through the instrumentality of one such worthy person, whose family had been resident in Bosham for two hundred years, a most interesting discovery was made in the church, verifying the truth of a tradition that a daughter of Canute was buried just outside the chancel arch. Before this, the old gentleman had borne witness to the remains of a stadium or hippodrome, about 150 yards south-west of the Roman villa, and that members of his family had seen the excavated tiers of seats.

A small Roman bath was also dug up near the churchyard.

This is evidence enough of Roman—and the Claudian head of Imperial—occupation of Bosham. And, even so far as its foundations are concerned, the present chancel is supposed to have been the Court House or Basilica itself, which, enlarged westward, became the present church so far as the nave and tower, which are Saxon. But the most interesting remains are the bases of the two Roman pillars, which support the pillars of the present Saxon or Norman arch.

When Warlewast, Bishop of Exeter—who remodelled the College

M

of Bosham—enlarged the chancel eastward and added the aisles, he also raised the floor of the nave. When the church was restored in the sixties, these bases were discovered, and although differences of opinion are held, the consensus is in favour of their being those of the original Basilica. Otherwise, it is difficult to account for

BOSHAM OLD MILL.
(*By Fred Davey.*)

their presence, the existing arch and its pillars being complete in every particular, even to bases, which rest on the Roman ones. I made recently a minute examination of them, and am inclined to believe that the Saxon or Norman bases were carved from the Roman pillar itself. I formed this opinion upon a fragment of stone still remaining and forming part of the southern Roman base, as if the workman who raised the present pillars had used as much of the original as possible and had not thought it necessary to destroy the origin of the work. Fragments of Roman pottery were also found, under all parts of the nave flooring, and Roman tiles and herring-bone masonry exist in the chancel walls.

It is claimed for Bosham, and with reasonable justice, that the Basilica existed in the fourth century, a date which eclipses the antiquity of St. Martin's, of Canterbury, where St. Augustine preached, which only dates from the close of that century There is little doubt that Christianity had attained a good foothold in Britain under the later period of the Roman occupation, but the Saxon invasion swept it away until 596, the date of Augustine's arrival. The lamp was probably relighted in Bosham soon after, for Wilfrid in 681 found a small monastery there, into which he breathed new life. Smyth's Manuscript History of the Manor of Bosham, written in 1637, says it belonged to the See of Canterbury. But the lay brethren Wilfrid found there were Irish under Abbot Dicul, and may have represented the earlier Christianity of Roman days. Wilfrid's action was again imitated by William Warlewast, the Bishop of Exeter, who founded a small college of prebendaries in 1120. Whether Herbert of Bosham, Becket's secretary, who wrote of his friend's martyrdom, having witnessed the murder, was one of these canons or prebendaries is not certain ; but that he was a native of Bosham is a fact. Tennyson makes Becket say of Bosham what is true to-day—a picture in little—

> " Better to have been
> A fisherman at Bosham, my good Herbert,
> Thy birthplace—the sea creek—the petty rill
> That falls in to it—the green field—the gray church—
> The simple lobster-basket and the mesh."

" The green field ! " This has reference to the little plot of grass which abuts upon its equally diminutive wharf, where the road ends by the church, and is one of its attractions. I know of no greater pleasure than to spend an idle hour on this sweet, uneven tract of turf, watching the water come or go, the changing lights, and the peaceful traffic of the little port.

" One of its attractions ! " After giving it full credit for these, it is but fair to say that a tinier spot cannot well be imagined. The village has but one or two really old houses. It is the hundred yards or so of dwellings fringing the margin of the creek ; the old mill ; the bridge across the mill-stream and the wharf with its Raptackle ; the ship-yard ; the green, and last, the church, which form the ever-abiding delight of the lover of Bosham. Well does

Kipling say—and one is proud to know that he says it of Sussex—

> " God gives all men all earth to love,
> But since man's heart is small,
> Ordains for each, one spot shall prove
> Beloved over all."

Bosham is the one " fair " spot for hearts—large or small ! Its attraction is out of all proportion to its size. Yet few who visit it escape the spell it wields. To me it seems, in its most literal sense, a very " haven of rest." Not the dead quiet which reigns in some of the old-time villages of Normandy, for instance, which so oppress the spirits with a sense of desolation ; but the gentle

BOSHAM QUAY AND RAPTACKLE.
(*By W. H. Bond.*)

movement which the sea brings, however far into the land it stretches its arms ; the sparkle of the water ; the coolness it exhales, let the sun shine never so hotly ; the rocking of the boats moored in the seaway ; the colour of the vast expanse of weed-covered creek when deserted by the tide ; the looked-for return of the flood, and the change it brings over the scene—these are a few of the elements which go to form the restfulness of the place.

But the fame of Bosham is not wholly due to its charm and kindly quietude. It is also because of its almost inexhaustible possibilities in an artistic sense. Not, of course, Bosham village only. The whole estuary is haunted by painter-folk. E. V. Lucas, in his abrupt and humorous way, after dwelling on its charms, says—" At high tide Bosham is serenely beautiful and restful.

But at low tide she is a slut ; the withdrawing floods lay bare vast tracts of mud : the ships heel over into attitudes disreputably oblique ; stagnation reigns."

I should be sorry to accuse so keen an observer as the gifted author of *Highways and Byways* of colour-blindness, or lack of the sense artistic ; but I am afraid that it is when she is "sluttish," i.e. at half-tide, that artists are most enamoured of Bosham.

I recollect my first visit with a friend who was neither an artist nor desirous of making its acquaintance. His face, when the place fully dawned upon him, was something to be remembered. It was as blank as the harbour mud was bare of water, but I cannot say it was disappointing—the face, I mean ! I sat me down on a wayside stone, and smiled so loud and long that the owner of it— the face, again I mean—came and knocked me off to finish it in the roadway. Certainly the action was excusable. Mirth of that description, on a hot and dusty day, the greyest of the grey, was out of place. The first view of what appeared to be an endless mud-flat, exhaling the odour peculiar to it, not exactly of the musk-rose order, was certainly a little trying.

And he was hungry, too—though this was a point in my favour, as the sequel proved. I supported him into the hostelry, took Mr. Punch's advice and "fed the brute." We lingered over the meal, and when we turned out again, a pleasant breeze was chasing the clouds across the face of the sun. But more than this, the sombre flats were almost covered with sparkling water, reflecting all the tints it was capable of, which are more than it is generally held to possess.

The shadows of the clouds made gloom where light should have been, and light fell where sombre hues, according to accepted notions of colour, ought to have held sway. Purples, blues and greens were everywhere, and the mud-flats, changed to golden-brown, glowed up at the old houses, whose ruddy complexion was such that one might well doubt if they were built of brick, or had been ochred-up to order.

There was a double transformation that day. The face of nature and of my unappreciative friend were alike brightened, and he now speaks as reverently of Bosham as if he were a mere painter.

The colour the estuary can exhibit, under the play of light and movement of the tides, is not to be described. It must be seen to be appreciated.

Talking of artists, it may not be generally known that Yeend King's "Lass that loves a Sailor" was painted from the corner of the churchyard looking south-west across the green and down

the harbour, and takes in a portion of the little Georgian house
by the mill-stream, that stands on the site of Bosham Abbey.
The only remnant left is the doorway in its garden wall.

It is the church, of course, which is Bosham's chief glory. A
building which is almost an epitome of English history, must
have more than an ordinary interest for every Sussex man. It
almost coincides with the foundation of the Christian faith. If
the Basilica really forms part of the present building, not many
years separate its erection from the date represented by the letters,
A.D. If it did not disseminate our faith from out its walls at first, it
was concerned with one of its greatest characteristics, viz. : Justice.

It is of noble proportions. The Saxon nave is large, and the
chancel is worthy of it. Nor do the aisles fall short of space. The
east window is a delightful example of five Early English lancets,
with Purbeck marble shafting. May it enter into the heart of
some generous and patriotic man to fill it with *good* stained glass !*
Here is a church intimately connected with " our rough island
story," with Harold and Canute, which might (and should) be
filled with fine stained glass, but is without a single specimen
—unless it be of grisaille pattern.

The tower is also Saxon. There is Saxon " long and short work "
to be seen in various parts, notably in the tower arch, which has
one of the rare triangular-headed windows above it. The Saxon
walls of the nave were pierced by Warlewast with handsome Early
English arches, and it was he who lengthened the chancel and
put in the beautiful east window. The unusual crypt, for whatever
purpose used, was also added then. The font is a fine example of
late Norman. There are other features of interest, among them,
the six piscinæ, the tomb near entrance attributed to Herbert
of Bosham, the tomb in the chancel, date of Edward I, which has
a recumbent effigy of a young girl, and the old oak chest, with four
hasps, in which a secret drawer or receptacle has recently been
discovered, and in it a coin of Edward I (1272–1307). The chest
itself is of about that date, and the little coin has lain hidden in
it for over five hundred years !

The spire is of shingle and rears itself as a landmark far and
wide. It gives a distinct character to the view from every direction. It bears eloquent witness to the force of the south-western
gales, being some ten inches out of the perpendicular, towards
the north-east.

The most interesting discovery during the restoration in the

---

* The emphasis is necessary. Better for Bosham and every other Sussex
church to be barren of painted glass, than to possess what many of them
do to-day ! Unhappily our cathedral of Chichester is, with a few exceptions,
a case in point.

sixties was the finding of the stone coffin and remains of the little Danish princess, Canute's daughter. The tradition, previously mentioned, which was firmly believed by Bosham folk, and ridiculed by more "superior persons," pointed to a certain spot in the church as her resting-place. The late vicar determined to test the truth of it, and sure enough, a massive stone sarcophagus was found, and in it the remains of a child about eight years of age. A sketch was made by Edgar Varley, the artist, and it was re-interred. Some later hand has painted a large tile with the Danish Raven, and inserted it over the spot ; and lately a memorial stone has also been placed there by the children of the parish. Of course, doubters still exist, but the verification of an old story, so exactly as to position and remains, would seem to be a notable point in favour of oral tradition.

While on the subject of scepticism, it is only fair to say that the Roman bases of the chancel arch are believed by Mr. Baldwin Brown, in his work *The Arts in Early England,* to be the original Saxon, with the present Norman bases superimposed ; but other authorities disagree.

Bosham was the port on the south coast where people embarked for the Continent, even before the Conquest. Harold spent the night in prayer in its church, before setting out on his ill-starred journey to Normandy. Also Canute, who ruled or held possessions in Denmark and elsewhere, and was a noted traveller, may often have sailed from here. He could scarcely have chosen a more convenient spot for one of his residences. The exact site is supposed to have been the square plot of ground to the north-east of the church. This is surrounded by a moat to this day.

The information given above does not exhaust the history of Bosham. Little has been said of its natural beauty of position.

If time allows, you cannot do better than trust yourself into the hands of one of the boatmen and drop down with the tide, and take in the beauty of Bosham and its harbour on the way. In doing so you may transport yourself into the very atmosphere of the remote past, if you are imaginatively inclined, for by this water-way came the Danes of old, intent on raiding the great bell that hung in Bosham tower, whose mellow tones had reached their ears as they crept along the coast ; and by their action gave Bosham more, perhaps, than they robbed her of. They endowed her with an undying legend. What matter if a similar story is told of at least three other Sussex churches,* and probably of nine out of ten estuaries on the south and east coasts ! From her point of view all the others are impudent fabrications. Nothing is wanting to render the story inviolably and unassailably true ; for not

* Arlington, Isfield and Hurstmonceux.

only does it reach us from those far-away times, but to-day bears witness to its veracity!

I have heard many versions of it. Truly, a tale does not lose in the telling. Probably the raid varied little from similar acts of piracy. Whether the bell was the sole object of the raid, is doubtful; but that Bosham tower was despoiled and the bell shipped on board the galley on its way to the open sea may be conceded. Also, that a catastrophe might result in the bell finding its grave in the profound mud or silt of the harbour, those familiar with its navigation will also allow.

But in the interests of wonderment and legendry, such a prosaic explanation is out of the question. The event happened in the days when prosaic details were the exception. The friars or brothers of the abbey, who had probably tucked up their gowns and fled incontinently on the approach of the Danes, returned only to see the galley on its homeward way. Little time was lost in solemnly cursing, by bell, book and candle, the pagan despoilers, and in ringing a peal backwards on the remaining bells at the psychological moment the Danes arrived at what is known as the Bell Hole down the harbour. No greater surprise could have met the eyes of the astonished warriors, than to hear the bell toll in answer and then sink through the bottom of their ship, whelming all in one common, watery grave.

This would seem to be the retribution, sudden and complete, which should end the recital. Another wonder, however, remains to this day. The submerged bell still answers the call of its brothers in Bosham tower, whenever a peal is rung. Alas, that such convincing evidence of the truth of the legend should be capable of any other explanation than the supernatural; and that despite should be done to a legend so favoured by fact! To destroy our most cherished beliefs and play havoc with romance, seems to be the vocation, if not the delight, of the man of science. This unwelcome interpreter of occult happenings says the mysterious sound of the missing bell is to be explained by the theory of " resultant tones " or harmonics, and is caused by our old friend Echo in conjunction with wood and water!

And, perchance, if we could follow the unseen working of the eternal law which produces this eerie sound, we should find it more beautiful in its operation than the legend itself. But that time is not yet; and you will find it difficult to persuade a native of Bosham of any other explanation than that handed down for ages, and corroborated by the evidence of his own sense of hearing. He will also refer you to the attempts made to raise the bell, by the employment, in proper canonical manner, of pure white oxen, and of the near success of the operation; the bell being grappled

and dragged to the edge of the hole.  It was on the point of being
restored to the devoted searchers, when the ropes broke, and it
sank back to profounder depths than before.  The cause of the
disaster was plain—a black hair on one of the oxen had been
overlooked !

The impossibility of finding the requisite number of purely white
animals, and the futility of further operations in consequence,
decided the matter ;  and the bell of Bosham still sleeps beneath
the flood, until it is aroused by the necessity of proving its existence
and completing the peal.

One, not an unbeliever nor a cynic, might suggest that Bosham
bells numbering but six, even miracle may find it difficult to make
a seventh very satisfactory in a melodic sense, but this would be
to inquire " too curiously," as Horatio says.

Few localities in Sussex have more stories connected with them
than Bosham ;  and it is only right that such hoary old age should
gather fame around its grey head.   It is claimed for it that Canute
silenced his flattering courtiers on the edge of its creek.   The proximity of his palace gives colour to the claim, and when the sou'-
westers blow there is set of tide and waves enough, to provide even
that object-lesson in rebuke of toadyism.

Again, a story is told of Earl Godwin, father of Harold, which,
however far-fetched, accords with what we know of that forceful
and astute nobleman.   In obedience to St. Paul's exhortation, he
asked of Archbishop Aethelnoth, " Da mihi basium "—" give me
a kiss," and on receiving it in solemn fashion, declared that the
holy man had sealed his consent to his request—" Da mihi
Bosham " :  one of the earliest examples of what is vulgarly known
as " besting " on record.

Bosham was also the scene of the treacherous betrayal of Biorn,
the nephew of Canute, by Sweyn, one of the Earl's sons, which
goes to show that " like father, like son," was as true then as
now.  Sweyn had forfeited lands by disloyalty to Edward the
King, which Harold and Biorn refused to restore.   Sweyn, with
guile, begged Biorn to sail with him to the King at Sandwich,
and having decoyed him on board ship at Bosham, took him to
Dartmouth, and " caused him to be slain and deeply buried."

# CHAPTER XVIII

## ITCHENOR, WEST WITTERING AND SIDLESHAM (9 Miles)

### FROM BOSHAM

### With Illustrations by the late Joseph Diplock and Arthur B. Packham.

THIS walk is too far to be included in one day's visit to Bosham. Why not spend a night in that quaint seaport? The "Anchor" has a low-pitched but spacious bedroom to let, clean and wholesome, and for hospitality the *soubriquet* of mine host, "Hearty Martin," speaks for itself. He will also, for half a crown, drop you down the harbour in a boat and land you at Itchenor. It is a trip well worth taking. You see Bosham and its surroundings from quite another point of view, with a foreground—save the mark!—of sparkling water, and a background of most gracious hills.

You get a glimpse, too, of other pleasant spots, such as Chidham and West Thorney—where there is a most interesting church, with a beautiful old tower—as well as an insight into harbour navigation, should the tide be falling. This is one of the most difficult of inlets to negotiate, owing to its being so broad and shallow, and I mind me of a cruise up and down its smiling but deceptive waters in a certain yawl called the *Kingfisher*. The crooked channel is indicated to those familiar with its navigation by certain things coming into line with the church spire and flagstaff at West Wittering point; and by poles or wands surmounted by quaint objects to distinguish them in the dusk. Thus, one has a bush, and another an old ship's bucket, or two wands in place of one, according as the wit or wisdom of the local navigators may suggest.

The downward voyage to the harbour's mouth was made in a beautiful yellow sunset, and I shall not soon forget the many charming views—nor forget the grounding of our vessel on the returning tack; the eight hours' sojourn, stuck fast in the mud; the coming of the blackest of nights and the rising of the fiercest of south-west gales; the freeing of our boat by the top of the tide; the labour entailed in hoisting sail, and in keeping to the channel

CHICHESTER CATHEDRAL.

(*By the late Joseph Diplock.*)

in the greyest of dawns and choppiest of seas ; the strength of the tide and the language of our skipper ! If anyone thinks these almost land-locked waters cannot be rough, let him try Bosham Harbour in a gale !

*Your* journey will probably be made in a small rowing-boat, with a tiny mast and sail to expedite the going. Don't forget the view of Chichester spire, western towers and campanile, as you get into the fairway of the harbour on leaving Bosham.

Itchenor has a little Early English church with three good detached lancets at the east end. A tiny tower and spire have been added. There is a Norman door in the porch, but the font is the most interesting object. It is octagonal, with shallow panels, resting on a centre pillar, and has four smaller pilasters with capitals and bases. The Norman door may have been carved, but the arch is now cemented. The drip-stone ends with two grotesque heads. Two slabs in the porch floor have geometrical crosses in relief.

The village has something of the charm of Bosham, except that it turns its back upon the sun, and therefore has less of that sparkle and glitter with which the water runs up the harbour at the latter place. But then it has less of the winds, and that may be an advantage.

Distances are long in these level districts, owing to the limitation of the view. One cannot stand on high ground, and even ordinary hedges may be high enough to form a screen. These seem to be trained up on purpose. You will find it a long three miles to West Wittering. Once there, however, you will be glad that you have come. A similar, but fiercer, exultation probably filled the breasts of Ella, his sons, and horde of Saxon warriors, who landed on this very spot, and by the capture of Regnum, founded the kingdom of the South Saxons. Their joy was prompted by the prospect of victory and the lust of spoil ; yours by the view to be seen from the shore of the harbour, across and beyond Hayling Island and Langston Water to the distant hills. At the full of the tide, on a day of sunshine and floating cloud, few sights are better worth seeing.

I wonder how much the view differed from what we gaze on now ? So many centuries of ceaseless sap and scour, accelerated by strong south-west winds, must have largely increased the expanse of water since those far-off days. A great deal of land is now represented by small islets and wide shoals. Probably all the inlets were more like creeks into which the streams brought water from the hills. No doubt these inlets were the channels by which these reached the sea. Invaded by the scouring tides, they are now the broad waters that you see, or the miles of mud and silt at the lowest ebb.

Here I would like to correct the usual impression that it is the ebb-tide—the water running out—that forms the scour, and does so much damage to the banks and defences of an estuary.   It is the flowing tide, backed by the great weight of water—as eager to invade the land as were those Saxons of old, and even more rapacious—that makes such havoc on fence and dyke.

Strangers to Bosham and the neighbouring district must be struck by the width and formation of the roads running south. They are sunk below the level of the land, as if by excavation, and each is bordered by fair green strips of grass and accompanied by a stream.   These are locally known as " lavants."   They are formed by the drainage of the Downs and are subject to floods, and in these we recognise the agency by which the shallow depressions have been made.

Historians have wondered why Ella did not sail farther up Chichester Harbour before landing.   Probably, he preferred to beach his galleys on this very narrow neck of land, where they could easily be defended or launched, rather than trust to the unknown and treacherous shoals farther up the inlet.   The peninsula, moreover, was largely forest, which he would desire to clear of opponents, before making his attack on Regnum—afterwards changed to Cissaceaster, or Chichester, in compliment to his son. The Romans, who did nothing by halves, had protected the city, especially on the western side, with earthworks, many of which remain to this day.   Its relative importance in those days was far greater than now.

\*       \*       \*       \*       \*

West Wittering has one of the most interesting of Sussex churches. It has characteristics shared in most part by all, and which may be described as " being native to the soil "—to use a homely simile. We have no such church as Hythe, in the sister county of Kent, the contemplation of which, I am told, so powerfully affected the imagination of Streete, the great architect, while resting awhile within its walls, that he forsook the profession he was studying and registered a mental vow to devote himself to that art, and, if possible, to restore the church, which he either did, or left designs for the doing.

I know of no Sussex church—not excepting Boxgrove—that could inspire such a resolve, which has its origin in a sense of exaltation and religious fervour.   The feelings stirred by our homely interiors are more human.   They are such as well up in the heart of a wanderer on seeing his native village again after long years. Not exaltation, but warm affection fills the heart and dims the eyes.   So of our village churches, it is not their beauty, but the charm which always clings to home and homely things, which attracts us.  Except in parts, few of them can be said to be quite beautiful in an architectural sense.  They are none the less entirely beautiful to us.

West Wittering Church was either built on the borderland of a change of style, or was soon altered.  From the quaint admixture of modes I incline to the first view.  The nave arches are pointed Transition, with different carving to each capital, the fleur-de-lis and more conventional scrolls being apparent.  This arcade is continued in the chancel, but with semicircular arches springing from Early English corbels and marble pillars, as at Boxgrove. The chancel arch also springs from corbels, and two others show where the original roof had its support.  The east window of two lancets, finely proportioned, has pilasters and mouldings on the internal jambs, which is unusual.  The other windows are mostly lancets, in one of which are the Earnley arms.  There are two canopied Perpendicular tombs with Renaissance details, to this family, on one of which the Annunciation is sculptured, more meritorious in design than in execution.  The archangel Gabriel is on the left with a scroll of the divine message in his hands.  God the Father is seen in the clouds, while the Dove descends in rays of light on the Virgin, who kneels with books of devotion before her. The detail which will attract most attention is the miniature form of the crucified Christ, among the blossoms of a vase of lilies, each outstretched arm nailed to a lily-stalk and flower.  In this one seems to see Holman Hunt's picture of " Nazareth " foreshadowed.  The other tomb has the Resurrection equally rudely carved, but has a less spiritual feature—the family arms supported by angels !

A broad-arched piscina, Jacobean altar-rails, two old oak stalls with Tudor rose and leaf carved on the misereres, and an ancient oak chair, are to be seen in the sanctuary.  The south aisle of the chancel is really a chantry or chapel.  It has two tiny lancets high up by the king-post of the roof, and a recess with the coffin-lid of what is supposed to be a boy-bishop carved in relief with a pastoral staff.  In the south aisle and elsewhere are the original " poppyhead " or fleur-de-lis seats.  During the restoration mural paintings were found, but in too damaged a state to restore.

The staircase in the tower is of the quaintest kind, with solid steps nailed on to risers, and oak supports to the bell-floor, with cross-beams to strengthen the uprights.  This is the kind of honest, unconventional work which is apt to offend the eye of the powers that be in these days of superficial education, and is often put to its primitive use as firewood.  There is also an old carved table which should be preserved.

The tower itself is also quaintly placed, standing apart from the nave. It probably had an eastern chapel, as there is an archway containing a lancet window. It is also entered by a pointed arched doorway. The porch is spacious, and although restored, it has been done on the old lines.

One other quaint possession had Wittering Church when I was there—a bees' nest in the roof. Their dull drone was, however, musical compared with that emitted from the organ, which my companion, T'other, with the confidence—or impudence—of youth essayed to try. Damp, in churches, is the great enemy of the king of instruments, and the " syphers " on this one were many and painful to hear. A large wooden pipe was also dangerously out of the perpendicular. T'other, who knows little of anything else, but knows much about organs, promptly repaired the defects, and replaced the pipe, to make amends for the trespass. I wonder if anyone else wondered what Robin Goodfellow had been there— or was it put down to the weather !

On your way to East Wittering you will pass two inns having queer titles—" The Dog and Duck " and " The Old House at Home."

It is nearly three miles to East Wittering and nearly another three to Earnley. The former has a derelict tower mill, with the quaintest of caps, supported on oak ties and beams, but the sails are gone. The key of the church was nearly a mile away, and we were assured by an old clergyman coming through the churchyard that there was " absolutely nothing to see inside ! "

It is Early English all but the south door, which is very beautifully carved with a kind of feather design—or fan—twenty of which complete the arc. The capitals are fluted. It has also a well-designed modern bell-turret, with a three-light foliated window in oak. From here to Sidlesham is quite five miles, and there is a path across the fields, which are very open ; but in this present year (1910) the growth of weeds and wild grasses, owing to the wet summer, was so unpleasantly profuse, the track was completely overgrown, which made it very hard work. Owing to the sparse population, field-paths are being rapidly obliterated.

On your way you pass near another mill—Earnley—which has an exterior platform, adding greatly to its pictorial qualities. Two of its sails had canvas stretchers, a feature I have only seen in Holland.

As Sidlesham tower can be seen long before you reach it, you are not likely to lose your way. It is a pretty village, and has a large unrestored church, difficult to understand, unless the chancel has at some period collapsed. As it stands the ground-plan of the building forms a T, with the transepts as the horizontal limb.

It has probably been a large cruciform structure.   There are lancets in both transepts, and a good blocked-up archway in the north arm, and a fine Early English arcade in nave.   The restoration in 1890 left much of the " churchwardens Gothic " untouched : an embattled tower ; an old carved muniment chest ; an altar-tomb to Dame Betrix Braye (1532) ; the original font (much battered about) and old bells.

When Pagham Harbour was a reality, there was a tide-mill here.   It still stands, and is a picturesque, ruddy building of brick.

A short distance north-east of the church is the " halt " on the

WEST STREET, CHICHESTER.
(By Arthur B. Packham.)

light-railway plying between Selsey and Chichester. You will probably have had walking enough and will prefer to reach the cathedral town by this means. True, there is also a station at Donnington, which has an Early English church, with an embattled tower. It was dark when we arrived, so I have not seen it. The guide-books dismiss it in few words. As it was " restored " in 1847, I fear little of interest is left.

Hunston, just south, had a very ruinous church when Nibbs etched it in 1851. He spoke of it as almost beyond repair, so I suppose it has disappeared.

Rumboldswyke, close to Chichester, has a Saxon chancel arch, and Roman bricks are to be seen in the walls, which have the characteristic " herring-bone " work. It seems to have been rebuilt in Early English days.

# CHAPTER XIX

## MID-LAVANT TO KINGLY VALE, STOUGHTON AND THE MARDENS TO SINGLETON (15 MILES)

### BY RAIL TO MID-LAVANT

### WITH ILLUSTRATIONS BY DOUGLAS S. ANDREWS AND A. S. C.

SITUATION will sometimes contribute more to the designation of a place than anything else. " Men love to call the lands after their own names," but both Mid and East Lavant get their titles from the little stream upon whose banks they lie. It is the local name for these watercourses. Insignificant in themselves—the one running from above Funtington through Bosham has *no* title—when in flood they can cause much inconvenience, especially as the period of overflow is known only to themselves. They are the outward expression of the hidden source—the swollen springs beneath the Downs, and although generally presenting a dried-up appearance in hot weather, have been known to issue forth in flood in the height of summer, to the great discomfort of the low lands about Chichester. These visitations are described as " the lavants are out."

Both villages are near at hand. East Lavant Church is the larger, and has undergone " restoration." A low tower stands on the south of the nave, and the west door is Norman with fine zigzag mouldings, but the church is mainly Early English. So many of our churches exhibit these features, that one is apt to wonder whether an earlier building ever existed, or whether the older style died so slowly that such an ornamental adjunct as Norman doors generally are, was purposely included in the Early English design.

There is an altar-tomb with canopy, and an ancient slab of Sussex marble to a lady of mediæval times. These, a brass, and a handsome new reredos complete the list.

Mid-Lavant Church is also Early English, but has been almost rebuilt. A small Norman window and two lancets are all that is left of the original building. There is a tomb with effigies to Dame Mary May of 1681. Lavant ladies would seem to be of greater importance than the sterner sex in those days.

To the north-west you can see " Stoke Clump " prominent on

SINGLETON CHURCH.

*(By Douglas S. Andrews.)*

its down something short of two miles distant. If you make for that you will be near the site of the recently-discovered Neolithic flint-mines, which lie on the slope just east of it. They are nineteen in number, and are indicated by depressions of the mouths of the shafts long since filled in. These have hitherto been supposed to be shallow pit-dwellings, but now are known to be similar to those on Cissbury and Caburn. One of them was excavated, in 1909. They are 12 feet wide and 15 feet deep, and are extended at the bottom in quest of the flint strata. Flint knives, cores, wedges of bone, and a well-preserved miner's pick made from the antlers of the red deer, were found. Deep marks made by the deer-horn wedges still existed in the chalk sides of the pit.

" As hard as a flint " is a phrase often used by us, and would seem to admit of no qualification. But the Stone Age can teach us otherwise. Hearts harden as they come in contact with the world and flints are similarly affected by air. The new flint, if not softer, flakes much more easily. Hence the reason for excavation.

Notwithstanding all that has been discovered, the true period of these pits, as of the great hill forts that crown the Downs, is still an enigma, and in her great range of hills Sussex offers the best opportunities for research into the life and habits of Neolithic man.

\*   \*   \*   \*   \*

But if you elect to visit West Stoke, two miles directly west from Lavant, you will find a prettily situated Early English church. It is usually dismissed in a few lines—a traceried window, piscina and Jacobean tomb comprising its apparent attractions ; but after the story told of an equally tiny and simple church (Ford) by a " seeing eye," there may be more here than one would credit.\*

The surroundings of West Stoke are quite beautiful, and a half-mile further west a grass-grown track, long and pleasant, leads north and loses itself in Kingly Vale. The gates at intervals remind one of the more formidable barriers which romance loves to interpose between the Knight-errant and his quest, and much of the glamour of romance clings to Kingly Vale.

It is a great down coombe forming the south-eastern slope of Bow Hill. The steep western and northern sides are thickly wooded, but the hollow itself is a beautiful lawn of natural grass, except for a central grove of yew trees of such enormous girth, that the two thousand years of growth with which they are credited seem likely enough. They surround the remains of an equally mighty oak tree, shorn of half its bulk by lightning or decay.

Tradition, that well-spring of romance, claims this dark yew

---

\* *Ford and its Church.* By Philip Mainwaring Johnson. Vol. xliii. S.A.C.

grove as Druidical and the oak tree as sacrificial, and also invests the hollow with the story of the " dread arbitrament of war." Here Saxon met marauding Dane in battle and prevailed ;* and the barrows and mounds that break the sky-line of Bow Hill as you gaze up from below, mark the resting-places of the vanquished kings. Hence the name, Kingly Vale.

The world may wag its wise head doubtfully, but tradition makes its converts on the spot. Silence and solitude are inseparable from these Down valleys—are indeed among their chief charms ; but here the solitude is oppressive, and the silence too unbroken. It is impossible to stand in this great coombe and not to feel the difference. Alone among the valleys of the Downs, this has a brooding, sombre air as though a mist of dark memories hung above its grove, and dimmed the sunlight. You feel that there are ghosts and unquiet spirits about it, and when you enter its gloomy recesses no doubt remains. The daylight now is dusk, and it is not hard to imagine the dark rites of the pagan priests amid these giants with down-stretched, bony arms, and this dull red flooring of dead yew spines, dyed as if with blood.

It is no common sight. The trunks are gnarled beyond belief, while the writhed, fantastic branches, misshapen and knotted at the joints by growth of livid fungus, borne to the ground by their own weight and the snake-like ropes of hoary creepers, take root, and again reach up towards the air and light. Many of these gaunt arms are dead ; but death brings no decay, any more than to the tusks of the mammoth. In vista, the whole scene is weird and strange. It has been compared to the interior of a great cathedral—a most inappropriate comparison. In some woodland aisles this simile may be used, but here is no airy vault supported by ordered shaft and column. Nor does the atmosphere of holiness which pervades a noble church reign here. The light is " dim," indeed, but in no sense " religious." It filters down through the sombre foliage on to a confusion of limbs and branches of every size and shape, sinister, threatening, thrust out from ribbed trunks as if demanding the blood of the victim lying beneath the knife of the pitiless priest at the foot of the mighty oak.

Not to Arden, but to " the wild woods of Broceliande " this grove belongs. Merlin might well be prisoned in one of these great trunks, and the spells and magic he wielded would seem to cluster here in kindred shades vainly awaiting his release.

Of such are the thoughts and visions born of Kingly Vale, and I do not think they would be otherwise had tradition never invested the spot with its deathless story. Such grave and sombre haunts are the home in which strange legends have their birth.

* Saxon Chronicle, A.D. 895.

Having given the rein to fancy, I am in no mood to descend to detail, and, in fact, of archæological data there are next to none. If I have prevailed upon you to visit this secluded valley for its own sake, its natural attractions will amply repay the trouble; and if you give yourself entirely to its influence and associations, few hours so spent will bring a rarer sense of satisfaction; but if you are of mind material and unimaginative, be advised by one who, for good or ill, is neither—and don't go!

If you come direct from Lavant to Kingly Vale, Stoke Down stands at the south-eastern side of it.

Stoughton lies in the valley beyond Bow Hill, a little north of west. It is not only a stiff climb, but the woods clothing the slopes are very thick and low, and the rabbit warrens make it a rough way. If you are wise you will cross just south of the wood; but you will miss the barrows and the view from the top, which are worth the toil.

Bow Hill is shaped as its name implies, a mighty curve four miles in length, its crescent facing the cradle of the setting sun. One would think that its name was also emblematical of war, for besides the battle of Kingly Vale, it was the scene of the struggle between Edelwalch and Ceadwalla, the exiled noble of Wessex. The South Saxon king was vanquished, and tradition says was buried in the southernmost barrow. Some of these have been opened, but not very carefully. Much probably remains to be discovered. An altar-slab and urns, and portions of a comb were found in one.

As you look down into the valley, Stoughton lies immediately below. It is probably as little visited as any village in Sussex, lying on a by-road, which, if it does not lose itself among the hills, leads to nowhere in particular. In times gone by agriculture made places relatively important, and from the size of its church, Stoughton has probably "seen better days." One of its patrons was St. Richard of Chichester, and he honoured it by presenting the great tithes to the canons of the cathedral to find them in ale! There was indeed a "National Alliance" then, but it favoured the beverage, and the old rustic who averred there was "beer *and* beer," probably "spoke wiser than he was ware of!"

The fine Church of St. Mary is cruciform, lofty and spacious within, and of an ugliness almost unredeemed without. Restoration, with its usual perversity, has left the exterior untouched, and has ignored one crying evil—the vandalism perpetrated by a former generation in lowering the chancel roof, and cutting off the arch of two fine Norman windows in either wall. As these were of equal size with the east window and had pilasters at the angle of the splay, the loss is great.

The great height of the roofs of Norman churches is specially noticeable here. There was a good opportunity also missed in not rebuilding the tower, which is absurdly stunted.

The body of the building is Norman, with later insertions. The chancel arch is fine, but plainly moulded. The transepts have pointed Transition arches with good carved capitals, and two piscinæ, one with dog-tooth ornament and the other trefoil-headed, of a good type.

The font is similar to many in Sussex, square and supported by a central pillar and four pilasters—a very dignified design. It

EAST MARDEN CHURCH.
(*By A. S. C.*)

has a plain recessed arcade on three sides, and on the fourth a foliated pattern. It is of Sussex marble, and so hard that the edges of the panels have the appearance of new work.

A modern reredos is of beautiful work in alabaster, mosaic, and gilding, but is hardly in character with the building, although this is a point I would not stretch too far, otherwise our churches would fare badly for decoration. There are modern stalls and pulpit ; rather heavy oak seating throughout ; one stained-glass window— poor—and a copy of Leonardo's Last Supper, once the altar-piece.

The road runs north-east from here into the heart of the crescent formed by Bow Hill, and has a grand view of the Down to the right, and a wood on the left. A mile ahead you enter the wood and take the first turning on your right, which leads to East Marden. It is a pleasant track through the trees, too rough to be called a road, but "'twill serve," as Falstaff says. You emerge into more open country some little distance from the village. It is one of four bearing the same name, and are locally known as "The Mardens." Probably because they are so small, it is necessary to group them together, although fairly scattered. As if to accentuate the matter, only the dedication of one of the churches is known.

East Marden is a very pretty little place, and its Church of St. Peter has the merit of having been left alone, except for necessary repairs. A late addition is the oak panelling in chancel, which is in excellent taste. Encaustic tiles and alabaster are now seen to be out of place in our homely churches.

The triple set of divided lancets at the east end is quite in keeping with the modest design of the building. There is a large plain Norman door in the north wall with Perpendicular stonework on the outside face. The nave is Norman, the chancel Early English. The font is fashioned like a portly bowl.

West Marden was specially favoured by St. Richard of Chichester. The spring of water, which never fails, was drawn out of the hill-side by the saint, in answer to the pleadings of the villagers. Gratitude is of short life. The chapel it possessed has disappeared !

North Marden will add a good two miles to your walk, but it is worth the trouble only to see its simple, but delightful Norman church. It is one of the smallest in Sussex, being merely composed of nave and apse, with no dividing arch, and is a perfect specimen of the style, excepting that the sedilia or piscina by the altar is Early English. The three Norman windows are of the tiniest type, and there is a similar "peep-hole," as the children say, above a larger window at the west end.

The south door is its most attractive possession, having zigzag and other mouldings, with a Greek cross at the crown of the arch.

A simple bell-turret at the western gable ends the list, unless it be well to call attention to the rare feature of the apse, and the fitness of the whole building to meet the wants of a small community.

Mr. Hilaire Belloc, in his charming poem of " The South Country," speaks of

" Our Sister the Spring,
When over the sea she flies ;
The violets suddenly bloom at her feet,
She blesses us with surprise."

North Marden would seem to be the spot where her foot first touches ground, if one may judge by the profusion of white violets fringing the waysides last Easter. Whether its retired situation accords with the known shyness of the modest flower, certainly I have never seen such a wealth of blossom, nor ever smelt the like perfume. Truly does the Elizabethan herbalist, old Gerarde, speak of " violets, which are delightful to looke on, and pleasant to smel to, speaking nothing of their appropriat vertues, yea, gardens themselves receive by these the greatest ornament of all, chiefest beauty, and most excellent grace, and the recreation of the minde which is taken hereby cannot but be very good and honest ; for they admonish and stirre up a man to that which is comely and honest ; for floures, through their beauty, variety and colour and exquisite forme, do bringe to a liberall and gentlemanly minde, the remembrance of honestie, comlinesse and all kindes of vertues, for it would be an unseemly and filthy thing (as a certain wise man saith) for him that doth looke upon and handle faire and beautiful things, to have his minde not faire, but filthy and deformed."

Of its " vertues," he has much to say, and many simples may be distilled from its root, leaves and flowers, among them a draught " that comforteth the heart " ! There should be much use for that medicine in the world to-day.

The uses of violets for dyes is not overlooked.—" Dyers boil dried violets, and steeping the liquor with dried earth of Erethria, do make the Azure colour of Athens." " After the same manner they temper Vaccinium, and putting milk into it do make a gallant purple colour." The old herbalist transports us to Ancient Greece in those two extracts.

The 1636 edition of his monumental *Herball*, fully illustrated with woodcuts, is to be seen at the Brighton Library, and will amply repay study by those who love quaint English and old lore. It verily deals with " the Historie of Plants," not merely their botanical structure. It embraces mythological legend and names, and the uses of herbs in classic days both for medicines to assuage pains, or draughts for " hurts." Whatever the medical value may be in the eyes of modern physicians, there can be no question of its catholicity and scope. In these days of light and ephemeral literature, the industry and research it bears witness to, should put us to shame.

To encourage others, I cull some of its quaint information.

Of the " Ginny-hen Floure " or Chequered Daffodil, he says— " It is greatly esteemed for the beautifying of our gardens, and the bosoms of the beautiful " ! Gallant old Gerarde !

Of true Galingale—" The smell comforts the too cold braine, and being chewed sweetens the breath." Of mental and physical benefit, truly.

Not the least amusing are the evidences of self-suppression, a necessary quality in a work of 1,700 pages ! Speaking of sugar-cane and its uses—" The which to write of would require a peculiar volume. It is not my purpose to make my booke a Confectionary, a Sugar Baker's furnace, or a Gentlewoman's preserving pan " ! He is not sparing, however, in description—" Tulips of grete beautie, and very much desired of all, with white floures dasht on the backside with a light wash of watchet colour." Watchet is a beautiful old name for light blue.

Gerarde first found the " Double Yellow Daffodil " growing in the garden " of a poore old woman, in which place formerly a cunning man (as they terme him) had dwelt." We, who know what marvels are daily being worked in flower cultivation, can see by this that the " cunning man," or expert gardener, is no new product.

Of the " Flour-de-lace " he says quaintly—" It smelleth like the Hawthorne floures, being lightly smelled unto."

" His root is made of many thrummie threds," is said of " Spike Flote-Grasse." Of Dog's Grasse—" That hath spoky pannicles."

Note the poetry of his description of the Red Wortle—" Abiding greene oll the Winter long ; with berries of an excellent red colour and full of juyce, of so orient and beautifull a purple to limme withall, that Indian *Lacca* is not to be compared thereunto."

Many homely, but beautiful names, such as one hears when country children speak of flowers, are treasured in his pages. " Lady-lace grasse " is one of these—" It has white veins or ribs, and silver streaks, fashioning the same like to laces and ribbons, woven of white and green silke, very beautiful to behold." A sufficient justification for its name, and, for a mere man, a right feminine description !

Of the down of Cats-tails he says—" It is used to make mattresses for plowmen and poore people " ; both of whom he evidently thought deserved a soft couch.

His remarks upon Mushrumes—" whereof some are very vene-mous and full of poyson, others not so noisome ; and neither of them very wholesome meate "—are prefaced by this quaint opinion : " Many wantons that dwell neere the sea, and have fish at will, are very desirous for change of diet to feed upon the birds of the mountaines ; and such as dwell upon the hills or champion grounds, do long after sea fish ; many that have plenty of both, do hunger after the earthly excrescences, called Mushromes."

He quotes Horace to show that the Englishman's dislike of all mushrooms but one is of old standing :

" The medow Mushroomes are in kinde the best,
    It is ill trusting any of the rest."

Of Roses—" Though it be a shrub full of prickles, yet it had bin more fit and convenient to have placed it with the most glorious floures of the world, than to insert the same here among base and thorny shrubs, for the Rose doth deserve the chief and prime place among all floures whatsoever ; being not onely esteemed for his beauty, vertues, and his fragrant and odoriferous smell, but also because it is the honor and ornament of our English Scepter, as by the conjunction appeareth in the unity of those two most Royall Houses of York and Lancaster."

But that which entitles old Gerarde to our " high commendation, true applause, and love," is the fact that to him we owe the beautiful name he has given to the Wild Clematis, in its habit " of decking and adorning waies and hedges, where people travel ; and thereupon I have named it the Travellers-Joy."

I wonder whether he is also to be credited with the name of " blow-ball " given to thistledown.

*     *     *     *     *

The road leads east from East Marden, and brings you into one of the most beautiful valleys of downland—Chilgrove. Its beauty, we may suppose, has always been its attraction, for not only is it the site of a British settlement with earthworks and a double vallum, but the foundations of a small Roman dwelling have been traced, the home probably of the officer appointed to supervise the native village ; and near this, in 1845, bronze armlets, rings and glass beads were discovered beside the bones of a young female, possibly his child.

Fine trees overhang the valley, but its hollow is like a lawn, without its formality. The valley was once served by a chapel dedicated to St. Margaret, of which there are slight remains. It was part of the parish of West Dean—rather a long tramp for the priest on a hot day, but duty was duty then as now.

There is also a hostelry of an old-fashioned sort providing " entertainment for man and beast," as the phrase goes. I have a vivid recollection of the fresh butter ! It was " food for a King," but I doubt if even kings get quite such butter as that !

Lest it be urged that a mere inn scarcely needs notice, it may be as well to say that among the Downs they are so few and far between, that Captain Cuttle's advice—" When found, make a note of "—becomes a public duty.

From Chilgrove to Singleton is a good three miles as the crow flies, but four and a half by the road. This central zone of downland, far removed from the sea and the salt winds, better pleases the average man, by reason of the woods which not only fill the hollows, but brave the summits of the lower hills. The scenery here, as at Slindon, might have inspired the verse :

> " The great hills of the South Country
> They stand along the sea,
> And it's there walking in the high woods
> That I would wish to be."
>
> BELLOC.

It has not the peculiar attraction of downland proper, that expanse of unending, undulating green, void of almost everything but gorse, which so delights the hill-man, and so exasperates the forester, and makes them mutually pitiful towards each other. Here they can meet on more equal terms, where neither trees nor downs predominate. In his heart of hearts one will feel that the prospect loses more than it gains by the presence of trees and woods, and the other will wish the bare spots were less bare. One will regret that his outlook is sadly restricted, and the other will be thankful that it is ; but both will confess to beauty of its kind. Both will agree that few villages are more charmingly situated than Singleton. Our forester will be quite satisfied. The valley in which it is deeply sunk is very wooded, and the surrounding hills almost lose their character as downs, owing to arboreal encroachments.

The village itself is delightful, and the church, as our sketch shows, is picturesque. The tower has a dignity all its own, derived from simple lines of early Norman or Saxon design. The rest of the church is Early English, and of this the pillars in the nave are graceful examples. The love of change has replaced all the windows of the earlier style by Perpendicular ones, but this is not an uncommon feature in our churches. The porch and font are also of the later style. The stairs to rood-loft are lit by a tiny lancet, and are quite the best in Sussex. Two old tombs, a good stoup, and a quaint inscription to a worthy huntsman remain to be noted, as well as the old wooden gallery which gives that homely character to the interior, which I have called attention to elsewhere. There is a little ancient glass in the window over the chancel arch.

SOUTHEASE CHURCH. (Page 211.)

(*By Arthur Ellis.*)

# ROUTES EAST OF BRIGHTON

INTERIOR OF RODMELL CHURCH.

# CHAPTER XX

## ROTTINGDEAN, THROUGH TELSCOMBE AND RODMELL TO LEWES (9 MILES)

WITH ILLUSTRATIONS BY ARTHUR B. PACKHAM, ARTHUR ELLIS, THE LATE JOSEPH DIPLOCK AND A. S. C.

DEAR H——" What can an artist do here ? Can any good thing come out of—Brighton ? " I am not in the mood to argue to-day, or I could point out its undoubted, if modest possibilities, in an artistic sense, but instead, I answer, " Many good things come out of—a stay in Brighton ! " And not the least among them is the vigour which impels one to foot it over these delightful South Downs, and drink in their scented breezes, which may have inspired the poet's phrase—" airs from Heaven " ! It has been known to inspire people to paint the Downs—and in doing so has made many sadder and wiser men ! And yet it is the only medium, apart from word-painting, which comes near expressing their breadth, atmosphere and charm. And this nearness is only comparative. The line and curve is so subtle, the colour so delicate ; and yet these things are easy when compared to that which portrait painters know so well and find such difficulty in catching, especially in placid subjects—fleeting expression. There are not wanting those who declare that it is impossible to paint the Downs. Few paint them well : Hine, Aumonier, Grace, and our Clem Lambert being the chief of these. Engraving and etching, no less than pen and ink, can do little, and photography utterly fails. The balance is in favour of painting, especially water-colour, so come and try ! Go the walk that T'other and I did last week from Rottingdean to Lewes. There is a 'bus from here that will land you, after a breezy ride, in Rottingdean.

\* \* \* \* \*

In like manner it deposited us a few days since. T'other may be said to represent the majority of folk who inhabit Brighton, whether visitors or natives, in that the Downs are almost an unknown land to him. Many, of course, know and love them—

an increasing number—but with the exception of that part traversed on the way to the Devil's Dyke (drawn thither by the cockney pleasures that crown the hill about the hotel) very few have but the most superficial idea of their charm and beauty. Like calm and quiet natures among humanity, they do not bestow all their secrets to the casual inquirer, nor to any but the friends knit to them by years of mutual communing.

There is much to see in Rottingdean, but our immediate goal was Telscombe. The usual white road winding up the hill north-east of the church brought us to the opposite descent—a spacious valley with a farmstead below, beyond which we could see a path climbing caterwise across the cornfield. Between us and the farm there is a wide stretch of grass scored with a dozen or more cart tracks gradually converging on the farm. It is the downland way! Where there is room enough and to spare, why spend time and flints in filling up the ruts, when you can find level going at the side! So the single track becomes one of many, with less disfigurement than one would expect, because the curves are but a horizontal repetition of the prevailing lines of downland.

Nor does the patient Mother—Nature—seem greatly troubled at these thoughtless or calculated violations of her virgin turf. Filling the hollow ruts with little pools of rain-water, she fringes the edges with stronger growths of grass and flower, heeding not the time spent, and with her hand smooths the scars away. Only the older among her lovers know how unceasingly she practises the healing art. For many years now, owing to agricultural depression, much land has gone back into her care. Nor does she lose a moment. It is as if she had been watching the last reaper or gatherer depart, to begin her loving work. Late in the year though it be, there are yet some weeks in which to begin. The autumn winds waft thistledown across the deserted field. The ever-present weed-growth adds its seeds, and the grasses shed theirs as well.

The next spring and following months will find an increasing wealth of knapweed, scabious and herbage of every kind which have taken possession of the lately cultivated plot, it would seem for good, so strong and vigorously do they flourish, But if you look down among these ranker plants, you will find that shorter growths—wild thyme, trefoil and clover to wit—are also flourishing about the roots and among the stones. So time goes on, and in a few more years these latter, requiring less moisture than their more succulent companions, begin to prevail and spread until there are large patches of each showing all over the field, and lading the air with perfume.

Look down again among these and you will find that Nature's

final word is being said. The down grass is asserting its sway and will not be denied. Its texture is astonishing. The finest moss is coarse by comparison. To call these closely-matted, minute spines, "blades of grass," is almost to mis-name them. Only in its prime or in summer is the term applicable, but language is limited and of far slower growth than even grass. Slow as this is, the time arrives when the other plants and herbs are but incidents in the universal carpet of greensward—Nature's velvet pile.

T'other listened to this very patiently as we strolled along, but was more interested to hear that a team of black oxen used to be kept at the farm, but were now a thing of the past. Few sights of rural life are more attractive than the oxen ploughing. The deliberate motion and bowed heads of the beasts, slowly plodding their way along the hill-side, or standing out black against the sky, always with an accompaniment of foraging rooks or seagulls, made a picture peculiarly appropriate to the scenery, the loss of which is as great as that of the vanishing windmills.

Now we began to climb, but soon pulled up to get our own breath and that of the Downs as well. "Oh, the duplicity of the Downs," puffed T'other; "in the apparent smoothness of their hollows, what 'ups' there are! At the Dyke now, you look for a wide area and get it. Here one gets the wide area without looking for it."

"True," I replied; "it is not your melodramatic villains, dark and scowling, that entrap the innocent and unwary, but the sleek faced, smiling deceivers. Such are the Downs, with their atmosphere of enticing charm."

"Charm!" echoed T'other, who hasn't a soul above a "near bit"—"unmitigated monotony, you mean. In form they are as exasperatingly eloquent and resourceful as the variations of a Scotch reel. You can't tell one from another, and get tired of all in turn!"

I mildly rebuked the unwisdom of seeing all things through the medium of a camera, and enveloped in the focusing-cloth of prejudice. It did not follow, because the lens "levelled up" everything it did not flatten down, that therefore these "Everlasting Hills" were not worth looking at.

"Well, I don't see any beauty in them," said T'other.

"No, nor on them!" I retorted, "or else you'd see yonder those dewdrops, strung on threads of gossamer, flashing like jewels under this low sunlight."

"Oh, no doubt your precious Downs are nice, but aggravating! They would be nicer if they were not both," grumbled T'other enigmatically.

By this time we had breasted the hill, and passing an old barn

O

and ruined cottage built in a sudden dip for shelter, came at last unexpectedly upon Telscombe. It is usual to speak of it as " quite the most secluded village in the whole range of the Downs " ; but after a long acquaintance with the solitude and aloofness of various spots, in my opinion West Dean, beyond the Cuckmere, is even more removed. Be this as it may, Telscombe is sequestered enough, in every sense. One stumbles upon it with surprise, where it lies nestled in its hollow. There was a charming picture on this occasion owing to the play of light and shade. Caburn and the back of Firle Beacon can be seen over Telscombe. The former was deep blue-grey, the latter rather lighter, but the village in the foreground and the hill beyond it were bathed in sunshine, while the sky was

TELSCOMBE.
(*By Arthur B. Packham.*)

one that always gives a beautiful aspect to the Downs—a sky of broken clouds.

There is a pretty picture just as you descend the road into the village, having the cottages built along a bank near the church as a subject, with the latter to close the view. The church is very old, and with our forefathers' unbending habits where religious ideas were concerned, is built regardless of situation, so that the eastward position might be maintained. Like Rottingdean Church— but less steeply—it climbs the hill. " And in doing so adds greatly to the view," said T'other, preparing his camera with unwonted alacrity, having found his beloved " near bit."

To me the little fabric is beautiful in its simplicity. We look at these things with different eyes. The midland churches are generally larger, because later, and a Northants man, with the splendid example of his own county in mind, would pass our tiny structures by.

"Each to his choice, and I rejoice," that these are what they are. Telscombe is almost wholly Norman and Transition ; the nave of the former, the chancel and tower of the latter style. The font, like many in Sussex, is beautiful, and the capitals and stoup are worth seeing. The Jubilee or Coronation enthusiasm is responsible for the rather ornate stencilling and frescoes which now adorn the church. No subject is of greater difficulty than this of decoration. As a general principle, it seems to me that only wall spaces should be dealt with, especially in old churches—the tints left on pillar and arches by age being considered sufficient. Here at Telscombe the whole of the walls and arches have been colour-washed, and the stencilled patterns are imposed on the stones of the latter also. The pillars only are without ornament. The instinct which led to this reserve should have extended its influence to the other stone-work. The panels of fresco are beautiful in themselves, but too full of detail to be quite in character with so simple a structure. Still, it evidences a desire to beautify the house of God, which is preferable to the cold neglect so often to be found to exist.

The village is so tiny, that it is entirely contained in the cup-like hollow of the down. The road curves sharply through and rising out of the coombe runs gently north-east along a lower ridge which slopes at last to Southease on the Ouse. All the way there is a beautiful view, with Lewes, Caburn and Firle Beacon and the Weald towards Crowborough for background.

To see Southease you must turn a little to the right—a tiny village, the houses to be counted on the fingers of one hand. It is a pretty place, situated well above the pools and backwaters of the level, half-way across which a bridge over the Ouse leads to an old farm-house among trees, called Itford Farm, and to a "halt" on the railway line, at which a train bound for Lewes or Seaford occasionally stops.

At first sight the little church will not impress you. Rather does it raise a smile which the poor interior with its "church-warden's" chancel arch of wood will scarcely chase away. But when you look for detail and have seen what it has been rather than what it is, a feeling of reverence for age will take the place of amusement.

The quaint round tower is its chief feature, being one of three situated on what was an estuary of the sea in old days, and probably used for beacons to guide the shipping. It is now surmounted by a spire, even more quaint in form, which our sketch most faith-fully portrays. It is difficult to tell the age of this tower. From the rude character of the work, I incline to the belief that it is older than any part of the building, and may well have been a beacon tower before the Norman church was erected : for that the body of the church is Norman may be gathered from the existence of a tiny blocked-up window on the north side.  On examination, you will find that north and south of the chancel, which probably ended in an apse, there were chapels or transepts.  The arches can be seen, and a piscina on the exterior of the north wall.  The little building may have been cruciform.

Unless the poor substitute of wood was meant to commemorate a vanished chancel arch, there was probably only a wooden screen dividing chancel from nave in olden times.

The font is Norman, of the plainest type, square, with a smaller base having four pillars at the angles without capitals or ornament,

SOUTHEASE FROM THE MARSH.
(*By Arthur B. Packham.*)

and there is a modest holy-water stoup let into the thickness of the wall, cheek-by-jowl with the door latch !

The square pews are equally unassuming ;  those near the chancel being carved on the top and cross rails.  Were the restoring fever of a few years back to descend on the rather dilapidated structure, these would probably have been banished.  I hope they may be allowed to remain—although a little of the abundant solicitude shown at Telscombe might well be expended here.

Turning back along a pleasant road you come to Rodmell. T'other and I took a short cut across the fields, trespassing unlawfully, I fear.  As we went I stopped, for at my feet was a hare in its " form," crouched closely, probably just awakened and hoping it might be unobserved.  As we stood over it, its eyes looked so " glazed " that T'other said it was dead.  So I gave it a little tap on the head with my stick.   In a second it bounded up and away followed by a hearty laugh.   Like most Down ramblers, I have been close to hares before, but never quite in such " hand-shaking " proximity.

You find the first inn (since leaving Rottingdean) at Rodmell. Please note the last syllable.   In company with such worthies as Lower and Durrant Cooper I have committed a grave offence in my sketch by spelling it Rod*mill*.   A proof of this sketch found its way to this brookside village, and although approved, its welcome was almost discounted owing to this error.   The murmur of disapprobation was so emphatic its echoes found a way to the ear of the offender.   He, poor wight, could only plead ignorance of the true orthography, and shelter himself under the above names, and the authority of old maps, as well as the possibility of its reference to the mill that is so prominent a landmark.

The late vicar, the Rev. R. M. Rosseter, however, kindly wrote thus to me :—

" All official ecclesiastical documents connected with the Benefice are spelt ' Radmell.'   The word has passed through many terminations ;   thus originally Radmelle—mele—mel—mell, now mill. There is no doubt the proper way is Radmell, converted at present into Rodmell.   Whether ' melle ' or ' mell ' means mill I will not say, but there is no doubt the word Radmell or Rodmell means ' the road by the mill.'   The road from Newhaven to Lewes through Rodmell is one of the oldest in the county, originally a British track made into a road (' Ermine Street ') by the Romans who used the port at the mouth of the Ouse.   The road ran all round the lagoon or arm of the sea which used to come up to Lewes.   The former inhabitants of the brookside villages were fishermen.   Northease is a hamlet in the parish of Rodmell, Southease being on its other and south side in the next parish.   Of course, to be truly logical, if the latter part of the word is altered the same may apply to the first part, and it should be in English ' Road-mill.'   ' Rod,' I think, has little meaning.   However, the usual way is Rodmell, and though the ' Rad ' is changed to ' Rod,' it is best to retain the ' mell ' as showing its Saxon origin."

" You will be interested to know that the chancel door of our church has never been locked within the memory of man."

This last note might be taken to heart by many of our country churchwardens.   We all know how often an otherwise uninteresting village is redeemed in the eyes of the casual visitor by its church, but alas ! how seldom is the key easily obtainable, and disappointment results.

There are many richer, but I can conceive no worthier House of God than Rodmell Church.   It is the frontispiece to this article

and speaks for itself.   One of its notable features is the " squint,"
with its beautiful fluted shaft of Norman work on the right of the
chancel arch, which is also richly carved with billet, lozenge, and
zigzag mouldings.   The fine pillar with foliated corners is typical
of several churches about here, showing how fashion or the same
architect influenced a neighbourhood.   Telscombe, Beddingham
and St. Anne's, Lewes, all have this kind of pillar.   There is a
brass to Agatha Brooke, 1433 ;  and the little lancet and two circular windows in the gable are novel features.   The only fault is too

RODMELL CHURCH.
(*By Arthur Ellis.*)

heavily stained-glass windows, making the interior somewhat
dark.

Faithful to the Sussex characteristic, although it does not follow
the high road, Rodmell is practically one long street ending in
the marsh.   Soon after leaving the village there is a path across
the fields through Iford to Lewes.   Of this walk from Newhaven
to Lewes I cannot do better than quote Coventry Patmore, so
that you may have a choice of enthusiasts (I being admittedly
one).

*" I do not know a lovelier walk of eight miles.   It is on the
banks of the Ouse—a broad river towards its mouth—a good

* " The Sussex Marshes." From *St. James's Gazette*, July, 1886.

part of the way ; . . . During the last half of the walk Lewes is always in sight ; and if there is the setting sun upon it and the evening is calm, the views have a quality of quietness, peace, humility and pathos, which I have rarely seen elsewhere, and which it would take a long while to analyse—if, indeed, analysis were possible or desirable. The character of this scenery, in common with the rest of the Sussex Marshes, is altogether on a higher level than the ordinary scenery of England. You may travel from the South Downs to Scotland by any line you like, and you will not catch a glimpse of anything to compare with it artistically in the hundreds of miles of pretty rural prospect you may pass through. But truly beautiful scenery, like the best art, is not to be enjoyed without a certain amount of capacity a n d culture, and is moreover, like good art, not to be enjoyed in haste."

RODMELL STREET.
(*By Arthur Ellis.*)

" A pilgrim once boasted to St. Carlo Borromeo that he had just made the round of the 'S e v e n C h u r c h e s.' ' How ? ' asked the Saint. ' In m y carriage, of course,' was the reply. ' O happy horses ! ' answered the Saint. You must ' do ' such scenery upon your legs if you want to get at the heart of it, stepping out of your way here and there, and now and then sitting down to smoke a pipe over it ; and you will enjoy it all the better if you happen to be in love. For, truth to say, nature, in these regions, is passionate, though full of repose—a combination of qualities which no true lover of art, nature, or anything else will deny to be possible."

After this it is mildly amusing to see what one of the " Guides " says of this level, that " the one eyesore in the panorama from Lewes Castle is the ugly strath over which the Ouse makes its way seaward." One opinion comes of sight only—and sight from a distance—the other of intimate knowledge. This is the touch-stone which distinguishes the lover of Nature from the rest of mankind. Of the two voices echoed here, it is good to know that of the poet prevails. He is the better "guide"! "The ugly strath" is being found more and more attractive among artists. Rodmell and Southease have a summer colony of these, and one told me recently that he found so much to do close at hand, he had been quite unable to get as far as Tarring Neville just below Southease. It is here, perhaps, that work for the brush lies thickest, among the backwaters and windings of the older channels of the river, with the gentle slopes of the Downs on either hand. But, at the foot of these, there are many "road-scapes," by no means to be despised—nor less attractive because these highways meander in casual fashion, with reed-fringed runnels alongside. As seen from Lewes Castle, the Ouse Level forms, to my mind, the necessary foil to the flanking Downs.

Iford is another of the marsh villages stretching down towards the Ouse, and the origin of the name is evident. The Commissioners sent by William to compile Domesday gathered their information from unwilling and suspicious witnesses ; and not being familiar with local dialects and peculiarities of speech, were often at fault. It has been pointed out—whether correctly or not, I cannot say— that there is more than a little of the phonetic in the spelling of proper names given in Domesday. What the compilers heard, they set down, and we in Sussex know that "things are not always what they seem," when they fall from Hodge's slow tongue. It would seem to be so with Iford, which is "Niworde" in Domesday.

Iford is part of the Hundred of Swanborough. Alfred the Great—which adjective also implies the "Wise"—was the author of the sub-divisions of "Tithings" in Yorkshire, etc., "Lathes" in Kent and "Rapes" in Sussex—into these "Hundreds." The "men of the Hundred" were presided over by an alderman, and all of them were pledged to bring any offenders to justice, *or pay the fine themselves.* To this simple expedient we may ascribe the love of "law and order" which rules in England. Juries are generally fair, because fairness has become a tradition among us by long usage, assisted by the fillip to probity which self-interest gives.

The proceedings of the Hundred Court have much to interest us. The president was generally the resident Thane, and as the members came armed it was the custom for each to touch the spear of the president with his own in token of submission. This Court could fine but not imprison, and it had a number of things under its supervision which were eminently practical and useful. What a short way of dealing with certain offenders was the ancient Tumbrel or cucking-stool ! The baker who gave short weight or adulterated his bread, or the brewer who dealt in liquor which was anything but pure beer, were tied therein and ducked in a stinking pond! Rough justice, but probably very effectual. There is much need of the cucking-stool even now.

The pillory with its complimentary adjuncts of eggs and vegetables not over sweet, was also in the gift of the Court. Idle folk, land hunger, ways and water turned or stopped, unlawful games or fishing, all fell to them to remedy, and well they did it until Norman times brought the triumph of might over right in the feudal system.

IFORD CHURCH IN THE RAIN.
(*By Arthur B. Packham.*)

Although Parliament has gradually drawn these old-time powers into its net, there remained almost to this day the shadow of these Hundred Courts in certain usages of Courts Leet and Courts Baron. Even now the felonious demolition of a church brings a liability on the inhabitants of the Hundred to rebuild it. This leads by an easy stage to our illustration, which portrays the venerable pile of Iford Church under a visitation of rain. It was drawn beneath an umbrella—the sketch, not the church—by the only one found faithful to a tryst of sketchers. Looking at it, one wonders which to admire most—the graphic delineation of deluge, or the pluck of the painter who penned it under the penthouse of a parapluie !

The church is an interesting little building, probably cruciform when erected, and was served in Domesday times by *six* ministers. Populations were larger then—or better Churchmen ! The Lord's Day is often taken too literally now, no other day of the week being dedicated to His service. Although there is nothing striking in the interior, yet the plain, bold mouldings of the chancel arch are pleasing to the eye. There was no frittering away of effect in ornamental trivialities by these old builders. Many a satisfying piece of furniture of two or three hundred years ago has the simplest of mouldings. What we seem to have lost is the sense of proportion, which renders many simple things so pleasant to look upon.

Very little common sense seems to have been expended on the restoration of our churches some forty years ago. The chancel windows of Iford, for instance, are very narrow and small, and yet they are filled with stained glass of deep colour, so that even on a sunny day the light within is indeed " dim, religious." There are windows, beautiful in design and colour, which scarcely intercept any light. Such would have been inserted nowadays. So low and dark is the chancel that it is like walking into a tunnel. When your eyes get accustomed to the light, or the want of it, you notice a very low arch of unusual span on the north side.

Restoration disclosed the arches of a vanished north aisle, and traces of mural paintings, and opened up some tiny Norman windows. The bells are dedicated to St. Botolph, St. Katherine, and St. Margaret.

The " Constableship " of the Hundred, in 1597 and onward, was filled by an Iford, Kingston, and Westout man in turn ; but as the population decreased and only one yeoman " fitt and able to discharge the duties " lived in Iford (although there were a dozen able men in Kingston), the steward, that there should be rotation, elected one of these holding lands in Iford to fill the post. " Some have greatness thrust upon them." The recipient of the honour " complayned as of a wronge and breach of custom," but in vain. *Noblesse oblige.* This shows the elasticity of conservatism. In like manner, although the cottages had no common, they had the right of feeding their cattle in the Down valleys " *when the brooks be drowned.*"

The Hundred Court of Swanborough was only abolished in 1860, after an existence of nearly a thousand years.

Like Steyning, Lewes was at one time on an arm of the sea. Excavations at Iford show that the sea once washed its shores— when it had them. A paved Roman causeway was found some time since in the Levels. Swanborough Manor House, besides its lovely situation and view, has a long history to boot, and is specifically mentioned in the preface to King Alfred's Will, as the place where an oath was taken by himself and nobles to hold the lands against the heathen, and pass it on to their children. This circumstance alone renders the spot deeply interesting to all who pass by—not alone to Sussex men. It adds the halo of chivalry and romance to the surroundings of the humble marsh village, undreamed of by those who do not study the history of their own county.

The Manor House has a fine view from its lawn eastward. With Caburn and Firle Beacon rising on each side, it may be said to face the gates of Dawn. There is much Early English and Perpendicular work, the fine roof being of the latter style. It has also new work in the old style, but not in the old spirit. The ancient work is instinct with the spirit which can be at once original, beautiful, nervously strong and bold ; the spirit by which alone all these excellences are embodied in lifeless material, then " as lively stones are built up "—the spirit of creative genius, which of old designed wondrously, and built nobly, because in architecture the mediæval mind found its truest expression, and aimed at the highest ideal—the service of the Creator Himself.

By this spirit alone do men rise to the highest effort. To the Divine Ideal have all the really great works of man been offered. Egyptian, Greek, Roman and Gothic Art had its inspiration in this motive. It shall be so whether we will or not. The world is old and men are apt to say that " Art decays and the Beautiful perishes." This sounds strangely from the mouths of Christian men. How can the Beautiful vanish, while the Good—that is, God—remains ? It is we who are at fault. It is man's heart, not the source of inspiration, that is dried up and barren. All effort shall be, and is, rewarded ; but the holy men, Abbots, Priors and Fathers of the early Church, who invented the Gothic styles, and built our cathedrals and abbeys, sought inspiration on their knees. Do we still need to be reminded that " all things come of Him " ? When men again fully realise this, then will the Lamp of Architecture, now dim, once more burn brightly.

\*　　　\*　　　\*　　　\*　　　\*

Thus " moralising on the times," our walk and the day drew towards its close. The delightful path before mentioned bringing us to Southover, which is part of Lewes. Here stood Lewes Priory, where William de Warenne and Gundrada, his wife, were buried, to be unearthed by the excavators of a railway-cutting—an invasion undreamt of by the famous invader and founder of the monastery.

# CHAPTER XXI

## OVINGDEAN TO ROTTINGDEAN AND NEWMARKET

## HILL (8 MILES)

WITH ILLUSTRATIONS BY THE LATE FRED EARP, ARTHUR B.
PACKHAM, F. J. SAWYER, AND W. H. BOND.

OVINGDEAN can be reached either from the Race Hill, by
following the Course until you see it truly "nestling" in
its hollow, or by the path beyond the Kemp Town Golf
House. The first is the longer and pleasanter, but the last
takes you by Roedean College, which is well worth looking at. It
forms a noble pile in itself, and its situation facing the sea is
almost unique. Advantage has been taken of every opportunity
presented by the rising ground, with the happiest result.
The quadrangle, with its low central tower, is delightful to look
upon.

The whole building makes a fine picture as you approach it also
from the race course, with the gleaming sea as a background!
Ovingdean lies at the back of the School, over the brow of the
hill. Few abodes of human life could better express the silence
and solitude which are the chief characteristics of downland than
the village of Ovingdean. Village, quotha! If the title were held
by virtue of counting houses as men "count noses" in a crowd,
it would fail to qualify for the name; but, fortunately, dignity
cometh of worth, and not by numbers, and the possession of a
"Grange," to say nothing of a church and parsonage, would justify
a more resounding title, even were the houses fewer than they are—
and they could scarcely be less in evidence, without risking the
plural number! It is a village without a shop or an inn!

Ovingdean does not rely on any striking loveliness of its own to
render it acceptable to the lover of beauty and the Downs. There
is a want of homogeneity about it. Although it cannot be said
to "sprawl its length along" like so many village streets, it has
a strong smack of the casual order, as though the tenements grew
at haphazards, like the mushrooms. Notwithstanding its affinity,
the parsonage turns its back upon the church as if scandalised by

THE SAXON CHURCH OF OVINGDEAN.

(*By the late F. Earp.*)

221

the unavailing efforts of the sacred structure to climb the hill and take " a whiff of the briny " ! The Grange looks askance over its shoulder at both, and the humbler homesteads stand irresolute which way to face, and by no means " at ease."

Pausing in its midst, the visitor looks in vain for any other human being, and thinks aloud—" what an odd little place " ; but, looking back from his halting place on the slopes around, he unconsciously murmurs, " How peaceful and pretty it looks ! " This is the memory he carries away into the turmoil of life, and this is his last and lasting impression of Ovingdean. The peace of the Downs is wrapped about it. Under their shadow and influence it has been ever sleeping. So tiny a place, the little copse fringing its hollow seems to envelop it like a cloud of grey mist.

Its history is as somnolent as its situation. Absolutely the only item is the interesting but unlikely sheltering of the Merry

OVINGDEAN CHURCH.
(By Arthur B. Packham.)

Monarch, unless the following extract from the Parish Register of 1686 can rank as such : " There has been no Communion at Ovingdean within the memory of man. The steeple good, but no bell in it. The small bell that belonged to it is lying, without a clapper, in a private house ! " Could any words be more eloquent of slumber and disuse than these ?

Ovingdean and its " little church " are mentioned in Domesday, but spelt " Hovingdene." In the same book " Arundel " is spelt " Harundel." There is no suspicion of cockneyism about Domesday !

The church itself is of great age. There are those who count it purely Saxon, and I agree—except perhaps the tower. The tiny, round-headed windows and north doorway are of the most primitive type, and the triplet of low, plain chancel arches are only a shade less ancient, if at all ; with a diminutive, old oak screen to match. Everything is on the smallest scale. Even the church-yard (beautifully kept like the church), although reverently called "God's Acre," falls far short of that measurement. The lich-gate, though modern, is beautiful. If Ovingdean wanted greater proof of age, it is supplied by the recent discovery of a Roman burial urn.

I cannot forbear quoting from Harrison Ainsworth's *Ovingdean Grange* here :—

" Grey and old was Ovingdean Church at the time of our story, for its architecture is Norman and Early English, but upwards of two centuries older now, and somewhat greyer in consequence, though Time has dealt kindly with it, and touched it with a hand so loving and tender, that if he has robbed it of aught, he has only added to its beauty. Peace rests upon the antique little fane, and breathes from out its hoary walls. Peace rests upon the grassy mounds and carefully tended tombs lying within its quiet pre-

BACK OF THE GRANGE.
*(By Arthur B. Packham.)*

cincts. Nothing more hushed, more sequestered, more winningly and unobtrusively beautiful can be conceived than this simple village church. The walls that surround it and shut it in like a garden, the trees that shade it and completely shelter the holy edifice on the north, give it a peculiar air of privacy and tranquillity."

A path at the eastern entrance to the village leads over the hill to Rottingdean. On the right as you go stands one of the old hooded mills, which owes its immunity from destruction to the fact that it forms a landmark to fishermen at sea.

Rottingdean, being so near, scarcely asks for description. Most people like its street—which is not too straight—and varied tenements, some partaking of the country sort, others smacking of the sea—although there is but a small " gap " here, as these narrow clefts in the cliff leading to the beach are locally called.

There is a type of house (it can scarcely be dignified by the

OVINGDEAN CHURCH IN 1899.

(By F. J. Sawyer.)

name of domestic architecture) in all seaside towns, especially where exposed to the force of the gales from seaward, which is a thing apart from ordinary fashions in houses. Small, as if to offer as little surface as possible to the gusts, and small of window also, to keep out the glare. Compact and absolutely destitute of any ornament other than green paint and whitewash, varied with frequent coats of thick tar on weather-board or porous wall, they lay no claim to distinction, except as to their tiny garden plots. Here the dogged English character peeps out. Let the salt winds blow as fiercely as they may, there are yet several months in which wallflowers, nasturtiums, stocks, London pride, garden daisies, sweet-williams, and such lowly plants will flourish, under the protection of the fence composed of flotsam and jetsam of barrel-staves and timbers cast up by the waves. Flints from the chalk, and scallop shells, plentifully whitewashed, make a brave border to the formal beds, and the brick-paved pathway leading to the doorstep is red-ochred as if to deny the right of the sun to do all the " tanning."

The same exposure to weather probably accounts for the huddling together of boats and boat-houses, raptackle and capstan. One would think that some phenomenal " ninth wave " reaching beyond the bank of beach, tossed them all together, and leaving them high and dry, had sunk back and returned no more.

These remarks apply more, perhaps, to such a place as the Raptackle at Hastings, rather than to Rottingdean, but they are true in degree of all coastwise towns.

Poets and painters have found Rottingdean pleasant to live in. Kipling and Burne-Jones have added the prestige of their name and presence to the little town. Both found inspiration here, and have left enduring works behind them, the former in his Sussex poems, and the latter in the glorious colouring and design of the windows in the chancel of the church. These alone are worth going to see.

It is not perhaps generally known that the Duke of Wellington was at school here. It is pleasant to think that some small part of his strong, imperturbable, and patient character was due to the influence of these quiet hills, and the natural caution and reserve of the Sussex rustics he would come in contact with as a boy.

The church is entirely Early English, and has a central tower. It climbs the eastern hill, and the effect of the different levels internally gives a dignity and appearance equal to that which size would give. There is a novel feature above the eastern lancets. On the exterior each is surmounted by an unpierced quatrefoil.

The Burne-Jones windows darken the chancel somewhat, but one forgives that in the beauty of the colouring. This is noticeable in

P

all, but most perhaps in the two side lancets of St. Margaret and St. Mary, which are in opposite effects of blue. The halo round the head of each saint is of a most luminous ruby. Note, too, the colour of the serpent under St. Mary's heel, and the whole scheme of tints in the eastern triplet—St. Michael, St. Raphael and St. Uriel —or St. Gabriel.

The prevailing idea of Burne-Jones's art is that it harks back to past methods of colour and design. Yet he himself considered it too modern and therefore unsuitable for insertion in ancient buildings.

T'other and I took refuge in the church from a thunderstorm on

RUINED NORMAN CHAPEL, BALSDEAN.
(*By W. H. Bond.*)

one sultry day in August. The atmosphere inside was so oppressive that T'other remarked that " the Dean must be revisiting his church " ! Youth is incorrigible.

One road to Falmer is the same as that to Telscombe until you near the top of the hill. Here you turn off on to a wide green way beside the cultivation in the valley on your left. There are usually hay or wheat-stacks on this grassy strip. You set your face due north, and soon a path will be found catering across the crops, regaining the turf by the side of a long strip of brambles and gorse. An old flint-pit, a barn and an empty pond are next met. Here you are on a wide stretch of grass which stretches right away to " Norton Top," part of Newmarket Hill. It is used as a galloping ground for race-horses. On either side is a broad valley, that on the right winding far away to Kingston Hill, where it begins— or ends.

Balsdean, a most retired farmstead, with a modest Georgian house set amongst trees, lies half-way up this valley ; and its elms and buildings make a pleasant patch of darker colour, and a good sketch. It is but the shadow of its former self, its capacious barns having fallen to decay quite recently. Its hey-day was of long ago. Few wanderers among the Downs to whom the place may be quite familiar, know that there is a ruined Norman chapel here. Small circular-headed windows and doorway betray the religious char- acter of what might otherwise be deemed a roofless stable. On the western wall there are traces of colour. One would fain see the remains of a fresco in the faint lines, but, as a ship is figured, I fear that some shepherd boy, inspired by nautical leanings, and aided by sheep-ruddle, is responsible for the rude design.

This chapel may have been served from Falmer, Rottingdean, or Kingston—whichever parish it is in. The recent purpose to which the sacred edifice has been put—that of a cowstall—suggests comparisons which may be soothing, or sorrowful, according to the view you take. Of suchlike humbleness, perhaps, was the stable at Bethlehem, and over similar, if more stony hills, the wondering shepherds came to see " the thing that had come to pass." Or, the gaunt walls, roofless and broken, and the neglected graveyard, choked with nettles, may point to sadder memories. Liberty of thought, and freedom to worship his Maker as each man wills, are privileges bought with blood and much suffering, and however many sects and denominations fill the world with jarring creeds, the principle is right. With such a mighty upheaval as the Reformation, it stands to reason that centuries must elapse before comparative calm and mutual tolerance can ensue ; but the pity of it is this, that such a cataclysm should have been needed.

The picture this humble chapel affords to the mind's eye, of care for the spiritual wants of the poorest of her children—when there was indeed " one fold under one Shepherd "—prompts the reflection that had the Church been true to her primitive shepherding of the souls of men, she might still be reigning supreme over their hearts. Who can tell ?

There are probably a good many of these small chapels con- nected with farms and isolated homesteads hidden away among the hills. I discovered one by chance at Old Erringham Farm in the Adur Valley, which appears to be unrecorded in the Sussex Arch. Coll., but is noted on the Ordnance Map. It has one round- headed window, and a two-light Transitional lancet in the east wall. Indications of a holy water stoup remain, but it was getting dark, when I realised the character of the little building. It was used as a fowl-house then, but the calves are now sheltered in it ! The woman at the farm-house told me it used to be called " the Synagogue "—of all names in the world !

*    *    *    *    *

Retracing your steps up from Balsdean, you go straight forward to the highest point—Norton Top. Being centrally situated in the range of Downs, the views from it are fine in all directions. The Romans appreciated its position and one has only to stand here to see why. It is not steep enough for a camp, like Hollingbury or Caburn, but they had a station on it. In 1889 a labourer

FARM IN BRAKY HOLLOW.
(By W. H. Bond.)

gave me a Roman coin unearthed while trenching for flints. I went the next day and obtained the rest. They represented a small hoard, buried in an earthen vessel, as one of the coins was found adhering to the inside of what had been the foot of a vase of yellow ware. They were chiefly of Hadrian's reign. I picked up fragments of pottery of various kinds—black and yellow—and one piece of Samian ware ornamented with the honeysuckle pattern in relief, together with part of a bronze fibula and a broken quern.

The huts of the soldiery were probably of wattles daubed with clay, or plaited with furze, and these fragments were the contents of a midden or refuse-pit—except the vase with money. This would be hidden by some soldier in the safe " Bank of Mother Earth," until his return—an anticipation never fulfilled.

As you stand and gaze south-east over many a hill and vale, the subject of our sketch here, Braky Hollow, lies hidden in one of the coombes.  It is useless to give directions, you must find it for yourself somewhere between Iford and Telscombe !

In a former walk I have spoken of land going out of cultivation. The summit of Norton Top has lain fallow for the last ten or twelve years.  It was a miniature jungle of wild growth last July, prominent among it being the superb spikes of the viper's-bugloss.  In the cart-ruts crossing it towards a little shanty, probably not unlike the Roman huts, I still found small fragments of pottery.

The path from Rottingdean runs just below the summit on the west side.  Here you come to another broad, rutted track.  It sprawls, an untidy, but flowery way, from where you stand, to the race-course at Brighton, and eastward—but more smoothly— to Kingston Hill.  This is one of the few walks which our towns-folk take upon their downs—from the Tenantry Down to Falmer, and even on to Lewes.

Brightonwards are small holdings, with ugly little buildings for the accommodation of pigs and poultry, guarded by kennelled, and consequently noisy, dogs ; but look beyond these surround-ings, and the view will make amends.  There is one of the most comprehensive prospects to Worthing, Cissbury, Chanctonbury, and to the Isle of Wight beyond.  But if you see the island, bad weather is impending.

It is worth the walk to see the variety of wild flowers and plants which fringe the derelict wheel-ruts.  The burnet moth, with its rich black wings splashed with red, may be found in thousands here in July.  The caterpillars feed on the clover and birds-foot trefoil, and the chrysalides enclosed in shuttle-shaped cocoons may be seen on the stems of grasses where the sun can reach them.

The hamlet below on the right is Bevendean ; merely a farm-stead, but of sweetest memory to a youth I wot of, when the fever of butterfly-catching was on.  There is a little shaw on a crescent bank just east of the farm, and here I have spent many happy hours on many days of the year.

The Down butterflies are chiefly blue—reminiscent of its skies— from the tender hue of the " chalk-hill blue " to the glory of the " Adonis."  This slope was the home of both in their season, besides most of the others, as well as the fritillaries and commoner species.  Facing the sun, it has never failed to provide sport, and when the scorching heat begins—for on the Downs there are practically no shadows when the sun is up—the little wood gave grateful shelter.

Here I have caught the first Clouded Yellow " newly arrived from Gaul," and its paler and rarer relative, *Hyale*, and the still rarer and paler *Helice*, comparable in fewness to black diamonds among jewels. But the catching of them! Their journey across the water (they may often be seen going out to sea) seems to strengthen their wings and accustom them to long flights. On hilly ground chase is almost hopeless ; but they are fond of clover and lucerne fields, and here stratagem may succeed where fleetness of foot fails.

Dark Green, Silver-Washed, and occasionally High Brown Fritillaries are fairly plentiful, and east of Firle Beacon, where a certain long, fine grass grows in patches, I have caught many Marbled Whites. It is not common on the Downs. Another handsome butterfly less admired than it should be—the Grayling, frequents the Downs, wearing a refined combination of soft brown, grey and buff, proclaiming the gentleman among lepidoptera. But of all broods and perhaps of all butterflies, the Adonis is, as its name implies, the paragon. It is indeed " of heavenly blue." The Common Blue is of a beautiful lilac hue, but it pales before the lovely and brilliant sky-blue of *Lycœa Bellargus*. It is strangely local. Many may be caught on such a bank as this at Bevendean, and nowhere else in the vicinity.

To reach the farm, there is a very steep descent by the mill, but this is no part of my plan to-day. You will follow the race-course to the top of Elm Grove, where the trams are—but do not wait for you !

# CHAPTER XXII

## FALMER OVER KINGSTON HILL TO LEWES (5 MILES)

### WITH ILLUSTRATIONS BY THE LATE LOUIS MEADEN, LOUIS GINNETT, AND ARTHUR B. PACKHAM.

THERE *were* two routes from Falmer Station to the village, but one of these, the longer but most pleasant, viz. into Stanmer Park and up a green walk to the fringe of wood on the crest, and then out by the park gate to the " Swan Inn," has been closed. The privilege of entering the Park was greatly appreciated by the people of Brighton, but the misbehaviour of the rowdy few brought deprivation on the many, and the Park is closed. Now that a salutary lesson has been administered, we may hope that some portion of the privilege may be restored. It would be a graceful act.

At present there is nothing for it but to foot the high road up the hill, which would be no great hardship were it not for want of shade—and passing of motor-cars, on what may truthfully be called, " The Dusty Highway." The title suggests an allegorical meaning, but here my purpose is not to dwell on this interpretation —often striking, and often inaccurate. It is of one of the realities of the highway I write now. It may seem paradoxical to say it, but one of the hardest realities met with on the King's highway is that seventh plague of Egypt—the dust. It has not the outward result that its famous progenitor had, but the " blains " it produces in the temper are none the less real because they are " suppressed."

Some, with a bad habit of over emphasis, common to writers, most unnecessarily add an adjective and call dust " impalpable." Would that it were ! Perhaps there is a foreign variety to which the term applies, but on our roadways the quality of dust is to make itself not only seen, but felt—not to say tasted ! How else can we account for the familiar flint stones the rude wind flings in our faces ?

One does not need an active imagination to conjure up the long length of hedge-girt roadway under a sweltering sun and a brisk east head-wind. O the misery of it ! It is doubtful whether the " weary wayfarer " is half as weary as he is exasperated. " The

LEWES FROM THE WATER MEADOW.

(*By the late Louis Meaden.*)

darkness which might be felt " would be preferable to a tramp. At least there is the hedge for him to lie under and sleep till morn, and of the " palpability " of night there is a doubt—the language of the quotation is more picturesque than true ; but of the cloud of dust bearing down upon him there is neither doubt nor unreality. Tramp or " gent," there is nothing for it but to turn your back and wait till it " blows over," returning thanks for the deliverance when it has gone. But should the coming of the cloudy whirl coincide with the passing of a motor-car, coach-and-four, or other " chariot of the mighty," turn again—and refrain from words. None but unholy ones express the situation. Silence is best.

Except the familiar statement that " March dust is worth a guinea a peck," probably because it announces the advent of spring rains, I have only heard one word in its favour. As a boy I accompanied Baring Gould, the novelist, part of the way to Hurst College, where he was staying. I remember him saying that he enjoyed walking without boots when the roads were deep in dust, and often did at night in the country. At Patcham he slung his boots over his shoulder and trudged gaily on.

But this was said of dust in repose. I doubt whether he cared for it more than anyone else, when it is on active service. In general neither man nor boy has a word to say in its favour, nor, by their patient cowering and closed eyes, do cattle like it either.

To Palmerston's description of dirt as " matter in the wrong place," dust would seem to lay the greatest claim. The " dust of ages " is applicable to spots where little or no movement, whether of life or life-giving breeze, enters. What deadness comes to such crannies and chambers ! Imperceptibly all things, however brilliant in colour, assume the grey garment of forgetfulness—the dust, until that alone is the prevailing hue. A parable this, warning us that movement is as essential to the heart and brain as to the body itself, otherwise they risk being choked by the dust of indifference.

The persistency of dust is great enough to give it the character of being maliciously alive. To call it inanimate matter is only true of it in bulk. In separate atoms it is busy enough—witness its antics in a sunbeam. It calls itself a " mote " then, but a poetic title and a little glitter does not render it less objectionable when it gets into the " wrong place."

For all that it is so lively, its instincts are gregarious. It much prefers to settle by its neighbour atom and have " a good rest." In some situations this is both permissible and useful, but in others it meets with objections, and a dire foe most insultingly named after it (the duster) effectually defeats the intention. Housewives regard dust much as our forefathers did the Wandering Jew, and give it no rest. And wisely too. Its destructive powers are

far in excess of its insignificant atomic constituents, but in gross
it is by no means a despicable foe.   Its ranks are being added to
each minute, and we have it on record that it is the Alpha and
Omega of our earthly frames.

Possibly it has charms—we know it has many fertilising uses—
but its charms are not self-evident.   It has certain artistic qualities,
and gives pleasure to many an artist in a painting—but not *on*
it !   It is always best when seen at a distance !   The otherwise
difficult composition of road-line may be shortened or softened by
its portrayal in a picture—a less hackneyed form of veiling than
the smoke of the familiar field fire.

FALMER STREET.
(*By Louis Ginnett.*)

A search for its charms is, I fear, foredoomed to failure—not to
say quixotic.   After taking thought, I have come to the conclusion
that it has no charm for anyone but a scientist or a farmer.   These
—and the artist as a distant relation—are its only friends.   The
one desire its advent inspires is to be quit of it.

However, few things are of good or evil merely.   Even dust has
its good points.   Perhaps this thought will help us to bear with
equanimity its least bearable visitation—a speck of it in our eye !

\*          \*          \*          \*          \*

Three wanderers—the Bookworm, T'other and I—" suffered "
Falmer Hill on a hot and dusty day last August and reached the

village.  " To look at a thing both ways " is generally considered
an advantage.  It does justice in landscape no less than in life.
Views are therefore given from opposite ends of Falmer Street.
Not that Falmer Street needs no commendation.  It is not *too*
picturesque.  It does not present an embarrassing choice.  Indeed,
to see a picture from either end of it requires a belief in one's powers
akin to making " a silk purse out of a sow's ear "—as the vulgar
old saw remarks.  Anyhow, it requires a fresh eye and hand, and
the illustrations exemplify the fact.  That they are not uninteresting
may be seen at a glance, but their chief attraction lies in their excellence as line drawings.  In certain qualities of colour and under
some conditions of light, a satisfying picture might be painted of
Falmer Street ;  but people would give the credit to the artist's
imagination
rather than to
the    place.
Wriggle as one
may in defence
of the common-
place, it is in
the vicinity
that   Falmer
pleases.  Unless
it has a crowd
of children just
out of school, or
a  bevy  of
cyclists stop-
ping—to give
their machines
a rest near the

YEW TREE COTTAGE, FALMER.
*(By Louis Ginnett.)*

inn ;  or the covered country carts halting—to water the horses,
there is a great want of animation.  " Dull " and " dusty," said
Bookworm.  " No trees," groaned I.  " No shades—except the
' Swan Inn,' " gasped T'other. . . . Two travellers only, and a
remnant of another, arrived home that night.  The joker sometimes
receives his reward !

When Falmer Street is left to keep itself company, and one turns
to right or left, there is much that is pleasant to behold and to
sketch.  Two lanes lead up to the pond.  If learned men are to
be trusted, Falmer derives its name from this lakelet or mere.  But
nowadays the tendency to " call a spade a spade," dubs the little
sheet of water " a pond."  It is difficult to say what makes one
word more acceptable than another.  Perhaps it is because " mere "
is more archaic and poetic in its use, therefore we deem it the prettier.

In sound it certainly pleases more than " pond." Anyway, whether it is conscientiousness or brutality—" pond " it is called. As to beauty, just rob " Falmere " of its last syllable, and replace with its rival of to-day. There is no doubt what the verdict would be. T'other added to his iniquities by contending that either word was appropriate, or both, for it was a mere pond ! After this the subject dropped.

For the sketcher or rural man—he who is happy in simple scenery —the surroundings are sufficient to give enjoyment. The schools and some cottages cluster near the end of the water, and across it from the south-east corner the church, with the farm close by, makes a good picture. A lazy afternoon may be spent under the trees with as much sketching as you have a mind to ; but cast your eyes beyond, and there stretch the hills ! If solitude is what you need, stroll up the lane and leave the world of Falmer to drowse along as it may.

FALMER POND AND CHURCH.
(By Arthur B. Packham.)

If botany were not so shunned by our modern young men it would add a charm to a jaunt quite novel and at-tractive ; but few know, or care to know, what " grows in the hedge." It is strange, when one sees how interested people are at the wonders of plant life described in lectures, or shown in the microscope, how few seek this knowledge for themselves. To see through the eyes of others is as prevalent as of yore. Very few care to take trouble, and therefore very few are happy in themselves. They want amusing, when they should be able to amuse.

The lane is cut deeply into the rise, to ease the gradient, and up the banks on either side grow many old hawthorn trees. It is a revelation in odour, to come here when they are in blossom. The hollow cutting retains the scent—a quarter of a mile of perfume !

As you ascend, the trees, more exposed, get stunted, and end near the head of an enormous coombe, which lies on your left—one of two great amphitheatres between here and Kingston Hill. Sweeping round the edge of this coombe and on to the next, there is a grass-grown trench, with a bank at the side, which may be either one of the protected ways for the Roman soldiery, or a track worn down by old traffic to below the level of the down. In any case, it is the pleasantest of pathways, and on either side, in russet-coloured patches, blossoms, near the end of the month, one of the most exquisite of the June roses—the burnet-rose.

It is not common, even on the Downs. Of a lustrous creamy white, with a yellow heart and tiny leaves of purple-brown, it grows on a little prickly bush a few inches high. When in full bloom, it is one of the most beautiful sights to be seen on our Downs. But like many beautiful things, it is very fleeting and frail. There is only one way to enjoy it. " Gather ye roses while ye may," only applies to the cool evening and then only to the opening buds of the burnet-rose. But do not root them up. Cutting will do but little harm to these great patches. Carry them home in a basket, and arrange them in a shallow rose-bowl with water. Then see what a joy awaits you the next morning, and for a week !

The great coombe below is famous for its " valley entrenchments," which are exercising the minds of our archæologists just now, in the endeavour to account for their age and use. Whatever they may have been, there is no question as to their extent and size, the whole of the hollow being mapped out by these mounds.

You follow the green track, taking mental pleasure in each of the hollows, forming minor coombes on the eastern side of the great valley, until you rise towards the higher slopes leading to Kingston Hill ; but if you are wise you will swerve a little and view the second mighty valley from the corner of the copse to your left. The view of Lewes from here is very fine. Skirting the edge of the great depression you find your green way once more, but here it is more level ; and giving a long look down towards the distant sea, which is seldom absent from view on the higher downs— you approach Kingston Hill.

On its southern slope there is a great stretch of gorse—or as Sussex folk prefer to call it—furze. (Disdainful of what he thinks unnecessary fastidiousness, the shepherd or his boy would call it " fuzz.")

" It is difficult to speak of common things, and not to seem tedious," I remarked to the Bookworm. " Every one knows what furze is, its perfume, its characteristic of perennial blossoming, which has become proverbial, and that it is very unpleasant to walk through, or to pluck ! "

" If there is little to say that is new," replied Bookworm, " don't try ! Gorse speaks for itself. Its perfume is one of those things to be grateful for—in silence. Words fail to do it justice."

\*　　　\*　　　\*　　　\*　　　\*

There is one of the steepest slopes in Downland on your left as you go. A fence has been erected along the brow to prevent the cattle falling down. Usually a horse or two and a flock of sheep are to be seen grazing by the pond far below. It is only when you can compare with objects like these, that you realise how considerable is the altitude from which you gaze.

Kingston Hill gives a fine range of views in nearly all directions. Newhaven and the white cliffs beyond Seaford, and the utmost limit of the Downs in an easterly direction ; while directly ahead is Lewes with Caburn to the right, and Mount Harry to the left, where was fought the Battle of Lewes between Henry and de Montfort, which largely loosed the bonds placed on the people of England by that other " stricken field "—the Battle of Hastings.

When you are passing the foot of Caburn yonder, it towers bravely up into the sky, but from here one is surprised to see how much lower in altitude it is, compared with Firle Beacon.

Just below lies Kingston, a sweet little village quite off the main road, with a simple little Decorated church, well cared for and airy. In looking on this quiet hamlet, nestling, so out of the way and protected, I am always reminded of a sheepfold, fenced round and secluded. A steep path leads down to it, but your way lies right ahead.

I always like the group of farm buildings and stacks at the intersection of the little by-road to Kingston, and have sketched it again and again, not for any great merit as a picture, but because the sunlight lingers about its lichened roofs and yellow straw stacks so temptingly. There are trees enough to give contrast and sheep and cattle to add life. Just beyond, a windmill helps the composition—or would do, if it were not six-sailed. It is the only one of the kind I have ever seen, except in Holland. Why should not more than four sails look well in a picture ? Probably because four is a medium quantity. Two is not enough to give form, and six are too many. It is interesting to note how generally the artist tries to place them at any angle but a cross, although I have seen good effects with the sweeps in this position.

Alas, like most of our windmills, this too is falling to decay. There are many things in our rural landscapes that could be better spared. Windmills seem a link between animate and inanimate nature, as they circle in the sunshine. No view can be called lifeless where a mill is at work. I once saw what seemed to be great flashes of light in looking towards Rodmell from Newhaven. It was sunlight reflected from the sails of the mill at work in a brisk south-westerly wind. Unless other counsels prevail and the mill is repaired, I shall never see it so again. It is now sailless.

One of the pleasant sights of our Downs in days not so very long ago, were the mills in motion on the skyline in various directions, as if impelled by the great cloud shadows moving so quickly over hill and dale.   Steam roller-mills, the supplanting substitute of our vaunted progress in civilisation, cannot fill the aching void the disappearance of the older method causes ;  for it is not the eye only that is affected, but the heart as well.   I feel their loss, much as a boy feels the loss of a playmate, where no other is to be found to take his place.

Windmills in Sussex are mostly of three patterns.   First, tower-mills substantially built of brick or stone, octagonal or round, and generally lofty.   They are very picturesque by reason of a railed platform supported on brackets on the first floor.   Usually crowned with what may be termed a spiked helmet of copper, they stand bravely up, with a military air about them, reminiscent of mediæval watch-towers.   The present tower-mill on Round Hill, Brighton, was a really beautifully proportioned structure before its sails " went by the board," and any enthusiastic young architect might have done good work for future reference, by measuring up, and drawing it in detail for one of the architectural magazines.   Only the tower is left now.

A fine example was the old Black Mill in West Hill Road, also in Brighton.   Of this only the octagonal basement walls remain.   Another " platformed " mill still stands and works by the little river Tillingham, on the west of Rye, and makes a good picture.*

Lambert's old " View of Brighton " shows four mills, three of which were on the east cliff.   With the Black Mill and those on the Dyke Road there must have been eight or ten.   I saw recently a very old water-colour by Thos. Wakeman, which showed a wind-mill almost on the Steine—about where Broad Street now stands.

The second type is the hooded or " bonnet " mill, like that on the Down at Rottingdean.   In both these types only the cap or hood revolves, by means of the graceful and clever contrivance of a fan-wheel, thus keeping the sails in " the eye of the wind," automatically.

The third, and perhaps the most usual shape are called " Smock mills," because they resemble the once almost universal and, happily, still familiar garment or overall worn by country folk. Of this garment much might be written.   I am glad to see many little town children in Sussex wear them in summer.   The needle-work is often very fine and beautiful, and the " gathering " is most scientific in its method.   Many quaint objects are embroidered on the collars, sleeves and cuffs, such as ears of corn, sickles, crooks, snails, and other emblems conventionally treated.   The material is unbleached linen or homespun, and good, old examples are eagerly collected.   It is almost the only remnant of peasant or

* See pages 253, 260, 337, 376.

country costume left, and seems the natural accompaniment to a rural scene.

One more note *re* windmills. If it were standing now, you could see from Kingston Hill the mill in which Richard, King of the Romans, younger brother to Henry the Third, took refuge at the Battle of Lewes, barring the door and defending it awhile. At length, amid derisive cries such as " Come out, you bad miller—you, forsooth, to turn of a wretched mill-master ! You who defied us so proudly and would have no meaner title than King of the Romans, and always August !"—he surrendered to Sir John Bevis.

\* \* \*

SOUTHOVER HOUSE, LEWES.
(*By Arthur B. Packham.*)

But to return to our route. The track leads along the comparatively low ridge —but steep enough on the left, at the foot of which runs the Winterbourne, a stream, like many of the Down springs, running dry in the summer—hence the name The hill gradually slopes and at last brings you into South-over, arriving at the same spot as in the walk from Iford. The old buildings and the street as a whole are well worth sketching. It has a medley of mediæval and later structures which are delightful in variety. Anne of Cleves is said to have lived in one of them. Southover Church worthily closes the vista. As the purpose of this book is to touch upon the less known features of Sussex archæology, I leave the deeply interesting history of Lewes to be read elsewhere, and only dwell on the available walks in the neighbourhood ; but digress for a moment to say that Southover House, at the foot of Keere Street—a very fine Tudor house—is picturesque.

To Sussex folk it would savour of affectation to insist on what is generally conceded when the situation of Lewes is spoken of as beautiful and commanding. Therefore, let me be content with pointing out those things which may not at once be evident to those who see Lewes, perhaps from one or two points only, and are content to admire its site in full measure even so.

Among Sussex views Lewes is unique, and in no way second to
Rye, Winchelsea, or even Arundel.   The beauty of Arundel is
known, and apparent to all ; but when it has been viewed from
one or two points, it has been exhausted.   Lewes is by no means
so soon exhausted.  It seems strange to refer those who love
natural beauty to the map ;  yet it is useful, if not entirely necessary.   It will be seen that the town stands on a long, narrow strip
of down, pointing like a huge finger to the triangular group of hills
detached from the rest, of which Caburn is one.   On each side is a
valley.   In the northernmost flows the Ouse, and in that on the
right the intermittent Winterbourne, having its source towards
Falmer.   By the side of this runnel rises another long stretch of
low downs (our walk of to-day, reaching from Kingston Hill to
Southover).

Below Lewes the Ouse spreads out, and one wide marsh continues to Newhaven.   Another goes by way of Caburn, past Glynde
and Firle.   Four valleys therefore meet at Lewes, and the variety
of the views, of which the town is the chief point, is remarkable.
A famous writer sang its praises in the person of Defoe, who says,
" Lewes is in the most romantic situation I ever saw."    Gilbert
White also writes, " The prospects and rides are most lovely."
Coventry Patmore, whose love for Sussex so colours his writings,
speaks thus :  " No one can have any idea of the extraordinary
beauty of Lewes who has only passed through the station.   Seen
from the ' Paddock,' a large field on the north-west, the town is
almost as striking in its aspects as Edinburgh or Durham ;  but
Edinburgh is hard and austere, and Durham dirty, whereas Lewes
is soft, homely and clean.   The castle, ' bosom'd high in tufted
trees,' stands upon the top of the almost precipitous hill on which
the town is built ;  and, from the parapet of the Keep, which, with
the Barbican, is still inhabited, there is a view of the southern
marsh and the great level on the north, and of the surrounding
downs, which is worth going a good way to see.   The downs here
have more of a mountain form than in any other part of the range.
Crowborough and Fairlight are a few feet higher, but there are no
other hills in Sussex which look so much like real mountains as
Mount Caburn and the eastern summit of the great down, the
highest peak of which is Firle Beacon.   These two hills rise sheer
from the narrow tongue of marsh, through which the South Coast
line runs to Hastings, to peaked summits eight hundred feet high ;
and on the other side, towards Brighton, Mount Harry rises to
about the same altitude.   The shipping at Newhaven bounds the
view on the south, and Crowborough, crowned, like Chanctonbury
to the far west, with a ring of trees, limits the view to the north at
about twenty miles' distance.   The hill on which Lewes is built

Q

descends so swiftly from the foot of the castle to Southover, which is not much above the marsh level, that the effect is that of an immediate drop from the parapet to the bed of the Ouse, which in very high tides overflows the whole marsh between Lewes, New-haven and Seaford.

"On the east of the castle, and hiding from sight the great Laughton Level, through which the train passes to Eastbourne, rises the magnificent mass of downs of which Mount Caburn is the most prominent point. It is partly scarped by great chalk quarries ; but its principal feature is the beautiful ' Coombe ' that faces you all the way as you go down High Street from the west and gives the town the chief element of its singular picturesqueness. It is an enormous notch, beginning near the top of the hill, and widening as it descends. The outlines of this and the many other coombes in the district are indescribably soft and sweet. They are wholly bare of all growth but short turf ; and at morning and evening, when the sun is aslant, they are like nothing so much as dimples with smiles and good thoughts in them."

Patmore claims that six weeks can be spent at Lewes, and "a long walk or drive every day would not bring you to the end of half the beauty within easy reach of it."

Those who only know Lewes as they see it from the railways, or the surroundings as seen from the town, do not really know them at all. Let anyone approach it from Newhaven, or on the Downs above ; from Falmer by Kingston Hill, or the valley to the left with the Winterbourne for guide ; from Mount Harry or from the road or path below Offham ; by the river from Hamsey ; by the roads to the north-east or from Ringmer ; by Caburn over the hills or by the road circling its base ; and last, take a long look from the Down above Beddingham.

In short, Lewes is like a star, whose rays are many and beautiful, and of the first magnitude in the eyes of every South Saxon.

It only remains to say that the picture of "Lewes from the Water Meadows" is from another point of view *not* enumerated in the itinerary given above, which is proof of its possibilities as a sketching ground.

# CHAPTER XXIII

## FALMER TO PLUMPTON PLACE (8 MILES)

### WITH ILLUSTRATIONS BY FRANK GEORGES AND A. S. C.

THERE are two routes of which a choice can be made. To Falmer, as before, by train and up the hill to the village. The by-road next to the " Swan Inn," or the one beyond, both leading north, can be taken, for both bring you to the same point—a path to Balmer on the opposite hill.

To speak in a Sussex fashion, this is a " downright " path indeed, and almost an " upright " one too, so sudden and deep is the valley across which it goes " as straight as a die." As you descend don't forget to look at the view of Lewes on your right. It is one of many, but perhaps the finest.

Balmer, named also after its small mere or pond, is as isolated as any recluse could desire, and pretty withal. It may lay claim to be called a hamlet, as, besides the farm buildings, there is a cottage or two. Although on the top of a high hill, it has quite a wealth of trees—in the comparative sense, seeing how few there are in the neighbourhood. Of views it has no lack, in all directions. The artist ought to be at home here, if the character of the scenery appeals to him—and if he can paint it !

The track continues on right through the farm and neighbouring pasture fields until the last gate and line of old trees are passed, and before you lies Plumpton Plain, an immense expanse of down of which it may be said that it is anything but a plain, in the accepted term, being rolling downland with some fairly deep valleys to boot. Some two miles ahead lies a clump of fir trees on the north ridge known as Black Cap, the dark trees suggesting the name. West of this a gap in the skyline of the down is where your track turns to descend into the Weald. Two miles of springy turf lie between.

As you go there is another broad but shallow coombe on the left, and on the right the rolling plain where the Barons' army formed up in array for the Battle of Lewes. A cross to mark the struggle is cut into the turf ; but Mother Nature would fain let the

1893.

PLUMPTON PLACE, SUSSEX.

(*By A. S. C.*)

dreadful memory pass into oblivion. It is only when recut by those who will not let the dead past bury its dead—or, to be charitable, wish to commemorate deliverance from tyranny—that the cross is visible.

How many changes have these tranquil slopes seen in the affairs of man ? Wherever you go the old marks of cultivation are to be seen, banks or steps lining the hill-side, where the last furrow turned by the plough, assisted by the soil carried down by the rain, has raised a mound as the years went on, and where—gone out of use—the grass has healed the wound but cannot entirely obliterate the scar.

As you wander over the Downs, it is impossible not to observe the many mounds on the otherwise even surface of the grass. They arrest attention, because curiosity is aroused—not, alas, for the first time ! A great many show too evident signs of the untutored archæology of earlier days. A hole dug in the centre of the mound sufficed to satisfy the spirit of research then operative. It is highly probable that the secret sought for was seldom found. Archæologists of to-day know that the finds are often made just within the circle as well as in the centre of a mound. Perhaps it is as well that the unscientific use of the spade was thus restricted. Very few of the finds were properly recorded, and added little to the knowledge of mankind in general. A little local wonderment would be aroused, and with the passing of that generation, only the cinerary urn or votive offering in glass or pottery, uninscribed and often unregarded, would remain on some dusty shelf in the squire's mansion.

\*       \*       \*       \*       \*

East and west of the gap just mentioned, these graves are plainly visible. Some have been opened, small hollows marking the excavation. Others are mounds only. Some three years ago a friend of mine passing down to Plumpton, saw a round object protruding from just beneath the shallow mould in the cutting where the road begins to fall into the Weald. It was the skull of a youth or girl—one of the earliest dwellers on the Downs. How many years had it lain there—who can say ? One can only speculate, but probably long before the Roman Eagles appeared in Britain. I always examine these barrows, whenever I go by, and seldom fail to find small bones thrown up by the moles.

Immediately below the ridge, the road descends through a beech wood entirely devoid of undergrowth, and as you emerge there is a fine view of the steep slopes westward, with the winding road fenced with oak post-and-rail of a grey that only exposure gives, hedged with bushes and low trees. Just by there was an old kiln in its hollow, and following the usual sinuous course in descending you cross the steep field at the foot of the hill and come out on the high road some little distance east of the wayside inn—the " Half Moon." A gate close by the inn, and a catering path across the meadow brings you to Plumpton Place.

If artistic conditions only are considered, its situation would be called beautiful. Built on a knoll which has a spring rising at the foot, and almost forming a lake about it, embosomed in trees, so that its presence is unknown to the passer-by, it makes a good subject for the brush. Being so, it is somewhat strange how seldom the guide-books have pictured it.

Whether the somewhat stagnant water renders it equally good to live in is another question. If it were, I should expect to find other than farm labourers inhabiting the home of Leonard Mascall (who is said to have introduced carp into its moat and into England in the reign of Henry VIII). Nay, more, he is credited with greater gifts ; but the exigencies of rhyme are supposed to account for the last item of the following couplet—

> " Turkeys, Carp, Hops, Pickerell and Beer,
> Which came into England all in one yeare."

According to our view of things, Leonard Mascall deserves praise and blame for his gifts. Some would deem the last item a doubtful blessing ; but such a one would not be a Sussex " yokel." The product of malt and hops known as " beer," if finally banished from England, will surely leave it by the shores of the county which the couplet credits with its introduction—and then only by compulsion !

The house is Elizabethan in form, but is neither large nor fine in detail. It is a worthy yeoman's dwelling. If mosquitoes are to be found anywhere in Sussex during a hot summer, I should think Plumpton Place would have the doubtful honour of their first appearance. And yet the moat is not wholly stagnant. It is always running water and beautifully clear round the back of the house, and when the moat encircled it, was always moving. But now part has been filled up, there is a large sheet which in dry seasons is very shallow and green with weed. The moat overflows and forms the mill pool just below. Here again is material for the painter. It is a charming spot.

Plumpton Church was one of the most dejected-looking buildings forty years ago, but is not nearly so mournful now, owing to trees having been planted and a low wall built round the churchyard. It stood absolutely alone in the centre of an immense field without a bush to soften its lonely graveyard. Perhaps its proximity to the Downs, which are among the highest along the range, helped

to dwarf it. With the exception of the Place and Mill there is no
habitation at all near.

It has a sturdy tower and shingled spire. Its restoration in the
sixties left it—in some respects—poorer than before. True, the
wooden-framed windows of the domestic type were abolished, but
so were the frescoes found under the whitewash. I happened to
be there when they were stripped off by the workmen. They were
infinitely brighter and more complete than those at Clayton or
Preston, and were painted in red, yellow, black and white. They
promptly made way for the one substance churchwardens of that

EAST CHILTINGTON CHURCH.
(By A. S. C.)

day could understand—stucco, of course, grey and blank as their
minds. I begged the head of a saint, and treasured it until it was
accidentally destroyed. One of the Sussex archæological volumes
has an account and a coloured illustration of the designs.

One should not sneer at restorations, as such, because they are
often necessary; but what is so exasperating was the fashion
(things are better now) of making old churches new. Old age has
a charm of its own. To stand before work done by loving, if not
too skilful, hands, when our England was in its infancy, has an
indescribable attraction for me, as for most people. But I could

take you to Sussex churches that have been so scraped, scrubbed, and scarified that it is impossible to say with certainty if any part is really old. Where whitewash covers everything, I admit that removal is necessary ; but there are ways and means of doing this without recutting every moulding, scraping away every old chisel mark, and by refacing each stone, irreparably destroying the surface tints, which only age can give. This is the kind of " restoration " that makes one rage ! As a general rule, when a guide-book says a church is uninteresting, it means that it has been restored !

COTTAGE AT EAST CHILTINGTON.
(*By Frank Georges.*)

On the west side of Plumpton Place there is a pretty lane which gradually loses itself in the fields. Its cart-ruts become obliterated, but there is sufficient indication of a path running due north for more than a mile. It descends to the lower ground where a stream meanders, and rises again through a farmyard into the road that leads eastward to Chiltington (a private road, as the gates will show, but pedestrians are permitted to pass). The whole walk is pleasant, being just north of the Downs, whose graceful undulations rise above the intervening trees.

The village is of the straggling order, but is charmingly situated. The church stands at the winding of the road, and has a sturdy, squat tower with a cap that reminds one of the country boy with a hat several sizes too large. Restoration is probably responsible for the chancel arch and some of the Decorated windows.   As the north and south doors indicate, the original building was Norman. The south door has a pointed arch inserted under the circular one, and a good timbered porch has been added.   There is one fair stained-glass window and one poor.

There is a very fine yew tree, as the sketch shows.   These are often found in churchyards, and are supposed to have been planted to provide the archers of the neighbourhood with bows.   This legend is not universally accepted.

An old house stands hard by of which I should like to see the interior, and there are others in the neighbourhood.   The inn has elements of the picturesque, with its outside staircase and generally unsophisticated air.   Just before reaching it, a path leads west-ward to a large sheet of water fringed with willow and other trees. Water is generally lacking in Sussex landscape, and this mere taken in conjunction with the line of Downs, should provide an opportunity for the artist.

East Chiltington is almost unknown to the majority of Brighton folk, and yet it is only five miles from Falmer.

The same private road goes west to Street.   Its church is mostly Early English, but has also suffered restoration.   Street Place is a handsome Jacobean mansion, with fine panelling and fire-places. Nearly all these old houses have their traditions.   Here a Royalist horseman, hard pressed by Old Noll's Parliamentarians, was said to have ridden into a large hiding-place behind the hall chimney-piece, and never to have been seen again.   One can imagine a communication large enough between " the hole " and the blacker orifice of the chimney, by which the man may have escaped, but for his steed to have vanished into thin air taxes one's credulity.

From Street to Plumpton Station is about a mile.   I would advise a careful study of the time-table to ensure correspondence between the trains at Wivelsfield, to obviate that dreariest of penances—waiting at a railway station !

\*          \*          \*          \*          \*

The other route I spoke of, from Falmer, is to keep on the road where Balmer footpath tumbles down its hill, and follow its spacious curve by Stanmer Park instead, until you reach the grass.   Just below lies Mary Farm.   Drop down by the house and go straight ahead by the side of a long wood, and " on and on "—as the children say—till you reach the north ridge.   (The whole way is over grass, and a most delightful walk it is.)   Below, you will see Plumpton Church, and the clump of trees to the right, in which the " Place " is sheltered.   Between you and it is an exhilarating descent of a good many hundred feet—and steep !

# CHAPTER XXIV

## TO HOLLINGBURY CAMP, CLAYTON MILLS AND HASSOCKS (7 MILES)

### WITH ILLUSTRATIONS BY WALTER PUTTICK AND A. S. C.

I DO not apologise for pointing out the obvious. It is necessary to take in familiar spots on the way. Hollingbury Hill and Camp—now mis-named " Park "—is a fine eminence from which to view the Downs. It has the advantage of a middle distance of dark trees in Stanmer Park as a foil to the lighter tones of the undulating hills, as well as the interest of its ancient earthwork. Speculation runs rife as to the makers of these strongholds—for such they must have been before centuries of detrition and deposit robbed the mounds of height and the ditches of depth. Originally the deep trench and steep bank, crowned with oaken palisades, must have been practically impregnable, except against the engines and catapults of the Roman Legionaries. These latter are credited with the digging of Hollingbury Camp, as it appears to be square—which most Roman camps are. But it is only apparently square. The shape of these fortresses was determined by the shape of the hill-top. This camp, however, is but weak in situation compared to Cissbury, north of Worthing, or Caburn, near Lewes. Either of these with double vallum crowning almost precipitous slopes, must have been formidable strongholds.

Hollingbury is reached from the Ditchling Road tram. It is only a few years since the old Toll-House, sketched here by Mr. Walter Puttick, claimed the nimble sixpence from all wheeled vehicles. They were necessary but exasperating evils, and no one but the Artist regrets their disappearance. They supplied subjects in the early years of last century to the painters of hunting scenes and caricatures of that somewhat shallow age. This toll-gate stood just above the fringe of wood that stretches northward towards the camp. There are two ways of reaching the latter—by skirting the wood, or descending through it and up the valley. (A third path through the eastern wood—the prettiest of all—is now forbidden.)

The view comprises the whole range of Downs between the

OLD TOLL HOUSE, DITCHLING ROAD, BRIGHTON, IN 1892.

(By Walter Puttick.)

valleys of the Ouse and Adur, and a good deal beyond—to Chancton-bury on the west and Firle Beacon on the east. Its beauty is of the downland type, which only its lovers fully appreciate. Wide, spacious, and free, it stretches before the eyes, east, west, and north. Choose your direction and start. Only the growing crops will turn you aside, and at the edge of these there is generally room to go. Here and there a wire fence surrounds a rabbit warren, but on the north ridge the grass is everywhere as free as the air—and this last is óne of the delights of downland. Be the day never so hot, a breeze always fans the downs. (In winter, of course, the gales have full play also.)

" THE FORBIDDEN PATH," ROEDALE.
(By Walter Puttick.)

While on this subject, it may be stated there are a great number of bridle paths and broad ways—equivalent to cattle-ways in other counties. These are marked by the Ordnance maps and are generally respected by the holders of the lands.

\*     \*     \*     \*     \*

Standing on the camp and looking north-west you see Clayton Mills, once spinning merrily on the distant ridge, some miles away, but now, alas! silent. Although you do not fly like the rook on *his* journeyings, you go nearly as straight. As you regain the Ditchling Road, there is a line dividing the crops, which will take you down to a pond far below. North and west of this pond, a great expanse of turf—valley and hill—is given up to pasture, and

CLAYTON MILLS IN 1908.
(*By A. S. C.*)

253

it is seldom that the pearly sheep dotted about the green are absent.

I write for strangers rather than for those who are " native here and to the manner born," when I ask them to listen to the broken melody of the sheep-bells wafted across the slopes and hollows. The bells are of the rudest type, rough metal clamped and brazed, giving out, according to size, the merest tinkle, or sweeter sound, or a dull, arrested clang. But there are few sounds which charm the ear so much. Like the skyward song of the lark, or the drone of the humble-bee, it enters so completely into the spirit of the scene that often only those unused to the sound will hear it. To me it is one of the sweetest sounds in nature (I use the word intentionally). The unknown shepherd who first conceived the idea of keeping his flock from straying by the use of these bells, was the unconscious composer of the first " tone poem "—and no mean poet either !

*          *          *          *          *

To descend to the prosaic, it may perhaps interest some to know that there are fashions in sheep-bells, as in most things. I recently had a talk with the shepherd of this very flock which grazes to east and west of the " Ladies' Mile." He was the proud protector of nearly a thousand sheep and lambs—in one flock ! A younger shepherd had another five hundred yearlings under his care in the next valley. These were " bell'd " with " cup " and small " horse " bells, of cast metal, giving the usual clear ring, so unlike the liquid single note emitted by the genuine " canister " sheep-bell. The " cup " bells are mostly used with flocks of full grown lambs. They are shaped like a Chinese cup with a right-angled loop of metal through which to pass the neckstrap.

The " horse " bells are those once used to accompany a team drawing the great wagon, and were worn above the collar under a leathern canopy. There are fourteen to the " set." One seldom sees or hears them nowadays. They are cast with a ring of metal near the mouth of the bell. The " Latten " bells are plain cast. Why they are so called, I do not know, nor did my shepherd.*

But the genuine sheep-bells are called " canister " bells—obviously because of their shape. To those who think they have merely the one purpose to prevent straying, it may be interesting to learn that musical considerations enter into the custom. Thus, however haphazard the sounds may seem to the listener, the intention is to make music, and to form chords. It succeeds, as the sweetness of the sound bears witness. It is a singularly liquid note. I can only compare it to the falling of large drops of water into a pool or well, re-echoing from the rock or sides.

* I have since found out that " latten " is a term for bronze, or a mixed metal used for crosses, candlesticks, small bells, etc.

A flock should have a " set of bells." There are eighteen in a set, ranging from the tiniest tinkler through the gamut of sounds down to the clanging gong. A set costs £5—or did cost that sum. " They are not to be had now," the shepherd told me. As an article of commerce they are dropping out. I suppose a time will come when the sweet sound will no more be heard upon our downs ? The pity of it !

\*       \*       \*       \*       \*

The second valley lies just beneath a long slope of the finest turf, called the " Ladies' Mile," stretching from Stanmer Park to Patcham. It is, or was, before cycles and motors made their appearance, a favourite galloping ground.

In the valley is a red-roofed barn with a group of wind-blown pines to the north, old and ragged, but still capable of forming a good sketch, with the aid of a bank of gorse and the sheep. On the slope beyond, the smoothness of the turf shows the route quite plainly, and a steady rise leads to a great barrier of gorse and to a steep and sudden descent, at the foot of which the road to Standean winds. But turning neither to right nor left, you attack the formidable gorse (and find how prickly it can be) and plunge down the hill to your green way, again mounting the gentle slope in front, bringing you to cultivation once more. At the top you can see Clayton Mills ahead. Your goal in sight the way is one of choice. A detour to the right, past what may be a Druid stone, lying bare and solitary upon the sward, takes you in a long curve to the north ridge overlooking the Weald ; or a straighter drop into the valley brings you to a slanting track leading to the mills.

While you rest upon or by the stone, I may be telling you of a large number of these " grey-wethers," as they are called, encircling a pond just north of Standean lying behind you. Whether they were found in excavating the pond, or whether pre-existent as a Druid circle, I know not for certain. There they lie, and you may, if you choose, invest them with the romance they undoubtedly suggest, if not deserve.

We live and learn, and in the pursuit of knowledge some of our cherished theories, built up of much mental exercise on carefully chosen foundations, have the solid ground cut away from under them by inexorable, frigid facts. It is so with the theory of many so-called Druidical remains. These very stones at Standean formed recently the text for an attractive article—accompanied by a plan— almost convincing in its conclusions. But, alack, the plan was almost as imaginary as the conclusions drawn from the prostrate megaliths. In fact, it may be said that the only things positively _drawn_, were the stones themselves—by oxen or horses from the neighbouring land, to get them out of the way of the plough !

It is rather an amusing commentary on the confident conclusions of our would-be archæologists, that these Standean " grey-wethers " are still being added to by the same process of haulage. Various methods are used to dispose of these inconvenient masses of sandstone or conglomerate. The stones in Goldstone Bottom were interred by digging a grave by each, and incontinently rolling them in!

One point only remains in support of the " Druidical " theory. It is not impossible that many veritable Druid circles may have been destroyed by like means, i.e. burial or haulage. So there

CLAYTON FROM THE DOWN.
(By A. S. C.)

is still room to weave romance, if we will! There is, however, an even better way—for some well-qualified archæologist to thoroughly examine these " derelicts of Time " for any sign of human handiwork. Stonehenge, or other known examples of Druid remains, would supply data. An ounce of archæological fact would be worth any amount of speculation. It is, I believe, almost certain that these " grey-wethers " were used by the Romans to mark off distances, even as our Ordnance surveyors mark them with the " broad arrow " now. There may possibly be Roman characters and numerals awaiting discovery on some of them— and maybe Runic symbols!

\*        \*        \*        \*        \*

# PRESSING WILD FLOWERS

### By James MacIntyre

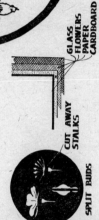

SPLIT BUDS

CUT AWAY STALKS

GLASS
FLOWERS
PAPER
CARDBOARD

**H**EDGEROWS and banks produce many types of wild-flowers all through the year. A permanent method of preserving the more attractive flowers is to press and mount them beneath glass. Trays, fancy box-tops, table-tops and framed pictures could all be utilized.

After the flowers and ferns of your choice have been collected, cut away all thick sections and stems which will never show. Now, take all the buds and heavy flowers and carefully split them with a sharp knife as illustrated. When all the flowers and ferns have been split, place them between sheets of blotting paper.

Next, lay over the specimens a drawing board or some weight that gives an overall, even pressure. After the flowers have been completely dried, choose the size of picture you wish to make. The glass, backing board and paper mounting should all be cut the same size. The paper mounting should be of a tone which will show off the flowers to the best advantage.

Now arrange the flowers in the most attractive way. A spot of quick-drying glue should be applied to the back of each subject.

All that remains to be done now is the framing. Passe-partout could be used or light wooden framing would make a more permanent job.

169

are ideal. If the young audience, when enthusiasm, crowd forward, it is a simple matter to get them to the far end of the room by warning that it will spoil the magic space.

All the following tricks are easily made at little expense. A smooth patter will make them more convincing in mystifying the children, and, maybe, the adults as well. A little practice beforehand will ensure perfection.

## The Magic Rope

For this trick you will need a quart bottle in dark brown glass, 1yd. of rope, and a cork stopper. Cut the cork into a small ball the size of a marble, so that it will drop easily into the bottle. Darken it with indian ink.

Explain that there is not enough room to do the Indian rope trick, but that you can stiffen an ordinary rope so that it will support a bottle. Give the bottle and the rope to your audience for examination. All this time you are holding the cork hidden between the base of the second and third fingers, on the underside of the hand.

As you take the bottle from the audience, put your hand over the neck and drop the cork inside. Push 1ft. of the rope into the bottle and withdraw it. Then push it in again, wiggle the rope about, and as you speak the magic words, quickly turn the bottle upside down and give an imperceptible tug on the rope. The cork will fall into the neck and wedge the rope securely. Reverse the bottle and swing it on the end of the

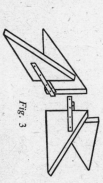

Fig. 2

Fig. 3

THERE is no need to feel apprehensive about your Christmas tree falling over if you use this adjustable stand (Fig. 1). It is much better than a flowerpot, and is not so unsightly as a tub.

The triangular pieces can be cut from the ends of a box, providing the wood is ¾in. thick. If the tree is only a small one, 12in. lengths for the base may be sufficient (Fig. 2). Four iron plates, ½in. wide, are

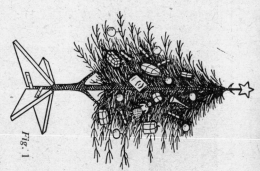

Fig. 1

required. Screw two of them, a little more than half way up, on one of the triangular pieces. Place the tree between the iron plates, and secure it firmly by screwing on another triangle (Fig. 3).

Complete the stand by fixing two more triangles. Here again, screw two of the plates on first, underneath the two already attached. It is then easy to screw on the opposite triangle. (F.G.)

Clayton Mills are the only ones now existing on the north escarpment, since Wilmington Mill was burned or blown down—and,
alas, these too have ceased working! One is a tower, the other
a " smock " mill. They form a fine picture, often painted, with
Wolstonbury or the Weald for background. Constable sketched
the tower mill. It is in the Print Room of the British Museum.
In his day the other mill had not arrived! It was moved, or
brought from the Dyke Road in Brighton, and re-erected here.

Whenever I see them they always remind me of a wordy war
I once had with the Bookworm, as we lay on the down above, and
looked upon the ancient church of Clayton far below. A stray
expression falling from my lips, of reverence for the age of the

CLAYTON CHURCH.
(By Walter Puttick.)

tiny structure, was the cause of the linguistic storm which hurtled
about our respective pairs of ears, and shook our quivering frames,
while it lasted ; but which made no impression whatever on the
doddergrass beside us, usually so sensitive to atmospheric disturb-
ances, nor did the hill-side generally seem at all affected.

The day was warm and we were warmer. I suspect the climb
had cost us more than we were willing to admit. The Bookworm
began it. He seized on the remark made between moppings, and
snorted : " Age, indeed ! What is the date and character of a
Saxon hovel such as that, to the least of the Greek temples, not
to mention the Assyrian or Egyptian ? " (It will be seen that the
Bookworm is of classic sympathies born of much study and travel.)

It is true that " a soft answer turneth away wrath," but the
matter as well as the manner must be conciliatory. To answer a

R

hot man in a cool manner, is like the strong wind among red embers
—it fans them into a blaze.  My suggestion that "hovel" was
ill-chosen to describe the building in question, and unworthy of
the polished "Age" he represented, seemed to jar some loose
chord of his nature, judging by the torrent of unmusical sounds
that followed.

He declared the Age which built Clayton Church to be but
little removed from the savage, and not worthy of mention in the
same breath with the classic days of yore.  Metaphorically, he
pulled the poor old structure to pieces, and left it a heap of rubble
on the ground.  He said the pillars and arch would do despite
to the shape of a tree-trunk, and no rudeness of construction could
exceed the rudeness of the times.  The one was a reflex of the
other, and both were bad !  The walls were of the poorest quality,
and were covered with "cock-eyed primitives" in the shape of
frescoes—a fitting ornament for such a structure.

"What was its crown of years—a bare eight hundred at most—
compared to the centuries which had rolled by since the meanest
classic temple, perfect in fitness and simple beauty, had risen in
honour——"

"In honour of the most imperfect set of deities the mind of
man could evolve," I interrupted.  "Deities who were human
to a fault, or rather, all faults ;  primitives who were truly ' cock-
eyed ' because their one attitude was that of winking at each other's
excesses, and who had less of the God about them than the statues
from Easter Island !  Culture and a sense of beauty were certainly
more general in classic days, but these were plants of long growth,
or gifts from God through Mother Nature, to whom her children
went for inspiration—for in 2000 B.C. men were nearer to the time
when ' God beheld, and lo, all things were very good.'

"We may suppose that the sense of beauty in form and fitness
was natural to that state of perfection, and however desperately
wicked men in heart became, the choice of things beautiful would
in some measure remain.  Perhaps this accounts for the fact
that ugliness was as rare then as beauty is to-day in things of
common use.  Certain it is that in the most archaic relics of ancient
days, beauty and fitness go hand in hand.  I go further, and say
that in culture and attainments your classic people were far and
away in front of the poor Saxon who built the ' hovel ' at our
feet, and, not to mention this our day, could even give points to
you, friend Bookworm, which is saying much ! "

Bookworm being contemptuously silent, I went on : "But if
you compare the general progress made by peoples in given periods,
that of our race during the last eight hundred years is greater and
more wonderful than any that went before, chiefly because we have

cultivated the heart as well as the mind and hand. Therefore, when I look at that lowly temple down yonder—rude and clumsy if you will—I see in it the earnest desire of our forefathers to turn again to the Giver of all good. I can overlook its ungainliness and should be inclined to applaud if a similar legend were adapted and emblazoned on its simple walls as that found on an old bell at Eastdean—'there is not a better bell under the sky!'

"Book-worm," I said solemnly, "what is your reply to all this?" But there was no voice, nor any that answer-ed, except a deep breath-ing. Book-worm was fast asleep! I couldn't brook this, so I stooped down, and shouted in his ear that "Clayton had neither in-cident nor history, nor any recom-mendation, but — Age!"

INTERIOR CLAYTON CHURCH.
(*By Walter Puttick.*)

He must have heard me, for he opened his eyes; but he did not thank me, which I thought rude.

\*        \*        \*        \*        \*

A descent by the Mills brings you to the village of Clayton and its Church, and a few steps beyond a squeeze-stile admits to the "Cinder Path," a really beautiful walk, notwithstanding it skirts the railway. The prospect on either side is fine, the chief hill to the east being Ditchling Beacon; that on the west is Wolston-bury. The path ends near a delightful knoll of pines that has a tiny stream at its base. Hassocks Station is close by.

CLAYTON TOWER MILL.—MOONRISE.
(By A. S. C.)

# CHAPTER XXV

## PATCHAM TO DITCHLING AND HASSOCKS (6 MILES)

WITH ILLUSTRATIONS BY R. G. GREYSMITH, ARTHUR B. PACKHAM,
H. SCHRODER AND A. S. C.

P ATCHAM is reached by the tram and the "Patcham Express," a leisurely 'bus (now a motor 'bus) that goes quite fast enough along the one *pretty* road out of Brighton, and lands you at the "Memorial."
I find the difficulty of enlarging on the charms of Patcham too great to be successfully overcome. It is too near home! Of a less attractive place more distantly removed it is possible to say flattering words on the chance that one of three things may happen. Either that your reader may not be familiar with the spot, and does not realise how thickly you have laid on the colour; or, your enthusiasm may fail to awaken in him the slightest desire for a better acquaintance with it; or that he may just look at your pictures, but studiously avoid a perusal of the letterpress! Of the three, I think I prefer the latter attitude, because he cannot complain that you have misled him, and has only himself to blame if he has missed anything worth reading.

One can hear the criticisms on any attempt to exalt the village of the Wellsbourne even before the attempt is made. "Thank you, we know Patcham quite well. Have several times driven there in a cab. Got a bicycle, you know; often go through it—dusty street with a Jubilee Memorial and no sidewalks. Hasn't any history, has it? Don't care much for it—too near the town, and not far enough out in the country for me. Only seen it from the road, but know it quite well. Not pretty, nor ugly, but passable."

Truth sometimes comes of itself! "Neither pretty, nor ugly, but passable." "Passable," truly—on a bicycle, or a motor-car! What if its charms are of the quiet order? It is charming enough for me. If it were "divinely fair," its proximity to our great town would raise up a cloud of fearsome things—pleasure-gardens where true pleasure is unknown; swings and roundabouts and

braying bands ; crowds of trippers and their noisy ways ; while
Nature's loveliness would make the poet's lines—

> " Where every prospect pleases
> And only man is vile "—

a keen and sorrowful reality.

Truth to tell, unless the surroundings of a big town are all alike
beautiful, whichever way one turns, it is a misfortune to possess
a " Fairy Glen " or " Crystal Grotto." I once spent a summer
morning of dreamy delight at Stonehenge, alone and wrapped in
the glamour of the place, until the midday hour had fled—and I

WESTMESTON FROM THE DOWN.
(By R. G. Greysmith.)

with it ! For coach and wagonette came tooling and tootling up,
depositing load after load of excursionists, to whom the antiquity
and mystery of the monoliths were as nothing compared to the
pleasures of the picnic. They sang songs neither of Arcady nor
Araby ; ate and drank gloriously ; sprawled all over the stones ;
lit a fire and boiled kettles behind one of them ; and when the feast
was over, used the circular cavities in them as wash-hand basins—
forms of sacrificial fire and libations not exactly contemplated by
the founders of the temple.

Around, all was as fair as before, but for me (" being but a
moonish youth " and sentimental) the sun seemed darkened, and
the beauty of the day was gone.

Let us not then think slightingly of the places where the quieter moods of Nature are only in evidence. Such a place is Patcham. Yet it can give pleasure to those who seek for it. From the hills around it has several views to offer by no means unacceptable to the artist; and more can be had for the looking. True, its houses are not very ancient or quaint; and its church is for the most part "clothed upon" with stucco, and has a conical and comical little extinguisher for a spire, which is neither elegant nor picturesque. Old pictures show that this usurps the place of a battlemented parapet, and should be disenthroned or made shapeable. Perhaps one day legitimate "restoration" may have a look in.

Within, there is a little Norman work, one or two Decorated

JUBILEE MEMORIAL, PATCHAM.
*(By Arthur B. Packham.)*

windows, and an ancient fresco of the Last Judgment over the chancel arch.

Above the church is Patcham Farm. The house is a very dignified brick and flint specimen of the style that superseded half-timber work. Its well-house, with donkey wheel and cistern, still stands— if to be very much out of the upright and on its last legs can be called standing.

It is not uncommon to see a quaint little red roof capped by a hood, peeping above the wall of a farm. It is generally circular, and covers a low building with sloping sides, not unlike a windmill cut down. This is a culver-house or dovecote. In the corner of the garden-plot of Patcham Farm stands one of these picturesque old buildings.

How old it is its condition bears witness. It has down-hill buttresses which are fashioned in a novel way, being adjuncts in one respect and part of the main wall in another. I was told that a dovecote exactly similar has been erected in the Isle of Wight by a lady, to whom the original was dear in childhood's days. She sent her architect all the way to Patcham to take its quaint plan. There are few older dovecotes than this in Sussex.

If you examine it you will find it has a door, but no windows, unless the hood can be so designated, its primary object being to admit pigeons, light being a secondary consideration. On entering you will find that the walls are very thick, and have, row above row, a number of apertures about a hand's breadth across. If you put your hand into one of them you will find them piercing the wall for a foot, and then turning at right angles to form a little

PATCHAM FARM AND CHURCH.
(*By Arthur B. Packham.*)

room large enough to hold a pigeon's nest and young. In the centre of the 'cote there will be a strong pole and framework, the latter fashioned like a ladder. This pole turns on a centre pivot, and by means of the ladder the nests can be reached when pigeon-pie is in season.

This dainty, succulent enough at any time, was almost a necessity in the olden days, when fresh meat was seldom to be had in the winter. Owing to the fact that hay was not known—or not used—cattle were seldom kept, except for stock purposes, during the winter. The animals were generally slaughtered in October, and "corned" beef was thenceforward more plentiful than our forefathers liked. Thus came the need for dovecotes. Now, alas—for still the phrase holds good—". the old order changeth." Now that they are less of a necessity, pigeons are found to be "more nuisance than they are worth. They settle on the roofs, and foul the tanks." It is an old story—the love passes with the need.

There are many still remaining in Sussex. The one at West Dean—minus its roof—is supposed to be Norman. The famous one at Lewes Castle, which was as large as a church, was destroyed at the beginning of last century. Most of the Norman strongholds had dovecotes ; and many and deep were the complaints from the Saxon farmers of the depredations of the winged inhabitants. But woe betide the man who took the law into his own hand against them.

I cannot forgo quoting here from Mrs. Ewing's charming story of *Daddy Darwin's Dovecot,* so faithfully and humorously illustrated by Randolph Caldecott (both writer and artist of tender memories).

It is the letter written by Jack March to the old and lonely man who was the last of the Darwyns who built the dovecote in the fifteenth century.

DOVECOTE AND PATCHAM FARM.
(*By A. S. C.*)

" HONOURED SIR,—

" They call me Jack March. I'm a workhouse lad, but, sir, I'm a good one, and the Board means to 'prentice me next time. Sir, if you face the Board, and take me out, you shall never regret it. Though I says it as shouldn't, I'm a handy lad. I'll clean a floor with any one, and am willing to work early and late, and at your time of life you're not what you was, and them birds must take a deal of seeing to. I can see them from the garden when I'm set to weed, and I never saw nought like them. Oh, sir, I do beg and pray of you to let me mind your pigeons. You'll be none the worse of a lad about the place, and I shall be happy all the days of my life. Sir, I'm not unthankful, but, please God, I should like to have a home, and to be with them house doves.

" From your humble servant—hoping to be,

" JACK MARCH."

" Mr. Darwin sir. I love them Tumblers as if they was my own."

" Daddy Darwin thought hard and thought long over that letter. He changed his mind fifty times a day. But Friday was Board day, and when Friday came he ' faced the Board.' And the little workhouse lad went home to Daddy Darwin's Dovecot."

*        *        *        *        *

Passing through the farmyard, the road ascends a gentle slope by half a dozen yellow stacks until it begins to turn down into a great valley. A look back will reveal the fact that Patcham lies at the mouth of several great valleys. The drainage of these forms the spring which supplies the well at the Memorial. In early days this issued in a stream which ran through Brighton and joined the sea at Pool Valley. It was called the Wellsbourne, and it is a commentary upon the liability of names to change with use. It gives its title to the Hundred, but " Whalesbone " is what it has arrived at in vulgar parlance.

Even as Brighton has rejoiced in being classed among " the noble ports and havens of the realm "—for thus old Andrew Borde of King Hal's days describes it—so the little stream has occasionally attained volume enough to give it temporary rank among the rivers of Sussex.

In old records the village is sometimes called by the name of the contributor of some of these sketches (Packham), which will be news to him, I doubt not.

The surroundings of Patcham are free and open enough to please any wanderer. There is nothing to prevent him reaching any part of the Downs. Hedges are unknown, and trees are only found in the hollows here and there. Wide, curving valleys wind away to the highest ridges fringing the Weald, narrowing as they go, but spacious even where they merge into the hill. If the Dyke were a rocky valley like so many in Sussex and elsewhere, we should make less ado about it. It is because it is so unusually sheer and narrow for a down valley, that we regard it as remarkable. The usual characteristics of these are breadth and space.

You turn from viewing the fair scene—for fair it is—comprising the whole of the well-wooded valley with Brighton and the shining sea for background—and follow the road into the coombe, an immense amphitheatre and all grass, except for one fine thorn tree immediately below, which, like a giant mushroom, gives shelter from heat or rain by the spread of its branches. I know of no finer specimen on our Downs.

As you go you can see the short cut which leads to Standean forsake the winding and much longer road, and strike across the green—a breadth of softest velvet upon a field of softer plush ! None but the downland man—and the cricketer on his well-rolled plot—realise to the full the joy of this turf. It is unlike any other greensward. Neither park nor meadow gives quite that sense of enjoyment or exaltation of spirit which springs unsummoned into play when the feet leave the hard chalk road and feel the grass beneath for the first time. It is a happiness not confined to youth alone, nor keener then. It comes to all alike ; but perhaps in greater measure to the frail of frame and tired of foot. I can promise this pleasure to all who trace this path.

A sharp rise leads along the border of a cornfield and between the crops to what is a rather unusual feature on the hills—a stile ! The descent beyond is not unusual ! Standean, in its valley, is as sudden a sight as Telscombe, and a charming spot to boot. It had an old Tudor house with stone-mullioned windows and arched door until a fire burnt out the front and roof some years ago, and robbed it of its designation. Of course, it was modernised in rebuilding ; but the eastern wall contains an indication of its former dignity, and "shows up" the poverty of the new work.

There is a very quaint well in front of the house. The winch is covered by an old grey weather-boarded cap, and is raised on a square platform approached by a well-worn stairway. Why it was raised is somewhat of a puzzle. Probably to allow water to flow by gravitation into the house from the two lead-lined cisterns by the side of the winch, or to prevent the cattle stumbling into the well, or the fouling of the water—the bank rising so steeply hard by.

The well stands under a fine chestnut tree. There are many old chestnut trees in the valley, the trunks of some of them but the merest shells.

By the way, why is the horse-chestnut so called ? Few besides the country-folk know—and yet a Londoner gave me the reason ! It is not because its somewhat bitter nut is a favourite with Dobbin. If you look above the brown husk just behind the sticky boss of the budding-shoot, you will discover a tiny, fairy-like horseshoe, nails, frog " and all ! "—as the children say ; and it is a delightful sur-prise to such, and to simpletons like myself. Look again, and you will find others more or less distinct, at every joint of the young branches, wherever last year's leaves have been shed. I deem it the best of " luck " to have made this probably well-known dis-covery. In this dainty semblance of a horse-shoe I have harked back to the pleasures of boyhood, when every day brought a new wonder to light ; and this late " find "—if I mistake not—is know-ledge also to most of my readers to-day. Nevertheless, in this derivation of the title of " horse-chestnut," I am quite prepared to have my judgment disabled by better qualified students of nature improving on the procedure of the " Seventh Cause," by reversing the accepted order, and giving me the "lie direct" to start with!

North-east of the house, a gate opens into an odour-laden lane, that, curving round, brings you into another mighty hollow, or rather, three, which will attract or repel in proportion to the love you bear the Downs, for they are thoroughly typical of the range. In two of them there is not a tree or bush to break the level monotony of green, and the only inequalities visible are the mole-hills overgrown with moss.  But in spring the turf is a carpet of violets, and in autumn a sheet of what is perhaps the loveliest and most dainty flower on earth—the harebell.  They grow more profusely the higher you ascend the valley.

Three coombes spread out before you from a common source—the valley you are in—much as a fleur-de-lis pattern spreads its leaves. They look very large, but the deceptive nature of the perspective will surprise, before you get to the end of either.  What the eye fails to grasp, the legs will acknowledge by the time you stand on Ditchling Beacon, which rises at the head of the midmost coombe. It is a fine hill, and has an equally fine view.  It is the highest point on the South Downs, so far as prospect is concerned.  Duncton Down, far to the west, is a few feet higher, but a thickset wood covers the summit, and it lies off the north ridge.  Here, at Ditchling Beacon, there is nothing to obstruct the view, and as far as the eye can reach, the hills on right and left fall gracefully away into the distance and the Weald stretches before you, mile on mile of field and woodland.

It is difficult to express in words the pleasure one feels in gazing on this almost limitless expanse of hill and coombe, bounded on the south by the shining sea, and on the north by " the blue goodness of the Weald."  But it has not always been so difficult of expression.  Here is an extract from a guide-book of " the sixties," now out of print, but too " precious " to be lost !—" The remains of a Roman encampment crown the summit, and recall to memory the grand old times when yonder rich and fertile Weald was an impenetrable forest ;  when tidal waters seethed and fretted in the broad valley of the Ouse ;  when Lucullus built his villa on the grassy slopes, and Aglaia wandered in love-musing upon the pebbly shore. . . . Here, on this breezy peak, etc., etc."

This is " elegant " food indeed, for simple down lovers !  And " breezy *peak* " may be referred to another and truer description— " our blunt, bow-headed, whale-backed Downs."  " Breezy height," if you will ; but *peak*. . . . Ye gods !

\*          \*          \*          \*          \*

Ditchling Beacon is so called from the warning fires which were kindled on its summit when dangers threatened the kingdom. From here, in all probability, flashed the signal in answer to those which blazed in rapid succession from westward, when the Armada was sighted in the Channel.

I was fortunate enough to see the beacon fires from here on the

DITCHLING POND.
(*By Hubert Schroder, A.R.E.*)

Diamond Jubilee of Queen Victoria, and a truly wonderful and beautiful sight they were.   It was a most tranquil, cloudless night. On our way from Hollingbury Camp the grass and the darkness were starred with the " pale, ineffectual fires " of the glow-worm ; so many, it seemed as if they, too, shone out to grace the occasion. And these little fairy beacon fires, as we saw them on this happy

night, led our thoughts onward to those other beacon fires, soon
to be the visible sign, from one end of England to the other, that
" the heart of the people rejoiced."

Hurrying on, we reached Ditchling Beacon, restored for this
night to its pristine use and glory.   As we climbed the hill, the
great pyre of faggots loomed darkly upon the summit, as in days
of old.   Westward, the horizon was scarcely visible, but at a dozen

OLD RELIGIOUS HOUSE, DITCHLING.
(*By Arthur B. Packham.*)

points the darkness was pierced by showers of coloured fires, and
the sky above Brighton alternated every hue in and out of the
rainbow.   We looked out over the Weald, but except for the
twinkling of a lamp here and there, or the ascent of a rocket, all
was wrapped in gloom.   On Wolstonbury there was a striking sight
—the Hurst College boys in torchlight procession, were winding
up its steep slope to ignite their bonfire.

Of the horizon little could be seen, for a dark haze of heat hung

over it and reached high above.    As the hour drew near we sat
and gazed out into the darkness.    There was a gentle wind on
the hill-top, and it brought with it the sound of music out of the
Weald.    Now, as we looked, there blossomed and grew out of the
darkness before us bright orange globes of fire, like beautiful flowers.
In every direction they burst forth.    Then with " shout and song "
the mighty beacon behind us roared into flame and made night
into day.    Except for this, the silence of it all !    To walk on to the
next hill eastward was to lose even the crackling and roar of our
own beacon.    Here the others seemed larger and brighter than

DITCHLING FARM AND CHURCH.
*(By Hubert Schroder, A.R.E.)*

when we were near our own fire ; and we could not help observing
the shape each took—an oval with a point towards the sky—
veritable " tongues of fire."    Against the dark heat-haze of the
horizon they were finely visible, so that those many miles distant
appeared quite close, and seemed to hang suspended in the darkness.
All were of a beautiful orange hue, and each preserved its oval form,
but they were too far off for us to see the moving flame.    As we
stood, we could count over a hundred, and by the aid of a glass
many more were to be seen, and the glow on the sky of others
below the horizon.

The Down fires themselves were a noble sight, as they flamed away east and west, each on his own hill far into the distance, growing smaller and smaller as they receded from the eye. A notable sight, my Masters !

\*       \*       \*       \*       \*

From the Beacon, a road, said to be cut deep into the side to allow Roman soldiery to pass unobserved from the Camp into the Weald, winds snakelike down. The hill is very steep, and at its base you can see the little church of Westmeston. If you choose

WESTMESTON CHURCH.

(*By F. Davey.*)

you can skirt the slope, and drop by degrees into the pretty village. The church is beautifully situated, but its charm lies mainly in this and its porch. Inside, the restoration some forty years ago seems to have taken all the grace of age and ornament out of it. The frescoes found were promptly effaced with grey stucco— "and there an end," so far as description goes. What the church has lost by the destruction of these mural paintings, one of the Sussex Archæological volumes will show. They were drawn and printed in colour for the work.

There is a delightful path over the fields from here, with a little stream to cross, and all the way you get pretty views of Ditchling and the range of downs.  The former lies on a " bluff " of wealden sand—the chalk ending a little south of it.  For this reason the air is said to be quite different, and even relaxing.  Certainly it is never very cold.

Alfred the Great knew it, and had a " park " here.  The building near the church is an old religious house, and is much in request by artists, and with good reason.  The outside stairway is novel in this neighbourhood, and was even more attractive when it went up from the roadway, as an old picture I have presents it— unless this is the position the artist thought it should hold !

The cruciform church is a worthy fane.  The Early English work in tower and chancel is quite beautiful, and although the nave is simple, the whole effect is good.

The village has an air of a small country town—perhaps would consider itself one—and there are some houses with elements of the picturesque about them.  This is as far as *I* dare go.  But *you* must go farther—in another sense.  There is a 'bus to Hassocks along a beautiful road lined with houses sadly out of touch with rural scenery.  Here and there are exceptions, and Keymer Church can be visited.  Once interesting, it is now " made new." Age may again give it what it has lost, but you and I will not " be there to see."

S

# CHAPTER XXVI

LEWES TO BARCOMBE MILLS AND ISFIELD (8 MILES)

WITH ILLUSTRATIONS BY WALTER PUTTICK, ARTHUR B. PACKHAM
AND A. S. C.

FROM the station you cross Lewes and descend into the Pells, where there is a gate leading on to the river bank, and come at last "by devious ways"—so spacious are the windings of the Ouse just north of Lewes—to Hamsey. You will not begrudge the doubling propensity of the river. To my mind, it is all beautiful, especially near South Malling, which is sweetly embosomed in trees—but lies on the other side of the stream. There is a handsome "Queen Anne" house below the church, and at Old Malling Farm there are the remains of an ancient collegiate church in the garden, where the Archbishop of Canterbury had a residence. In the *Memorials of Canterbury Cathedral*, Dean Stanley tells the legend of the table which refused to bear the arms of Becket's murderers, when they rested here.

As you go along the bank, look back at Lewes and see how finely the castle crowns the hill ; and forward to Offham Church, than which no bolder situation could be found. This was built "to bring the Church nearer to the people" in a literal sense. Hamsey is the parish church, but it stands on a hillock far away on the level, and has but one house—the farm—near it. So Offham (pronounced Oafham) was built to take its place, and though it lacks age, is a fine church finely placed.

But Hamsey is the artist's delight. Ivy-clad and "set like a beacon on a hill," flanked by its farm and yellow stacks and dark yew trees, and backed by Malling Down, it is a place of pilgrimage for many besides Lewes folk, with whom it is a favourite walk. Prehistoric floods, or a mightier river than the Ouse, must have swept round the northern side of the hill, for it drops as suddenly as Malling Chalk Pits yonder, and close to the verge the pretty old church stands, exposed to every wind that blows. A more picturesque spot can hardly be imagined.

The church is of nearly every style. The chancel arch may be Saxon, but it is certainly the earliest Norman, and the other parts

pass through Early English to Decorated, with a Perpendicular
tower and font.   The tower (which seems quite half of the church
and yet not " too big for its place ") has a larger window than the
chancel, and a sturdy squat turret on the north side ; and in the
centre of each face satanic horned heads which ought to be gar-
goyles.   Presumably, the association of so pure and cooling a thing
as water was thought to be out of character with such Gehenna-
like expressions, so they do nothing but scowl at the fair prospect
on every side.

The farm building on the river bank is heavily buttressed, and
the dovecote serves as barn and pigeon-house.   It has quaint
oaken bars to its windows and is roofed with Horsham slates.

HAMSEY CHURCH FROM THE LEVEL.
(*By A. S. C.*)

These are seldom seen on any but substantial structures.   They
are not " slates " at all, but thin slabs of stone, and need good
timbers and stout walls to support them.

From the river bank, away on the right, Ringmer Mill may be
seen, but the church is hidden among trees.   Barcombe, on the
left, with its low, grey spire and red roofs lies as sheltered as Hamsey
is exposed.

Unless there is an evident path, try no short cuts from bend to
bend of the river.   Unseen and undreamt-of backwaters and dykes
will bar your way, and turn you again on to the bank.   Nor are
paths always to be trusted.   When you are about level with Barcombe Church one such caters across the grass.   It leads to the
station, but you lose the river just at its prettiest part, where

the level also begins to get wooded, and the stream winds among the trees in delightful fashion.

Those who do not despise simple things, may be interested in the marsh bridges and locks, and the gates and their fastenings. Over the river itself the first are usually brick arches, glowing with red, and hung with moss and weeds, where the water rises and falls. Those over the runnels vary from the single oak slab, with or without a slight railing stretching from posts driven in on either bank. But those across the wider dykes are often the most picturesque, and like most beautiful things in this age of

OLD FOOT-BRIDGE AT BARCOMBE.
(*By Walter Puttick.*)

iron, fast disappearing. Two rows of shapely piles are driven into the bed of the dyke, and surmounted by a cross-piece. On these, long timbers in a gentle curve stretch from bank to bank, and carry the footway flooring of rough-hewn slabs, and a post-and-rail, not too upright, completes the bridge on either side—and artists bless the builders all their days! One such, in ruins, stands near Barcombe Mills, and there are others higher up the Ouse.

The locks are nearly all in decay, but make a far better picture than when they were in use. The aims of Commerce and those of Nature widely differ. Tar and paint are the only decoration the former allows, while a hundred feathery forms of greenery and mossy tinting are the latter's more artistic palette. The gates and their fastenings will interest those unused to river-side methods. They are of every variety, from the stile which must be clambered over, to the little wicket-gate with a puzzle-chain for fastening. Perhaps the most ingenious (and surprising) is the " tumble-down gate." It is constructed of poles, pivoted and weighted at one end with shaped blocks of oak standing one upon another, forming to the casual eye, an ordinary gatepost, and working in a slot at the other end. It looks " very like a gate " until you manfully mount. Then the whole five bars collapse and you find yourself over sooner than you expected, but not in an erect position.

The chief use of the " tumble-down gate " is to allow horses to pass over it on the towing-path.

The fastenings are many and quaint, ranging from the great wooden latch drawn back or lifted up, to the little, swivelled triangular catch for the iron finger attached to the gate—one of the most certain in action. But the puzzle-chain, so easy to unloose when you know how, and so exasperating when you don't, is perhaps the most or the least interesting according to knowledge. As there are collectors of most things on earth, so there are collections of gate fastenings ; and with better justification than of some articles, so many and ingenious are the devices. Sussex abounds in them.

The last loop of the river near the ruined foot-bridge finds you confronted with a barrier and turned off the river bank into the roadway leading to the station on the left, or to " Barcombe Mills " on the right.

The title has an inviting sound. It conjures up alluring visions. The sketch given later on may, without undue egotism, be designated as a " triumph of mind over matter," and goes to support the assertion that there is " a soul of good in things evil "—if Barcombe Mills will pardon the not too complimentary quotation. But with the greatest desire to respect so ancient and honourable an institution, the mention of which in Domesday may be termed a recent episode in the course of a long and useful career—it is impossible to speak of the present building as a " vision of loveliness," or even a " dream of beauty." Set in the midst of scenery that may truthfully be called sylvan and sweet, or any other epithet of a like nature, with the charms of running water and quiet pool to enhance its tranquil beauties, stands the eminently useful but painfully plain structure called Barcombe Mills. Dignity of a kind it certainly has, of the type which seems to intimate in unmistakable terms to its surroundings : " Ah, yes ! This is a pretty spot in its way. Trees and rivers are all very well, but it would be deadly dull without *me*. For real importance give me just such another mill as—Barcombe, for instance ! "

"Here's the mill! Find the view!" This was the problem in front of three Knights of the Brush on a certain August half-holiday, and no quest of olden days looked more hopeless. "Find the view!" exclaimed one—"Find the architect and crush him between the upper and nether stones of his own mill!" But Sir Oldun—a leader of forlorn hopes—drew his companions off from immediate proximity to the ponderous pile and counselled a careful inspection of its possibilities from a distance. He succeeded in getting at a distance, but not at a view.

Fancy—ye who know not Barcombe Mills in the flesh—a big, flat-faced structure built chiefly of wood, of the Georgian type (if the term will pass muster) with a sort of semi-classic façade painted wholly white. What ornament there is, is on the front, the other sides and buildings, with a shaft, being of the cotton-factory order of architecture. Beautiful surroundings fail to redeem its ugliness ; if anything, they accentuate it.

In face of great difficulty, it is said to be advisable to take up " a correct attitude." All that can be said is to record the fact that on this occasion every attitude was taken up, both correct and incorrect, and it led to nothing but waste of time, and a threat of proceedings for trespass from the miller. Had not an apology been promptly forthcoming, the offender, and not his " correct attitude," might have been " taken up " in a more literal sense.

After marching and counter-marching at the heels of the worthy but mistaken knight, after looking at it with lenient eyes from the north, with hopeful gaze from the south, with an honest endeavour to compose it from the western side, and with a set determination to " make it come " from the eastern face, we ended in cursing it all round the compass. With the worst intention, the prophet of old remained to bless. Here were three seekers after ever so little a sign of grace in the object of their search, anxious to think well of what was well-nigh hopeless, compelled to fall back on uncomplimentary adjectives, the least forcible being contributed by the most considerate of the three knights, who looked long and carefully, and then reluctantly ejaculated—"ghastly!" This term was echoed by all.

Then, when hope and the afternoon were nearly gone, " the soul of good " peeped out, and it was discovered that by assuming an attitude that was neither correct nor comfortable, exposed to the sun, by leaving out a gate and other sundries, by looking under the bough of a tree that was neither ornamental nor useful, it was possible to make a poor picture by dint of patience and long-suffering. Here is the result, which was not arrived at without much grumbling.

If it be urged that " much cry and little wool " would be the

appropriate title of this attempt to fill a page of these " Sketches,"
I can only point out that where history and incident conspire to
render Barcombe void of human interest, the only course open
to the chronicler is to chronicle small beer ; and when, in addition
to sterility, ugliness reigns supreme (except in Nature's handiwork),
it is little wonder that a fictitious importance is given to things
that make for " copy."   If it be further asked why Barcombe
Mills should have been chosen, if so unsuitable, I can only refer
the questioner to Sir Oldun, that worthy but mistaken Knight of
the Brush.   He will probably reply wisely that " it's a poor subject

BARCOMBE MILLS.
(*By A. S. C.*)

that will not repay study."   If the questioner is equally wise he
will refrain from pursuing the subject further, or he may arrive
at a dead stop of mutual agreement, and discover Barcombe Mills
to be the particularly poor subject which does not repay study of
any kind, and the conversation would end as suddenly as this
paragraph does—and be about as informing !

\*          \*          \*          \*          \*

But if the mills are disappointing, the mill-pools and the river are
just as charming.   One scarcely ever goes there, but an artist may
be found sketching either the bridge or the lock above it.   The

little wicket-gate just over the bridge to the left brings you on to the opposite bank, and the river between here and Isfield is even prettier than that already traversed. If you ask why I have not chosen the best route first, I answer that there is no Hamsey between the mills and Isfield, and that he who does the one walk is sure to do the other.

ISFIELD CHURCH.
(By Arthur B. Packham.)

You first cross another wooden bridge—which repair has not rendered prettier—and follow the bank through many beautiful windings to a second bridge delightfully set about with willows and bushes, until a ruined archway with no parapet conducts you to the western bank again, only to be transported once more to the eastern side near a farm—with abnormally lofty chimney stacks for so small a house—by which you can gain the high road leading to the station.

If you would see Isfield Church (and it is well worth a visit) it lies quite half a mile farther, on the east bank of the river, quite away from all habitations. It is a beautifully simple structure, which addition and restoration have not spoiled. The tower, which had a meaningless slate cap, has been raised, battlemented, and crowned with a small shingle spire, in perfect harmony with the surrounding pastoral scenery. The modern porch is beautifully designed, and the interior is one of the most interesting in Sussex, because of the chancel and the Shurley Chapel, the Decorated windows of which are noted for their originality and beauty. There is a fine piscina, and a " squint," besides beautiful monuments and brasses ; an altar tomb to Sir John Shurley and his spouses, 1631, with a quaint inscription, as well as a really notable canopied tomb, with a graduated row of children kneeling reverently along the side. Whether the piety of their attitude, or the number of the offspring is meant to be commemorated, I must leave you to judge for yourself.

Shurley Mansion lies north-east of the church and has a wall surrounding it with towers at the corners, and intermediate bastions, containing bullet-headed yew trees of the toy order, reminding one of our grandmothers' " samplers."

Whether the old village of Isfield has disappeared, I do not know, but certainly the church stands far removed. To prevent disappointment you must get the key at the blacksmith's shop on your way.

\*          \*          \*          \*          \*

I am loath to leave the river without saying that there is yet another charming walk above Isfield, starting from where you left the stream and crossing the newly renovated bridge, which has this excellent precept painted on a board at each end— " Endeavour to make a name for yourself, before carving one on this bridge ! "

You have before you the most beautiful reaches of the Ouse, especially near the lock. Isfield Church is a charming feature in the view. Higher up you cross the river again, and eventually come out by the little inn called the " Horse and Barge " (reminiscent of the time when the Ouse was a commercial highway). The inn, I think, is closed. From here are two miles of delightfully wooded road passing through rocky country to Uckfield Station.

FLETCHING MILL.—spring

A.S.C.

FLETCHING MILL IN SPRINGTIME.

(*By A. S. C.*)

282

# CHAPTER XXVII

## SHEFFIELD PARK STATION TO FLETCHING MILL AND FLETCHING (7 MILES)

### WITH ILLUSTRATIONS BY WALTER PUTTICK AND A. S. C.

THE road from Sheffield Park Station to the "Sheffield Arms," and right on to Wych Cross, is one of the most beautiful in Sussex. It was laid out or made when "earth hunger" was not the vice it has since become. From the entrance of the park northwards there is a very wide strip of green on either side, more than many a village green can boast. The view from the hill just by the gates—near which is a Georgian mile-post of unusual and chaste design—is, for a road-scape, charming. The "Sheffield Arms"—fronted by a clump of trees and an attractive sign-post—looks well from here, but nearer, is found to be rather of the workhouse type of architecture.

The path to Fletching Mill lies through the inn yard, and across several fields, growing more delightful as you proceed, and dropping down at last to the mill-pond.

I give this drawing of "Fletching Mill in Spring-time," because it is a privilege to know it, " and the demesnes which there adjacent lie." Lying right off the main road, it is known to but few—and happy are they! I rejoice to think that your roving rout of cyclists will have to leave their bundles of rubber and wire at the inn, half a mile away, and approach the spot, as pilgrims should, on foot.

To such I promise a rare sight. The precincts of the mill are beautiful enough ; but north-east of the mill-pool there is an upward hollow, rock-girt and deep with bracken, the entrance to which in later spring is perfectly blue with a carpet of hyacinths, diapered with daffodils, and the air is laden with the scent of pines, towering up a hundred feet. Nowhere in Sussex but here have I seen such firs as these. But everything seems to grow lofty in this hollow, even the beech trees. A rare spot for a picnic ! This rocky ravine is the result of some great upheaval. It is deep with silvery sand and dead leaves, and steep too ; but when you reach the top, you are on a rampart of rock which overhangs a much deeper valley, and on every side stretch hilly woods.

There are beautiful alleys to the right along the ridge, and primroses and violets galore among the trees ; but you must retrace
your steps down to the mill, leaving it on your right. The rough
woodland track will bring you out at " North Hall." Why it is
called by this dignified name I do not know, unless the quaint little
Gothic cottage owns it. Leading down the road are three or four
half-timbered houses that are good to sketch. As you come out
of the gate on to the high-road, immediately opposite (if I remember rightly) there is a field path—all paths are pretty about here—

ON THE PILTDOWN ROAD.
(*By A. S. C.*)

which will take you into Fletching village, through an avenue of
pines bordering a pool.

Fletching is where Simon de Montfort and his army rested the
night before the rapid march and ascent of Mount Harry, from
which his host poured down on the surprised army of the King.
As a proof of the unpreparedness of Henry's force, the watch on
Mount Harry consisted of one sentinel, and he was asleep !

Fletching is a model village, and some of the new houses are
very beautiful specimens of an older style. To destroy, rather
than to repeat, is too often the tendency now. As Mr. Clayton
has recently pointed out, there is much work to be done by the

Sussex Archæological Society, in making a list and description of the beautiful old homesteads and cottages of which so many are "improved" off the face of the earth every year ; and he pleads for their preservation.   He points out that although Sussex is not rich in the greater archæological buildings, it is very rich in the humbler yeomen's homes, erected by ancient craftsmen.   To pull down " the work of these unconscious artists," is little short of sacrilege.   Down Street Farm and Daleham Cottage are two near Fletching which may be cited as types of these modest homes. To reach them from Fletching you must go north-east across the fields.

The farm is nearest.   It lies in a hollow of its own just off the

DOWN STREET FARM.
(*By A. S. C.*)

road, and is very old.   Settlement, or the contour of the rocky ground, have made the lines anything but parallel, but gives an effect more than quaint.   I did not see the inside, but have little doubt that it fully bears out the irregularity of the outside.   It is difficult to estimate the age of these old buildings.   Parts of those more solidly built than others, in my belief, run some of our later churches pretty close.   Down Street Farm is one of them.

To spend a summer holiday in a farm-house !   This will always have a charm for the imagination.   It conjures up visions of new milk and new-laid eggs ; of the aroma of the wood fire, and the smell of the milking cows ; the busy chuckle of chicken and their ways ; the waddling ducks and the long line of geese ; the singing of birds, and many other interesting sights and sounds.   These are the attractions.  A sense of fairness compels me to point out that new milk is only obtainable by the severance of the calf from maternal love, and should it happen during the holiday month, day and night are filled with sounds of mourning both loud and deep ;  that the early egg is proclaimed by hysterical chortles, and that chanticleer and his like are earlier still and louder of lay ; and that the kennelled dog has been known to " bow-wow " at fancied footsteps as well as at real ones.

To youth these things are naught, but the city man takes time to become accustomed to them.  Yet weighed fairly, the

DALEHAM COTTAGE.

(*By A. S. C.*)

advantages overtop the noises, and the pure air and quiet days soon bring deep, unbroken slumber at night.

\*          \*          \*          \*          \*

Cottages such as Daleham are plentiful enough, although it has features which commend it in a special sense.  The quaint old bay window beneath the recessed eaves is attractive, as is the good Horsham stone roof.  The average labourer's cottage could un-doubtedly bear improvement and is being improved.  However picturesque they may be, the low, thatched roofs and rooms, the want of ventilation and light, are not conducive to healthful sleep, and they are often very damp.  But cottages like Daleham were originally yeomen's tenements, and have good rooms—sometimes panelled.

Fletching Church is large and handsome.  The Earl of Sheffield

"CARVERS," FLETCHING.
(By Walter Puttick.)

has spent much upon it ; but the result is scarcely commensurate with the sum. In the south transept is a fourteenth-century altar-tomb and brass of a knight and his lady. In the north transept are old helmets and gauntlets with the Neville Crest above ; and Gibbon, the historian, is buried in the Sheffield Mausoleum. Old stained glass found buried in the churchyard (probably to preserve it from destruction in Puritan days) fills three lancet windows in the transept. There is a fine Perpendicular screen, and a geometrical east window. The bulk of the church is Early English, but the tower is Norman, with a lofty shingled spire.

The park is very beautiful but difficult of access, except for Fletching folk. The Gospel teaching as to the reception of strangers has apparently not yet found its way everywhere in Sussex ; but this is no new thing. Our county was one of the latest to welcome the Gospel !

" Carvers," another pretty cottage, lies just off a shady road to the south, and inquiry will put you in the way of reaching the station again, by which time you will have literally " squared the circle "—and had a long walk.

# CHAPTER XXVIII

## LEWES THROUGH BEDDINGHAM AND TARRING NEVILLE TO NEWHAVEN (8 MILES)

WITH ILLUSTRATIONS BY A. JOBSON BROWN, ARTHUR B. PACKHAM AND A. S. C.

I MAKE Lewes the starting place, but would like to point out the view of Kingston Hill and the Downs generally, from the train about half-way from Falmer. The line is carried across the mouth of several coombes, in the first of which is a long fringe of trees. Just beyond these look towards the hill ! One sees the Downs and these only. It was at the end of March that the Bookworm and I took this trip, and the roller had been at work over the young crops, making wavy lines of dark and light green in graceful perspective across the intervening ground, which led the eyes naturally to the great Down.

It was also just after a snow-storm, which had shocked our faith in the eternal fitness of things ; blasted our hopes of an early spring ; made our rising spirits fall, and had again sunk the barometer into its boots.

A thaw—a sun thaw—had been some days in progress, and only the heavy drifts were left, but the wind had kept steadily in the north, and to-day brought a snow-squall every half-hour to whiten the surface, and melt again in the sun, which, owing to the clear air, was quite powerful, although the wind was so strong and cold.

I give these particulars, because a walk over the Downs after a snow-storm, for those who can face the wind, is by no means to be despised. The drifts gleaming in the sunlight, and the contrast between these and the inky clouds to the north ; the grass faded and wan, with here and there a dark patch of furze, or shadow from the driving wrack ; the belts of trees in Stanmer Park just purpling over before bursting into leaf—these are sights worth seeing when the opportunity occurs.

Dragging the Bookworm past all the shops in Lewes lest he should waste his substance and our time searching for musty tomes, we passed over the Ouse by the bridge, and turned to the right at the Cliffe.

TARRING NEVILLE.

(By A. S. C.)

It is said that the works of man generally deface nature. I cannot quite say this of the great chalk-pits with which the Downs are —I use the word without anger—" scarred." They bring a new element of form and colour to vary—again I use words with reluctance—the monotony of curve and sameness of tint. They are like nothing so much as gigantic escallop shells set in the face of the slopes, and are of the same pearly whiteness. The form they bestow has an element of surprise, always an attractive feature in landscape, while the colour is not common, except in cloud and sea. White, as brilliant as the chalk-pit gives, is an unusual tint, and in strong sunlight is nearly always accompanied with exquisite blue shadows in half the shell, and though nothing takes delicate colours like white, the effect is never " chalky," however entirely the pits may be composed of the substance itself. Sunset glorifies their artificial cliffs to the delight of the artist. Old age, and the stains of mineral deposits under the influence of rain, add to their charm, and many a beautiful, curving road leads up or down. In most of the pits cut into the steep north face there are picturesque, disused kilns, and even in these mighty excavations in the Cliffe the smoke from the live kilns is not altogether disfiguring to the landscape. (If, like Balaam, I have blessed where I ought to have banned, I do not extend this toleration to cement works, such as we shall see presently at South Heighton, with its leprous complexion, monstrous shafts, and rows of ugly tenements.)

Our next picture is to be found along the Cliffe. It is sometimes sketched in conjunction with the chalk-pits cut out of the steep hill-side—a favourite view with Clem Lambert ; but our Artist has preferred the bend of the river, with the boats moored to the wall of the little quay.

In due time we passed beneath Caburn, and saw it under unusual conditions. A heavy snow-squall was impending. The cloud-wrack north of the summit was black and awe-inspiring, and yet the hill, stretching its sunlit, burly form back and upward, with a sort of snow-cravat just below the vallum of the camp, looked almost ludicrous.

Here the by-road turns off to Beddingham. " Bedd-ing-ham," the Bookworm informs me, means " the home of the sons of Bedd." The sunshine even prompts him to gaiety, for he adds that the name follows a perfectly proper order—" first the bed and then the bedding ! " I gently hint that both must have been uncommonly damp, the " ham " or " home " coming last ; but the little conceit still surviving in the smile it had brought to his features, and fearful lest he should amplify, I hurried on to the church.

As said in another place, although the churches of Sussex cannot compare in stateliness with those in the midlands, they yield nothing in general interest.  Miss Lettice Grafton says—and says well—" Old Sussex churches have, one might imagine, cultivated the virtue of humility.  The country rambler comes upon them unawares, hidden among the valleys of the Downs.  They are rare examples of lowly strength, with their stout masonry, built to withstand the wildest gale and the more subtle attacks of gradual decay.  Their four-square towers rise to no great height, but for that very reason they will outlast many nobler triumphs of church architecture.  In another sense these aged Sussex churches know

THE OUSE AT LEWES.
(*By A. Jobson Brown.*)

no pride, for they are little known to any but antiquarians as treasures beyond price."

The great number of them, the hoary antiquity and little change—where change has been made—the delightful medley of styles, render them deeply interesting.  Very many have Saxon work somewhere about them.  Bedd himself and his sturdy sons may well have had a hand in the building of their church, to judge by the thickness of the walls and the tiny windows between the nave arches.  These arches have plain, flat soffits, and on one near the chancel there is a Virgin and Child in fresco.  The pillars are very massive, and the " four-square " Tudor tower is of comely size, with chequers of stone and flint—like Steyning—for ornament.

A carved oak panel in the vestry has " R. 1659. S." upon it—the
last year of the Commonwealth. Altogether, the Church of Bedd
is a worthy fane.

As we began to climb the hill, the squall burst, but we caught
the last glimpse eastward ere the sunlight was quenched. Firle
Beacon, the whole range of the Downs and half the valley were
almost golden with light, while northward, land and sky were a
perfect smutch of purple-black. The promise this gave was amply
fulfilled. The bitter blast made itself felt through one's overcoat,
and the frozen snow hissed and stung our ears. When we topped
the hill, the " smutch " was half-way to Newhaven ; the sun was
shining brilliantly, and no fairy wand could have changed the
scene more completely. The whole north face of the Downs was

BEDDINGHAM.
(*By Arthur B. Packham.*)

dazzlingly white and glistering, the only colour being in the bleached
blue of the sky.

From the summit down to Tarring Neville is a mile-long slope,
or more. On these downs between the Ouse and Cuckmere there
is much cultivation, so a good part of our way was over the plough-
lands, which made it heavy going. Tarring Neville is little known.
One almost doubts if the ubiquitous cyclist knows it except by
sight—by short sight, in his case ! Doubtless its importance is
sufficient for itself, and when the smallest affairs of life are great,
and great enough, in one's eyes, what matter how the world wags ?
And if the cyclist takes little heed of the village he passes so swiftly
through, be sure the village, in the person of its inhabitants, takes
a corresponding interest in *his* welfare. Time was when his coming
stirred the surface waters of curiosity to a ripple of sleepy wonder,
but like the wind he passed, and passes still—and is as little thought
of now.

It remains true of most things that unless they be self-advertised, or send a herald before them, their coming is quite a matter of unconcern to the home of Hodge. So it is with our wights of the whirling wheel. The humblest hawker's cart—not to mention the country carrier—is heard afar, or as distant as dull ears will reach. The "jogget" of his pony's hoofs, the grind of the wheels, the little cloud of dust, are all forerunners of his coming ; and the children stop their play a moment, and the good-wife checks her broom in its resistless sweep, to cast a look of more or less interest in the direction of the sound.

But, unless their eyes happen to be turned that way, the approach of the cyclist is now unheeded. Silently he glides into view—unseen. Silently the lifeless "roadscape" quickens with a note of life and colour—unnoticed. Almost as silently he flashes by—unobserved. A whisper dies into silence as he fleets away into distance—unregretted, for the best of reasons : no one knew of his coming, and no one saw him go ! And yet he has left his mark behind him—the pattern of his tyre in the dust ! A parable this, of wider application than it seems, for him who runs to read.

Is it to be wondered at that Tarring Neville and a hundred such inconsiderable villages should be almost unknown ? Yet it is not far from those who look for it, though not quite at our doors. One can hardly claim any special dower of beauty for it as a village. Like many another hamlet, its interests are centred—if the paradox be forgiven—in the long and dusty road. It clings to it as closely as its scanty buildings will admit, and only allows the church and a belated barn to stand apart—the former by courtesy, and the latter by indifference ! Its ground-plan is founded on the elementary principles of "dot and carry one," and the result is a straggling sparseness of tenements almost fatal to its title of village, had it not been for the church, true to its primitive profession of saving that which might have been lost but for its presence.

So Tarring Neville is a name on the map, as well as a habitation for men. Beyond this, the sacred fane, in outward show at least, does little else. It *was* Transition, with an Early English chancel, but is now chiefly of the style known as Churchwarden's gothic. There is a little aumbry with carved doors and traces of an aisle altar. Probably to make room, where there was already no lack of it, the font is built into the wall.

Truly a plainer structure might have been raised, but it would run simplicity itself uncommonly close. Within and without, the word "ornamental" is an inapplicable, impossible adjective. Apart from its present use, its justification will be found in the motives which prompted its erection in days gone by, and in the unknown records of its nameless dead. The joys and sorrows, hopes and fears that have clustered round its walls throughout the centuries, may have been of little moment to the wider world stretching beyond the Downs, and having its life in the heart of great cities. Perhaps because the scope for these is so small, therefore none was found to tell their tale. Tarring Neville has no history. It is hidden in the graveyard yonder. Yet the centuries must have brought their full sheaf of simple woe and weal, with here the joy of birth, and there the linen shroud ; with now a wedding or a home-coming from the wars ; with yearly round of uneventful toil, and many a loss and check, but ever ending with a harvest-home. Sometimes thankfulness and sorrow found vent within those sacred walls : at others, dull indifference held sway ; but still it stands and points its simple spire above, and bears upon its ancient bell the story of the Crucifixion, as if to hallow and soften the sound of its brazen tongue when it calls its children to prayer and praise.

In the village itself not many nooks and corners are to be found to sketch. A chess-board after a hard-fought battle is about as crowded. From the marshes, however, there is more to be seen and carried away on canvas or paper. Several large backwaters, or arms of the river and smaller dykes, help the foreground greatly, and the flowering rushes and water-plants are friendly aids ; while the hills forming the background above Tarring Neville are especially suave and gracious.

There is much sketching to be had in these levels, and now that there is a railway " halt " at Southease, I would suggest our artists turning their attention to this almost untouched locality. There are plenty of villages to provide housing, and the marsh is wide enough to give the breadth of view that is so dear to some painters, and yet the distances are bounded by hills not too high, nor rugged, nor wanting in colour.

More famous Piddinghoe—" where they shoe their magpies "—with its reputed ague and celebrated chalk-pit—" where they hang ponds out to dry "—lies opposite. To trace the origin of these local allusions and sarcasms would be infinitely interesting—and probably futile. It would make a fascinating record, for it is when the foibles and habits of people or places are described, that language is apt to be terse, not to say forcible. Probably there are few towns or villages in Sussex or any other county to which some humorous or caustic couplet or phrase is not applied by the wit or malice of their neighbours.

I hazard an explanation of the second of these Piddinghoe sayings (the first is beyond me, unless it be that the village lies in surroundings so low and marshy, that even its feathered inhabitants require footwear !*) There is, or was, much whiting made here, of chalk ground in water and then allowed to drain. The sediment is dug out, and deposited on shelves, under pent-houses, to dry. Hence the saying—" Where they hang ponds out to dry."

The advantages of a remote and little known habitation is expressed in a further couplet, which may hail from press-gang days :

> " Englishmen fight, Frenchmen too ;
> We don't—we live Piddinghoe ! "

Few places can boast of three quaint sayings.

Of Chichester, I have heard it said—" One half the city asleep, the other half on tiptoe lest they should wake them up "—a good description of the slumber that broods over most cathedral towns.

The respectable gentility and characteristics of Petworth are hit off in the following couplet :

> " Poor Petworth ;  proud people ;
> High church ;  crooked steeple."

Lewes comes off less favourably. Its inhabitants are accused by libellous detractors as willing to "skin a rat, for its hide and fat." " Flat burglary," indeed !

A prettier saying is associated with Heathfield, for " at Hefful Fair they turn the Cuckoo out." It is held on April 14, and is called the " Cuckoo Fair," at which, the story goes, an old woman lets the cuckoo out of her basket. This shortest of short stories, the setting of the seal upon the summer, like most Sussex legends, exhibits the kindly nature of its people. Few Sussex fairies are of the malignant type. One would like to see the subject em-bodied in a picture by a Sussex artist. We overlook the things that lie to our hands.

The habit of Sussex folk, for which they are noted, of leaving doors open behind them—probably originating in the love of fresh air—would seem to hail from Yapton, if the local saying means anything. The offender in this respect is greeted with the cry—" Do you come from Yapton ? "

Here is a weather rhyme about Firle Beacon :

> " When Firle Beacon wears a cap
> We in the valley gets a drap ;
> When Firle Beacon's head is bare
> All next day it will be fair."

Bosham is locally known as " Happy Bosham." Owing to intermarriage the entire population partakes of the nature of the

* For a similar reason, probably, Amberley women are said to be web-footed.

family ; but whether the adjective bears its proper meaning, or is merely sarcastic, the saying as usual, leaves vague.

" As black as the devil's nutting bag " is a Sussex proverb that most country boys know ; declaring that " if you go a-nutting on Sundays, Satan will come and hold the boughs down for you ! "

Lower asserts that when the rustic swears " by Job," it is the Anglo-Saxon for Jupiter, " Jobe " : and their use of " jobal " for " jovial " has the same derivation. If so, it is an interesting link with the remote past. The same authority says that Alciston and Alfriston were called " Ahson " and " Ahson-Town," probably a mediæval joke making them " a town of asses."

In the vulgar tongue a Brighton man used to be called a " jug."

I make no excuse for lengthening this paper. The information is gathered from various sources, and is certainly " off the beaten track " of everyday information.

Storrington folk are credited with being so simple that " they have to look at a pond to see if it rains ! "

An old feud between Arundel and Littlehampton boys survives in the gibes of " 'Hampton Shivers " and " Arundel Mullets "— the one referring to the ague prevalent before the brook meadows were drained, and the other to the mullet which still come in shoals up the Arun ; both sayings having a chill and watery origin. Ague is also referred to in the phrase, " Old Johnny has been running his finger down my back." The following charm was believed to be a cure for the " axey," or ague, to be written on a three-cornered piece of paper and worn round the neck till it drops off :

> " Ague, ague, I thee defy
> Three days shiver,
> Three days shake,
> Make me well for Jesus' sake."

Or a spider rolled up in a cobweb, and hung in a nutshell enclosed in a black silk bag round the neck.

" Gifts." White specks on the finger nails, supposed to herald the arrival of presents.

> " A gift on the thumb is sure to come,
> A gift on the finger is sure to linger."

" To beat the devil round the gooseberry bush " is to tell a long rigmarole without much point.

" To eat shorn-bug for dinner " is the Sussex way of expressing the extremity of poverty. " Shorn-bug " is a beetle.

The white-thorn is called " Cuckoo's Bread and Cheese Tree," and Chancellor Parish says, " It is very remarkable that this name should be given to the white-thorn, as among all Aryan nations this tree is associated with the lightning, while the cuckoo is intimately connected with the lightning gods Zeus and Thor."

The second Monday after Easter is called "Hock Monday."
It was kept as a festival in remembrance of the defeat of the Danes
in King Ethelred's time.

Old sayings are seldom complimentary, and are more often
aimed at the weaker sex. "Except where the missus is master,
the rosemary will never blossom," is one such remark.

Indolence is indicated in the following—"Old Laurence has got
hold of me." One would like to trace the origin of this phrase.

Easter Day was known in Sussex as "Holy Sunday," coupled
with the tradition that the sun dances at sunrise on that day,
but nobody has ever seen it, because the devil is so cunning that
he always puts a hill in the way to hide it! I shrewdly suspect
it was a unique excuse for the indolent "lay-a-beds"—in Sussex
phrase.

Small boys call the robin "Scutty," and this rhyme entitles the
songster and his reputed mate to protection, and also "Martins
and Swallers."

> "Robins and Wrens
> Are God Almighty's friends.
> Martins and Swallers
> Are God Almighty's scholars,"

Children in Sussex call the stinging-nettle "Naughty-man's
plaything." Another child's rhyme is quaint because of its child-
like phraseology, and its use of the Sussex word "threaddle"—
to thread.

> "Open the gates as wide as wide,
> And let King George go through with his bride.
> It is so dark we cannot see
> To threaddle the tailor's needle."

Owing to the muddy roads it was customary on "darks" (moon-
less nights) to send a man on in front with a lantern fastened
behind him. Such a one would be called "a Sussex moon."

Southdown folk call Pevensey Marsh "the Mesh," and the Weald
"the Wild"; and there is an East Sussex saying as to Romney
Marsh, which gives the local idea of its area—"The world is divided
into five parts, Europe, Asia, Africa, America—and Romney
Marsh!"

That churches show the road to heaven is expressed in the habit
of Down folk calling them "milestones."

"Mock-beggar-hall" has more than a local use, but it is peculiarly
Sussex, as a farm near Rye can testify, by which name it is called.
It designates a house which has an inviting external appearance,
but within is poor, bare, dirty and disappointing.

Again "Pucks Hall," or "Pookhale" (the fairy's cottage) is a
cottage at Selmeston (pronounced Simson), and one of the numerous
"ghostes" of rural Sussex is said to frequent the spot.

Withered or dry wood is spoken of as " sare," as the rhyme shows :

> " Burn ash-wood green,
> 'Tis fire for a queen.
> Burn ash-wood sare
> 'Twool make a man swear."

Some of these old words have a beautiful sound. It is a pity that the tendency is to let them fall out of use. This is because they have special meaning, or embody a legend or belief, and with the passing of the legend, the word perishes. Of such is the " Sheer-mouse." If it crosses a road trodden by man, it dies. This accounts (country folk say) for the number which are found without wound or apparent cause of death on the edge of field paths.

" St. Elmo's Fire," the phosphoric lights seen on various substances at night, are called " Fairy-sparks." The following proverb, if more general, is deemed a Sussex saying :

> " February fill the dick
> Every day, white or black "—

that is, snow or rain, an amplification of " February fill dyke."

Another general saying is certainly not dead in our county, that " if you go to the end of the rainbow, you'll find a crock of gold." Bavarians have a similar proverb, but it is only those who are born on Sunday that have any luck, and *if* they can retain the magic vessel in their possession, it will always contain three ducats. Certainly, as regards legends, there is little new under the sun. The widow's cruse and Aladdin's lamp are kindred stories.

County jealousies are to be descried in a Burwash description of a stranger—" a broken-down snob from Kent."

A quaint use of the word " tedious " is seen in expressing weariness, as " tejus tired."

I give two longer extracts, one of which is in the vernacular, on the word " spannel "—to make dirty foot-marks about a floor, as a spaniel dog does :

" I goos into the kitchen, and I says to my mistus, I says (t'was of a Saddaday), the old sow's hem ornary, I says. Well, says she, there ain't no call for you to come spannelling about my clean kitchen, any more for that, she says ; so I goos out and didn't say naun, for you can't never make no sense of women-folks of a Saddaday."

Shakespeare makes a beautiful use of the word in Antony and Cleopatra—" ' The hearts that spaniel'd me at heels.' "

As a final and appropriate paragraph, I give Chancellor Parish's humorous and witty remarks on a peculiarly local production— " Sussex pudding " :

" A compound of flour and water made up in an oblong shape

in a cloth, and boiled. There is a moment, when it is first taken out of the pot, when it can be eaten with impunity : but it is usually eaten cold, and in that form, I believe, it becomes the foundation of all the ills that Sussex spirit and flesh is heir to. It aggravates every natural infirmity of temper by the promotion of chronic indigestion, and finally undermines the constitution : for the first symptom of the decay of nature which a Sussex man describes is invariably that he ' can't get his pudden to set.' "

The Chancellor declares that " it promotes a dyspeptic form of Dissent which is unknown elsewhere " ! I would like to add that when " hissing hot " it can be eaten not only with impunity, but with profit. In my boyhood, children's first course at dinner was nearly always large slices steeped in gravy from the roast—coupled with the illusive promise that those who ate the most pudding should have the most meat ! It was not only economical, but far better than a lot of meat for juveniles. The custom might well be revived ; but I go hand-in-hand with the Chancellor in his indictment of " cold Sussex pudden " !

There are a number of quaint words used in the rural speech of Sussex, which are like the English people, derived from many sources. In the main they are of Saxon origin ; but Celtic, Norse and French can be traced among them. Who says to " hele " now, when talking of covering up ? I once met a countryman in the train between Brighton and Shoreham who did, and not for the first time in my life regretted that shorthand was not one of my accomplishments, so rich a vocabulary of archaic word and phrase his conversation with a friend disclosed.

\*　　　\*　　　\*　　　\*　　　\*

Piddinghoe lies on the other side of the river, and presents good opportunities to the artist. The church, the first of the three round towers, stands on a considerable hillock round which sweeps the river. The houses are gathered together on the little rise, and further north are several old kilns and drying houses on the bank, and a pool or backwater fills the hollows hard by.

To return to Tarring Neville. Not far ahead is South Heighton, to reach which you pass by the cement works. Let me be as charitable as I can, and call them " a necessary evil." The village lies on the side of the hill to the south ; but the proximity of the works has ruined it, and its once pretty neighbour Denton. Surely on such wide-spreading hill-sides separate cottages with gardens could have been erected. Instead, long rows of the ugliest sort appertaining to crowded manufacturing towns here disfigure the landscape. South Heighton Church is ruined and almost level with the ground. The churchyard only remains.

Denton, just over the brow, was once the prettiest of rural spots, but is woefully changed. It lies in a well-wooded nook, and has a little church of the unpretentious order consisting of nave and chancel only, divided originally by a screen and rood-loft approached by a winding stairway in the south wall. The circular font, of great age, is in imitation of wicker-work, with a plaited pattern at the base and rosettes in stone at the top.

NEWHAVEN TOWER AND APSE.
(*By Arthur B. Packham.*)

A beautiful canopied piscina and sedile, and an altar tomb complete the list, except this quaint inscription near the font.

HERE LYETH THE BODY
OF JOHN MINDER
AND SUN ROBE
RD. DESSESED
DECEMBER THE 9TH
1679.

The old lady cleaning the floor was very communicative, and told us, among other things, that the church "belonged to the Romans once"!

The road from Denton to Newhaven is somewhat flat, but the distances bounding the view, north and west, and the shipping in the harbour with Newhaven on its hill, redeem it from dullness. Of the port itself (for it is fast attaining the dignity the name implies) you must judge for yourself. It is responsible for the changing of the name of the place, which bore the rather meanly-sounding title of "Meeching" until the end of the sixteenth century. The interest it inspires is not that of the antiquarian, except the tower and apse of its church (the nave, rebuilt, certainly would not be ; it is most appallingly utilitarian). This reminds me that Nibbs, the artist, says, "The tower is surmounted by a comparatively modern shingle spire—a disfigurement to be found in so many churches in the county." It comes rather as a shock to be obliged to confess that probably he is right ; that these shingled spires of which we are certainly fond, and perhaps rather proud, are *not* very suitable, especially to a style so solid as the Norman. Where these are capped at all, it should have a pyramidical roof of stone, of a more or less acute angle. Custom has deadened the sense of style within us, or the beautiful silver-grey of the oak shingles has blinded our eyes to their lack of correspondence with many of the towers they surmount.

The church is said to have been built by the architect of a similar structure, Yainville, near Jumieges, in Normandy. I once came across it while driving to the Great Abbey from Caudebec, and it was like meeting an old friend on the road, so exactly does it resemble Newhaven even in situation, being on a hill above the Seine.*

* The same incident occurred to Lower, and is recorded in the Sussex Archæological Collections. It is corroborative evidence of the great similarity of the two churches. Lower gives sketches of both.

# CHAPTER XXIX

## GLYNDE AND FIRLE BEACON TO BISHOPSTONE (9 Miles)

### With Illustrations by Frank Georges and Arthur B. Packham.

TO Glynde by train. The village lies to the north of the line, under Caburn, and is one of the prettiest villages in Sussex. The church is quaint and unusual as a Sussex edifice, generally so hoary with age. It was rebuilt in the eighteenth century in the pseudo-Classic style of the day, and looks strangely out of place.

To reach Firle you must retrace your steps and cross the bridge. It is a pretty walk but dusty. The road is rather round-about, but there is a shorter way on higher ground—with a five-barred gate to climb at the juncture with the high road.

Firle is beautifully wooded and beautifully situated, but has no special feature as a village. The Gages' seat is here. They are descended from the Norman, but the house they inhabit has little antiquity. The park is very charming, and being on the slope of the rising downs, has lovely views.

The church is interesting, chiefly by reason of its tombs and brasses, to different members of the Gage family of the sixteenth century. One of the guide-books says some of these were lying at Firle Place, and were set up again in the church at the Restoration. Unless the older house had a private chapel, it is rather a puzzle to know why they were lying there. The tombs of one's ancestors are not easily movable. Perhaps they were translated during Puritan days, when so much iconoclastic fury was vented on what should have been inviolate. In any case, they are back again, and of considerable interest. One would wish to see greater consideration accorded them even now. One has the heating apparatus of the church in front of it, and church utensils and vestry impedimenta block the way to a close examination of others. The requirements of modern services find old churches lacking in accommodation, hence the apparent want of reverence in dealing with such things. There is some good stained glass and some— not good! A stoup by the south door is worth examination.

The church is reached by a long alley bordered with flower-beds. Retracing your steps to the gate and taking the road that leads towards the Downs for a hundred yards or so and then turning suddenly to the left along the park wall, you come to a woodland path leading directly up to the Beacon. The usual winding track (with a seat considerately dotted here and there for resting) brings you to the top of one of the most striking eminences of the range. It has the most mountainous form of all. In other respects its characteristics—view, tumuli, camp, etc.—are much the same. The view Lewes-wards is more attractive than usual, owing to the isolated range of Caburn ; but northwards overlooking the level

GLYNDE VILLAGE.
(By F. Georges.)

and the Dicker is less interesting. Southward, however, it is quite beautiful, owing to Newhaven Breakwater and the bold outline of Borough Head, Seaford Cliff and Cuckmere Haven.

These views are the reward for the stiff climb. When you have enjoyed them to the full, and perhaps have tired your eyes with the brightness of the sun and the sea, seek relief by looking down on the fading green turf, studded here and there with the dwarf-thistle, whose silken cushion of seeds awaits, perchance, another such a day of autumn sunshine, or a brush from the feet of the browsing flock, to set them free. It is difficult to see in them the beautiful object which children, and that other child of nature— the poet—delight to call " the blow-ball."

They lie in rather untidy profusion upon the grass.  Yet if you examine them singly, they are like nothing so much as the daintiest of folded, fairy parasols, until under the influence of the heat the delicate filaments expand as though instinct with life, and the breeze wafts them away to take their part in arraying the grass with the beauty of their amethyst jewellery in due season, when after much wandering, the seed each one carries has found its home in the soil and has fulfilled its destiny.

There are many plants whose seeds are distributed in like manner. An examination of these is deeply interesting.  Each varies in form and structure, and doubtless many a humble, hitherto disdained flower-seed has been studied of late years by those who are seeking the conquest of the air, for suggestions of aerial flight. One seed is the exact counterpart of the parachute, and there are many possessing special natural contrivances for flight.  Yet it must not be forgotten that they are all " heavier than air machines " to use the technical phrase.  Sooner or later they are bound to come to earth, otherwise their purpose in Nature's scheme would fail.

I would strongly advise all Nature lovers to provide themselves on their walks with a strong magnifying glass.  The marvels to be seen in flower and seed are astonishing, and the tiny flora of the Downs are especially fruitful in surprises.  The effect of dew or rain on the petals of these flowerets is one of the most beautiful sights the eye can gaze on.  These floating seeds of thistle, dandelion and the like, are also among the wonders of this world of ours.

\*          \*          \*          \*          \*

As you stand here on the Beacon you can see a white road, a little east of south, far away, descending a hill as it were towards you.  The ridge that stretches away towards that road is your path—several miles of grassy track.  It is also an exercising ground for racehorses.  On your way you pass the Five Lords' Burghs— great barrows, some of which appear to have been excavated in the careless manner of old, by sinking a hole in the centre.  Probably many of these, if properly examined, might yet yield archæological treasures.  Our energetic young society, the Brighton Archæological Club, might well turn their attention to such as these.  There is no lack of opportunities.  In every direction mounds are to be found

Still going south you come at last to a fringe of gorse skirting the cultivation.  If you look into this you will find much of it very old gorse, with massive trunks or stems.  This ancient gorse is growing over an old road, of which the ruts are quite plainly to be seen, filled with the dead spines of the furze.  This is an example of the age of some of these tracks.  Probably this very road has been used by Briton, Roman and all the many races which went to the

U

making of the men of to-day—of whom you are one! On either side, in spring, are great patches of violets, bluebells, and the unfolding shoots of the young bracken, which they enjoyed, maybe, as much as you will—notwithstanding that the Pax Britannica was yet to be. We can scarcely realise the liberty and peace of these days.

The track curves round towards Bishopstone, lying in a broad hollow at your feet. Here, for a thousand years, and probably many more, it has been an abode of man. Very few Brightonians visit it. It lies " off the track."

BISHOPSTONE.
*(By Arthur B. Packham.)*

Not a word too much is said or written about New Shoreham or Steyning Churches; but if Bishopstone were less isolated, another would be added to the list—that is, if the inside could be seen! On behalf of those who do come, I think I am justified in making a protest against so interesting a church being always locked except during services. The key is only to be obtained at the vicarage nearly half a mile away. That is to say, a mile and a half must be traversed, if the lover of Church architecture, or student, would see what ought to be easily seen—the interior of the House of God. Surely a key could be kept at the Post Office. Rodmell Church has not been locked within the memory of man. If one church can with impunity be left open, why not another?

It always seems to me that the minister of a parish whose church is always locked, except at service time, can seldom enforce the duty of private prayer upon his flock, for where better can they step aside from the world and commune with Him, than in the house where His Name is enshrined, surrounded by all things dedicated to His service ?

Whatever the differences of creed, the need of prayer is recognised by all alike, and it is impossible not to contrast the use made of our churches for the purposes of private prayer and those on the Continent. If the opportunity were given, and the duty pressed by ministers upon their people, many a heart would find relief in God's House from the pressure of daily cares.

One portion of the church has existed since before the Conquest, and no part is later than 1200. It is both notable and beautiful among Sussex churches. The south porch is undoubtedly Saxon, and has the characteristic " long and short work " at the angles ; but the sundial is its greatest glory. It is circular topped, and bears the name " Eadric " and a cross. It is placed at the apex of squared stone masonry forming the doorway, which later Norman workmen are supposed to have enriched with zigzag mouldings. (As a specimen of inept " restoration," a great part of this masonry is faced with Portland cement with impressed lines for joints !)

The Norman tower, like Seaford, has several stages or string courses, each story being a little smaller than the one immediately below. This lessening of size as height was reached enabled the Norman builder to dispense with massive buttresses. He relied on thickness of wall, and slight, flat supports at the angles, rising from the base, and each string course. Here at Bishopstone, however, there are no supports.

Within, the church is almost all Transition, and is a perfect example of changing style. Unless altered soon after erection as a Norman edifice, it is hard to account for the mixture. I would prefer to think that the change was a mental one on the part of its designer. In any case, whether evolution or decision is responsible, the result is most interesting to us.

The chancel is in two bays. The eastern portion—vaulted—is pure Norman and yet has a Transitional western arch. The west chancel is half-and-half, and the nave almost wholly Early English. When the Saxon church was altered or rebuilt, they seem to have begun at the eastern end. There is a curious carving, which may be Norman, of lamb and doves, and the font is of the plainest character.

A pleasant path across the low down will bring you to Bishopstone Station.

# CHAPTER XXX

## BERWICK, ALCISTON AND SELMESTON (9 Miles)
### BY RAIL TO BERWICK

### With Illustrations by E. Lucchesi.

IT is quite a mile and a half from the station to Berwick church and village, which are most beautifully placed among clustering trees at the foot of the Downs where they turn south to form the valley of the Cuckmere. The church, nestling among its trees, makes a picture from almost any point, with its spire of silver-grey—a tint that artists love. It is carefully kept, both within and without. The restoration, some forty years ago, was not such as we would wish to see now ; the new Decorated work "means well," no doubt, but seems incongruous. The whole of the north wall of nave rests on twin pillars of marble, which seem too frail to support it.

It is well that the departed are not troubled with the outward forms of sepulture. If they were there would be much perplexity among the ghostly visitants as to where they were originally laid, so much alteration has the exigencies of space demanded. It is only fair to say that small tablets, let into the floor, inform the visitors—mortal and otherwise—that certain busts and canopies have been removed from the superior sanctity of the chancel to the simple draughtiness of the tower, and, after all, it must be admitted that our forefathers were unconscionably fond of appropriating "the front seats," even when they could no longer sit on them, which seems unreasonable.

This liberty of removal would seem to have been exercised by the rectors of Berwick from early days, and was evidently symptomatic of the Reformation. Parson Nutt, in 1618, who has left a record of his parish behind him, removed the reading desk "into the boddy of the church." The fear of undue exaltation of preaching above praying caused George Herbert, at Layton, to make reading desk and pulpit of the same height !

The said worthy Rector of Berwick also built the wainscot pews which hid the beautiful canopied tomb in the chancel, surmounted by a cross of fine design. He and his wife were also commemorated there by marble bust and escutcheon. He can scarcely complain if—together with his "wainscot pews"—a like retribution has befallen them in being translated to another part of the church. Of such it may literally be said, "Their works do follow them."

Parson Nutt's *Remembrances* contain some quaint terms and phrases. He applies the word "forraners" to strangers; and "the eternal feminine" to a mill—"which paies me 40s. a yeere for the tithe of *her*."

THE GATEWAY, WILMINGTON PRIORY.
(*By E. Lucchesi.*)

The church was originally Early English. Perhaps to form a contrast, the additions are mostly of later style. The screen is old and quaint. Built into the tower is what appears to be a cottager's copper! It is the ancient font, while the chancel steps are edged with strips from the old altar-stone, found in restoration, and promptly sawn up for the purpose! In a chapel is a quaint, punning epitaph to one of the rectors (whose memory is said, in rather pagan style, to be " pretious to the Muses and Graces ") and to his son George, " both oregenal and transcript—the first unborne Jenua. 15, 1668."

" Oregenal and transcript," i.e. father and son; and " unborne," meaning " died "—certainly an " oregenal " kind of word, not lacking in poetry.

The stained glass is good, consideration having been given to the elementary fact that windows are to admit light.  In many of our country churches the larger part of them are treated as parti-coloured settings of vari-coloured saints, whose chief and passive occupation would seem to be the reverse of their whilom profession of " spreading the light."   The village—if so small a collection of houses can be so designated—is pretty, and being on a knoll, commands some charming views.   Across the river, some two miles distant, lies Wilmington, with its famous " Long Man " cut in the chalk of the shallow combe above it.   We are apt to be ignorantly scornful of the keeping of diaries, once so favourite a custom ;  but the grain of wheat among much chaff is sometimes enshrined in them, and many an obscure point made plain.   Would that " Remembrances " similar to Parson Nutt's had been left by some Prior of Wilmington as to whether the giant form on the hill-side was really the work of his monks.   As it is, controversy cannot settle whether it is prehistoric or mediæval ;  whether it represents some St. Christopher or pilgrim, or a Druid deity.   Opinion leans to the latter theory, probably because it gives greater scope to the imagination.   In any case it is of vast size (some 230 feet in length), and only religious enthusiasm, whether heathen or Christian, could probably have conceived or executed it.

Although no part of this ramble, you might make a mental note of Wilmington, if only for its ruined Benedictine Priory, of which the old gateway still stands, and some small remains, to be seen in the walls of the farm-house close by ;  its quaint church and fine yew tree ;  but chiefly to make a closer acquaintance with its " Long Man," and climb to the top, and get a view of the Cuckmere Valley and the sea across the great coombe which lies just behind the crest of the hill above the giant.   This, to my mind, is the finest valley in the Downs, being so much broader than the Dyke.

\*          \*          \*          \*          \*

The last time I was at Berwick, the dusk began to fall, and I was astonished at the number and size of the bats noiselessly circling about among the old trees.   That same afternoon I had seen a brood of ducklings, hatched under a sedate old hen in a distant field, being driven by the farmer to what would seem to be their natural element, the water of the duck-pond.   Instinct did not evidently suggest it, for they tried several times to escape the ordeal, until they were shepherded more completely, and perforce driven in, when to their evident surprise, they sat on the surface, instead of sinking in.   It was a most amusing sight to see the concern of mamma, but if ever satisfaction were expressed, it was shown in the wagging of their little yellow, fluffy tails.

Crossing the fields westward by a cart track will bring you to Alciston, lying immediately under a spur of Firle Beacon, which rises grandly at the back. Does anyone wish to see a village of George Morland the painter's day, let him visit Alciston. Such mighty thatched barns, granaries and farm-buildings, such as one sees in his pictures ; an old vicarage, once a manor-house ; and a simple little church, with one Norman window in the chancel, and remains of further eastward extension. Just below in the farmyard a dovecote of unusual form, like a cottage, stands in ruins.

The whole place has a forsaken air about it, as though the shadow of the Corn Laws, in passing over, had left it desolate.

There is a fine view eastwards from the churchyard.

Selmeston, called " Simson " by the villagers, lies on the edge of the comparatively level country a mile away. In these villages one naturally turns into the churchyard, and it follows quite as naturally that the church door is locked, barred and bolted, lest, I suppose, the fresh, sweet wind should disperse too much of the odour of sanctity which rises from mouldy matting and hoary hassock. But at Selmeston, another system obtains. Here, too, an odour met me, not the solid mustiness gathered between Sabbath and Sabbath, but the holier perfume of the flowers. If I remember rightly, the very porch was covered with jasmine or clematis.

The interior is most lovingly cared for. The church was rebuilt in 1867, but the oaken pillars dividing the nave from the aisle, an ancient and somewhat unusual feature, were retained.* There is some good stained glass, a rich sixteenth-century tomb " to one Betrix, wife of Sir Edward Bracy "—as it was quaintly put by the lady attending to the flowers—and a rough-hewn altar slab, with the customary five or seven consecration crosses on its surface. (" Supposed to be originally Druidical," the lady said, with more imagination than accuracy—from the favourite tradition, but un-likely circumstance, that stones on which human sacrifices had been offered were consecrated and put to use as Christian altars.)

If you desire to rest satisfied with the villages seen, you can make your way back to Berwick Station from here. If a longer walk, some miles more, making nine in all, commends itself to you, go north to Chalvington (called in the vulgar tongue " Chawton ") and Rype. The scenery through which you pass is of the more level type and lies much " off the track."

It is the fringe of the Dicker. What is the Dicker ? A large expanse of pasture, common, plough and cornlands. Flat ? No, slightly undulating. Walk through it when the hedges are snowy

---

* At East Guldeford, the most easterly parish in Sussex, the roof of nave is supported by a double row of oaken pillars.

with the new wonder of the "May," and it reminds one of the long swell of ocean's green bosom, with here and there a line of crested white. Dull? Yes, to those who prefer the mountains, because their clogged senses only discern in the sweet plains—

"the level waste, the rounding grey."

In my humble opinion, I hold with Coventry Patmore, that mountains are Earth's failures, the nakedness of which she vainly tries to hide by clothing their lower slopes with verdure. Mighty warts they are—piled up, scarred and arid-topped—disfiguring her fair face. Ever and anon, she gathers her robe of cloud about her head, and sorrow finds vent in torrents of tears, seaming and furrowing their way down her bosom, until the low round hills and grassy downs are saddened, and the smiling plains flooded.

All the humours of the earth-born mists cluster round the ragged mountain-tops, and the sound of their quarrelling is the thunder, and the flash of their swords is the lightning, until silenced by the tears of their mother, when they disperse in gloomy mood.

Mountains provide "holiday scenery," if you will, but not scenery to live with.

And wherefore "Dicker"? Ah, that, as the Ancient Mariner said, "I have not to declare"—which means, he didn't know! Probably it has a derivation, and antiquarians, who invent much when at a loss, can doubtless tell us what it doesn't mean, even if they fail in the true definition. Oh, this nailing down to the counter of dull accuracy every old coin which fails to bear the image and superscription of archæological fact—at least according to the latest antiquarian dictum! So long as I am happy in knowing where and what it is, let me remain in blissful ignorance of what the "Dicker" means. If I am asked any antiquarian poser, I reply that it is probably "Early English"—a useful designation which means any time from Alfred to Queen Anne. I recommend it to the puzzled.

I well remember the shock it gave my youthful mind when I discovered it was not—

"Wild shepherds watched their flocks by night."

It did not seem to me the wrong word then. That the uncouth, unkempt shepherd men, with their hard life of midnight watchfulness, should be called "wild," seemed perfectly natural. But the seedling syllables ab, ba, grew for me into the tree of knowledge, the fruit whereof was bitterness.

\*  \*  \*  \*  \*

Chalvington has a tiny church dedicated to St. Thomas of Canterbury—Thomas-à-Becket. Many Kent and Sussex churches are

dedicated to him, I believe.    The only architectural features are
some Decorated windows, in one of which some old stained glass
represents   the   saint.    Here   again,   antiquarians   differ.    Some
hold the church to be dedicated to St. Bartholomew.    The later
dedication accords with the architecture.    The whole village seems
to consist of two houses.

A pleasant path across the fields brings you to Rype.    After the
modest  proportions  of  Chalvington,  Rype  Church,  with  its  handsome  Perpendicular  tower,  is  large  indeed.    The  Pelham  Buckle
over  the  west  door  points  to  the  donor  of  it.    There  is  some  old
stained glass in the east window.    The body of the church is mainly
Decorated, and there are some curious recesses in the wall of the
nave.    It  appears  to  have  had  in  pre-Reformation  days  three
altars  and  a  rood-loft.    The  tower  stands  up  bravely  from  the
rather level surroundings.

Retracing your steps through Chalvington you make for Berwick
Station,  leaving  an  old  Georgian  house,  " Cobbcourt,"  on  your
right.

# CHAPTER XXXI

## ARLINGTON, MICHELHAM AND HAILSHAM (6 MILES)
### TO BERWICK STATION BY RAIL

#### WITH ILLUSTRATION BY A. S. C. : FRONTISPIECE

JUST outside the station on the north side, a wicket-gate and field-path leads into the Arlington road, thus saving a considerable detour. Again, just beyond the bridge over the Cuckmere, a second gate opens on another path to Arlington Church. On your way you have a good view of the Cuckmere Valley. The river is small and meanders through a fairly open country. In the distance across the Dicker Common the fine spire of Chiddingly is a prominent object to the north-west. Abbot's Wood bounds the view on the east.

Arlington village is quietly rural, with no special feature, but the church is of high antiquity. Many Sussex churches go back to Saxon days, as this does in the tiny window near the south door and elsewhere ; but few show Roman remains. An urn, fragments of pottery, tiles and glass found under the floor are preserved in a niche to indicate a probable Roman site. Indeed, it is claimed for Arlington that a Romano-British church preceded the Saxon building. The aforesaid window is arched with Roman tiles. One interesting speculation arises from the discovery of the urn. Did the Roman practice of cremation continue after they became Christians ? It would seem so. They were a practical people, quite uninfluenced by sentiment, and sentiment is admitted to be the only real barrier to a much-needed reform. In little country churchyards, the question may not be urgent—although Arlington would seem to show the way, even there—but in our great cities it is a necessity. It may be long in coming, but come it undoubtedly will.

To the Saxon building a Norman chapel was added north of the chancel. The original circular-headed windows and high-pitched roof remain. The tower has "long and short work" of Saxon origin, although it is mainly Early English or Transition. The shingled spire starts from much below the apex of the nave roof, owing to the squat tower ; but the effect is undeniably quaint.

The arch between the chapel and north aisle has the dog-tooth ornament on the capitals. Then a fire destroyed the chancel, which was rebuilt in the vogue of the day—Decorated. Finally, there are two Perpendicular windows and a font. It is interesting to see how leisurely our forefathers built sacred edifices, nor did they trouble if incongruities resulted. After all, it was at least Gothic : of different types perhaps, but none absolutely foreign in spirit. " Stone upon stone, line upon line, here a little, there a little," until Arlington, like many others, shows every style of architecture. Certainly, the interest to us is not less.

This is the rock on which our " restorers " have mainly come to grief. If is, of course, delightful to possess such a building as Salisbury Cathedral, practically pure and of one style, and where among our smaller parish churches such exist, as Poynings Church to-day, complete in the work of its builder, the heart and mind rejoices. But to pull down all work that does not conform to the main style of the building, as so many restorers have done, is to do grievous harm to the fabric, and wrong to posterity. It erases whole pages from the history of each church, and substitutes but two epochs, that of its building, and of its restoration—emphasising the piety of its founders, and the folly of its restorers—if that is not too dignified a title to bestow on them.

Arlington Church has other features of interest : a beautiful piscina, a tomb with cross under a fine Decorated arch, a screen carved by Sussex boys at Mayfield, and a " low-side window " with shouldered arch, in the south chancel wall.

These " low-side windows " are very fully illustrated and written on by Mr. Philip Mainwaring Johnston in vol. xli. of the Sussex Archæological Collection. It is strange that their origin and use is a matter of dispute. Some contend they were put in to enable lepers or other diseased persons to see the elevation of the host ; others that they were to hear the confessions and to administer the sacrament to such, and this view seems to have some point, because there is an opening and a seat at the bottom of some of these windows, and a sundial is cut on the stone at the side of others, as if to inform those outside of the time of elevation or attendance of the priest.

The other theories advanced are so varied and interesting that I give them here : viz. that they were used to ring the sanctus hand-bell through, at the elevation ; for ventilation ; for light to read the lessons ; for offertory purposes ; to announce by bell the coming of the priest ; for the acolyte to fan the charcoal of his censer ; for distribution of alms, in money or bread ; and last, and most attractive in suggestion—to symbolise the wound in the Saviour's side.

Whatever their purpose, the fact remains that there are many Sussex churches which have low side-windows. If one, it is mostly on the south side of chancel, and sometimes on both sides.

Arlington Church is dedicated to St. Pancras, and may have been connected with Lewes Priory, also named after the same saint.

On the north side of the churchyard, you will find a gate and path leading up the field. This takes you by the river-valley to Michelham, and it is a delightful walk. There is, however, little indication of a track. Nothing shows the depopulation of the country more than the disuse, and frequently, disappearance, of field-paths. You will find it "plain sailing" into a broad lane. Crossing this, an immense field lies before you. At the north-east end there is a shaw and a small stream spanned by planks. If you fail to find it, the river will bring you to a standstill. Follow its bank to the right, and soon Michelham tower will gladden your eyes. The phrase is an apt one, because of the charm which lies for you in the simplicity of design and beauty of proportion ; and for the poor wayfarer in mediæval days when food and shelter could only be obtained at the conventual houses.

Unless, indeed, the priory buildings stood up above the trees as boldly as the gateway, I doubt if the scene has changed in any particular. The sight of the venerable tower transports you to the fourteenth century. Far removed from any village, the priory would be liable to raids from marauders, intent on plunder, even if the poultry of the brethren were chiefly coveted. Thus the need for protection, amply provided by the river and moat ; the only entrance being through the ponderous doors of the gateway tower. This is of Perpendicular design, solid and imposing. With its equally substantial bridge and the neighbouring trees mirrored in the water, it is a great favourite with the artists who know it. The only drawback is the fringe of trees, whose envious lacery hides the best view from sight, except in winter, when a sketch can be made if you stand on the roots of the trees growing out of the water, and avail yourself of the artist's licence to omit the intervening stems and branches.

The old priory mill, hard by, is equally shy, and hides itself even more effectually from sight, but from the edge of the water on either side below the wheel, a picture can, with patience, be obtained.

Of the priory itself little remains. Early English arches are visible in the outer wall, and there are two old chambers, one possessing a fine double-canopied fire-place. These and a crypt are to be seen, if a written order is given by the owner, J. A. Gwynne, of Folkington.

It was founded about 1220 for Augustinian Canons by Gilbert de Aquila, the proud possessor of the title of "Lord of the Honor of the Eagle " of Pevensey, conferred upon the family by Henry the First on the attainder of the Earl of Moreton for rebellion.

These canons were of two classes, secular and regular, the latter being austere in rule of life ; the former possessing private property, with the right of marriage, although seldom exercised.  They also allowed their beards to grow and did not adopt the tonsure.  There were fifty-four priories of the order in England in the reign of Edward I ; increasing later to 175.

The " Lord of the Eagle " gave with no niggardly hand :  his " Park of Pevensey "—the boundaries of which can still be traced by an embankment enclosing it—with men, rents, marshlands, pastures, woods and pannage for sixty beasts and one hundred hogs ;  timber and fuel, " in pure and perpetual alms," together with the gift of Hailsham and Laughton Churches, and later the manor of Chington, near Seaford.  Even in our own town of Brighton the priors held lands.

The passing years brought " much grist to the mill," until the close of the fourteenth century.  Then the inconvenience resulting from so much of the real property of the kingdom lying in the " dead hand " of the Church, coupled with general corruption, called a halt, and dried up the springs of benevolence.

Defences against the inroads of the sea at Pevensey and elsewhere, and the maintenance of hospitality, owing to the priory being then on one of the high roads, and frequented by the nobility—and even royalty—so impoverished the foundation, that in 1398 the buildings were in a ruinous condition, and the churches of Alfriston and Fletching were granted to the Prior.  The King, however, made forty pounds out of the transaction, which later delays increased to fifty, with yet another ten before the final completion of the deeds !  This gift seems to have rescued the priory from the clutches of poverty.

Not that troubles ceased to vex the canons.  Exactions from unfriendly nobles, and forcible appropriation of their rights, caused them to have recourse to law, which was no cheaper then than now.  Disputes between churchmen were more obstinately contested than among laymen.  One of the Michelham Priors was so vehement against the Abbot of St. Augustine's, Canterbury, that the Chapter trying the case decreed " that it be buried among them that sleep "—the mediæval equivalent to ordering a letter to " lie on the table."

Even Edward the Second sued the Prior for the maintenance of some claimant of that right.  Forced loans to royalty, seldom repaid, also impoverished them ; but, on the whole, the priory seems to have held a tolerably tranquil course until the Dissolution, when it was swept away in the general ruin, although no great fault was alleged against it.   The King took it into his own hands until 1541, when it was given in exchange to Fitzalan, the Earl of Arundel.

This is, briefly, the history of Michelham Priory.   It has seen more stirring events than its present seclusion suggests.   It raises up visions of " the quiet life " more peaceful than the reality proved.

Retracing your steps, you take the road leading over the river bridge and gain the crossways, nearly a mile ahead.   The one almost directly opposite will bring you to Hailsham, through the " grateful shades " of Abbot's Wood.   It is a clean and pleasant town, with several good houses, and a large Perpendicular church, with a fine tower and peal of bells, of which the tenor still rings the curfew.   Love of things past is generally confined to matters of sentiment, such as this time-honoured custom.   I bring no railing accusation against those responsible for the fabric of Hailsham Church.   It is scrupulously well ordered, and was restored in 1870 !   1878 ! ! and 1889 ! ! !

# CHAPTER XXXII

## SEAFORD TO WEST DEAN, ALFRISTON AND
## BERWICK (8 MILES)

### BY RAIL TO SEAFORD.

WITH ILLUSTRATIONS BY ARTHUR B. PACKHAM, FRANK BAKER,
C. H. H. BURLEIGH AND A. S. C.

IT may seem gratuitous advocacy, but there are varieties of
mood even in that unwelcome visitor the east wind, or, perhaps, the wind that comes from the eastward; for it is possible, after a long spell of south-westerly and westerly winds,
that these may retrace their course, impelled by the still distant
tyrant himself, and a day, or even two, may waft a breeze almost
balmy in character from the east. There were two such days of
blessed respite this Whitsuntide (1910), and they brought special
gifts as compensation for what was to follow. This was just the
warm, dry air wanted to woo the perfume from the gorse. It is
in fullest bloom at the end of May, and its scent, in volume, is one
of those rare happenings the recipient is not likely to forget. Had
Shakespeare been a Downland man he might well have chosen
its odour instead of violets in that opening speech of *Twelfth Night*;
except that it is rarer and less known. Yet it is not only sweet—
which all love is—but passionate—which all love should be, and
is not. To me it seems to embody, as far as a perfume may, the
passionate fervour of requited love.

On such a day, and with such an odour to inhale, the road to
Chington Farm from Seaford loses some of its recent acquirements.
Time was when it left the town almost abruptly, a straight but
unsophisticated field-path. Now, half its length is built upon.
Chington Farm will bring you back to things less modern. A
typical farmstead crowning the gentle slope above the Cuckmere
Valley, it has a pleasant house and outbuildings clustered round
a large, clear pond. A big willow tree growing out of the water,
and other trees, help the view, and there is a quaint dovecote
and an outside stone staircase to one of the granaries close by.
Other yards, buildings and straw-stacks leave pleasant impressions

of this old Saxon homestead. The peacock seems quite in keeping and at home. It was humorous to watch a white rooster trying to combine dignity with retreat when the more aristocratic bird came

FRISTON MILL AND CHURCH.
*(By W. H. Bond.)*

too close. It was still more diverting to note the indifference of the hens to his presence. They kicked up dust into the eyes of the gorgeous creature. His beauty evidently did not appeal to them, and his chivalry under the contumelious cloud, passed quite unnoticed.

On reaching the limit of the farm, a short distance northwards brings you to a path catering across the crops to Exceat Bridge ; but on your way thither, stop and admire the view across and up the Cuckmere Valley.

Here again, our east wind brought us surprise. Under the sway of the veritable Fiend of the East, there is little colour in the landscape; but to day the river, a riband of royal blue, loosed as from a love-knot, lay on a carpet of tender green stretching from the bridge right away to the eastward cliff of Cuckmere, with the mighty shingle bank at its base, which cuts off that other blue of the Channel. These bends of the old river—the new channel lies on the western side and is straight and uninteresting—are a delight to artists, with the background of the Downs, covered with gorse and a farm embosomed in the only trees visible, to enhance the view.

Northward, the narrow marsh, with glimpses of the river intersecting it ; the spires of Litlington and Alfriston set in the midst of trees ; little Lullington Church on the slope, and Wilmington Down in the rear, form a charming picture. I have purposely brought you via Seaford. The Cuckmere Valley should be seen from the south ; being narrow, except at the mouth, it fails to do itself justice when viewed from the north. It is little known below Alfriston, yet it has a quiet, retired beauty for lovers of brookland scenery. Water has probably been the agency whereby the steep slopes of the hills on either side have been rendered steeper. On one of them, the White Horse of Newbury has been imitated in little by a former squire of Frog Firle, opposite Litlington, but time has nearly obliterated it.

\*　　　\*　　　\*　　　\*　　　\*

Your field-path from Chington will bring you to the bridge, and " the bridge will carry you over " to where the road turns north, passing the mouth of West Dean Valley. To my mind, West Dean is the most sequestered village in Downland. It is indeed " off the beaten track," and yet it cherishes memories of a more famous past, and aspires—if any place so lowly and lonely can be said to aspire—to have been a dwelling-place of the Great Alfred. Bishop Asser, his friend and secretary, " first met the King at Dene " in Sussex, whither he was guided by Sussex folk. Of course, there are several Deans in the county, and Dallaway thinks it was at the neighbouring East Dean, but has apparently no authority for the statement. Alfred had lands quite near at Lullington, and at Sutton in Seaford. Both these and " Dene " are bequeathed in his will, and this little spot has better credentials than any of the other places bearing the same pretty Saxon

X

word for a valley.  A dwelling so close to the Channel and so
hidden, would have great value in the eyes of England's first naval
king, who probably used the entrance of the Cuckmere.

Whether the large house West Dean possessed in earlier days,
occupied by a family of rank, the Heringods, was built on the
site of Alfred's palace, who shall say ?  Except for a fragment
or two and the roofless dovecote, this house " lies desolate " also.
The dovecote is said to be Norman, but is certainly mediæval.
It was complete twelve years ago.

But West Dean has other attractions than those of repute.
It is beautifully wooded, a characteristic of some Down valleys.
When not a tree, other than hawthorn, raises its head on the higher
ground, many are to be found clustered round the homesteads in
the hollows.  The village is tiny indeed, but nestled in its valley,
it is far enough from the world to be beyond its most stentorian
voices.  I know of no more peaceful spot—except for one peculiarity.  Telscombe is a surprise to its discoverer, but West Dean
is itself surprised to see *you* ;  and this wonderment finds undoubted
expression in the western face of the church tower as you approach.
It is unmistakable.  You need give little rein to your fancy.  Before
you, with a spice of malice prepense, grins a face surmounted by
a monk's cowl, as though a Brobdignagian friar had come to life,
and thrusting his head above the churchyard soil, gazed at you
across the rectory wall.  The illusion is caused by the lap-eared,
dumpy spire, and the disposition of windows and buttresses.  It
is not unlike the look the " native " is apt to greet strangers withal,
and in this sense is characteristic ;  but one drawback remains.
Having once seen it, it will not, like the " Cheshire Cat," fade
away !  It is a grin that will not wear off.  It greets you on your
arrival, and is apparently as pleased to see you go.  You become
obsessed with it.  It gets on your nerves !

The church itself, and its old priest's house or rectory, will,
however, make amends.

The former has no chancel arch, but the fine Norman arch with
clustered columns in the tower gives ample distinction to the
interior, even if the tombs did not do so.  Two of these are canopied
Gothic, and another, with kneeling figures, is elaborate Renaissance,
raised to the memory of the later dwellers in the ruined manor-
house.  A font on octagonal pillars ;  a scalloped piscina ;  remains
of the rood-loft staircase—the wooden screen, of course, destroyed
in the forties—and several interesting windows remain to bear
witness to the piety of various periods, and satisfy the cravings
of the archæologist.

The rectory, or " Priest's House," owing to its rarity, is the
greater attraction.  It has been pointed out, that while we have

many of the larger dwellings of our forefathers—castles, manor-houses and monasteries—remaining, there are few examples of domestic ecclesiastical architecture.  This humble habitation of two or three rooms is unique in Sussex.  Within walls, thick and well built, the upper room—approached by a " newell " or circular staircase, in an adjunct roofed over with stone—is perhaps the most attractive, as the original fire place with projecting funnel remains. The wooden shutters in place of glass windows are still *in situ.*

The plan of the building is simple, a parallelogram with the staircase, and a recessed cupboard or niche projecting at the south-east and north-west corners.  The main oak beam of the flooring is very massive, with substantial joists.  The pointed arch doorways and heavy oak doors of great age ; the original windows ;

a small cellar half sunk below the level of the floor ; a loft above the upper room — these make up a dwelling of exceptional interest, transporting one at once to the beginning of the fourteenth century.

ALURED'S CHAPEL, CHARLESTON.
(*By Arthur B. Packham.*)

West Dean Church was given to the Norman Abbey of St. Mary Grestein, and was under the control of the Priors of Wilmington, who may have built this rectory house.  In the early years of this century it was inhabited by labourers, but the rector now makes it part of his dwelling.  It is probably more quaint than comfortable !

\*          \*          \*          \*          \*

If it were not too long a distance to include in this ramble, I would advise ascending the valley to Friston, which lies exposed to every wind that blows, on the top of the hill.  The need for shelter is shown in the situation of the miller's house, which is half underground.  You go down steps into its little forecourt bright with flowers, nestled out of reach of the winds.  I am glad to give so accurate a sketch of the smock mill, now that so many are falling into disuse and decay.   The tiny Saxon church has many features of interest.

A path leads from West Dean into the next valley northward. It skirts a sloping field, and brings you to a steep green way, at the bottom of which lies Charleston Farm.   There are several " Charlestons " in Sussex.   The American Civil War familiarised the name, which sounds strangely modern ; but like many name-places in the New World, it is borrowed from the Old Country.   Except to the antiquarian its name scarcely suggests any great antiquity,

ALURED'S DOVECOTE, CHARLESTON.
(*By A. S. C.*)

yet the Conqueror's cup-bearer, Alured, lived there, and " built him a chapel," which stands to this day !   It is part of the farmhouse now as it probably was then, and a Transition window of two lights under a circular arch at the west end, and a small window in the east gable—a delightful specimen of a lancet with a filled-up head—remain to tell of its sacred use.   How many Sussex folk know of this relic of those far-off days ?   How few have seen it ! It arouses reflections of a deeply interesting nature.   Time seems almost to have stood still in this quiet valley while the drama of the Making of England has been enacted.   How little different it must have looked eight hundred years ago !

A charming valley too, with its spring and little lake helping to swell the waters of the Cuckmere. In the margin of this reedy pool grows that rare plant the golden dock, with its strangely congested fronds of seeding flowers, which a botanist tells me he has found nowhere else in Sussex.

In addition to the farm house, a dovecote, buttressed on the lower side, and having a stone kennel for that Cerberus, the watch-dog, stands most picturesquely on the steep slope under fine trees. I always mention these where found. Besides the quaintness of them, they are a link with the past by reason of their often hoary age and use. If Alured's chapel still stands, why not his dovecote, even more substantially built ? It is seeking for an unlikely thing, to expect evidences of architectural style in so homely an erection as a pigeon-house ; and some of them, built of native flint, may well be Norman without our knowing it. The doorways are often of stone, and determine the age, but here it has been replaced with one of the farm-house type. The clouds of winged, unauthorised gleaners among uncut corn, that issued from these squat towers, were one of the scourges of the Norman sway to the Saxon hind and small farmer.

You will leave this secluded, yet not remote valley with regret, and join the road which wanders by the entrance on its way to Litlington. On the right curves the steep hill side, and on the left a runnel, rush-grown and rich with water-loving plants. Cowslips thrusting up eager stalks, yet with bowed heads—like bunches of golden keys hung at hand for Spring to lose no time in unlocking the caskets of her latest treasures—colour the high bank as far as the eye can see. On this road, and within a few yards of the runnel, I found a dead grass snake nearly three feet long, evidently killed by a passing wheel. These green snakes are quite harmless —unlike the viper, with its chequer of dull, diamond-shaped markings. In my wanderings I have come across both, and although I know the harmless nature of the common snake, I cannot quite overcome the antipathy which is supposed to date from the Fall, but is far more likely to be engendered by the swift, sinuous character of its movements. Man has an instinctive dread of things slippery and crooked in movement, things difficult for the eyes to follow, and if to this is added a scintillating glitter and suggestion of sliminess, and the knowledge that some of the species carry certain death in their fangs—this is quite enough to account for the shuddering dislike most of us bear the snake. Other things such as the shape of the head, the rapid play of its unpleasant tongue, and the wicked eye,* also add to our antipathy. All its

* This does not apply to the green snake, which has an eye " like a bird's," as if to proclaim its harmlessness.

outward characteristics arouse the elementary and unreasoning sense of dislike and fear, which the undoubted, but evil beauty of its colouring only emphasises ; and even " the knowledge of good and evil " is almost powerless to overcome this aversion. Snakes like " Injins, is pison " !

The nearest acquaintance I have ever had with a live snake was on the Downs beyond Patcham, when, as a boy, I sat down on a clump of coarse grass, and one which seemed to my horrified gaze to be yards long, " slithered " out from between my legs and down the hill ! A quicker backward somersault was never indulged in by a professional tumbler than by the youth in question.

The road to Litlington winds its pleasant way to the village, and on to the church, which it passes. As I have been unable to find any records of Litlington, I suppose it is one of those happy places without a history. Yet much must have happened to influence its inhabitants since the original Norman church was built.

If these humble village churches alter but little now, time was when piety, or desire to be up-to-date in matters ecclesiastical, changed the Norman style to Early English, and later days have left their mark on the sacred building in windows, altar-tomb, or font. Two open and two blocked-up windows represent the earlier style ; sedilia and lancets the next fashion, and a tomb and font the Perpendicular.

The string course proves the Norman origin of the nave ; and the oak purlines, embattled round the walls, and shields on the corbels of roof, give distinction to the chancel, which has also a low-side window. The arches built of hard chalk—evidence of materials nearest to hand—are perhaps the most interesting feature ; unless it be the quaint and homely staircase to the belfry. It is what one expects to find leading to an upper room in an old farm-house, and would be out of place, were it not so convincing in its purpose. As you enter its ancient portal, you bow low. Not reverence, but necessity, compels the obeisance, the pitch being the reverse of lofty, and the tiny aperture giving light and air— " nine bobble square "—is of a piece with its proportions.

It is such features as these which form the special attraction of many of our little churches. They are not so distinctively architectural, as possessed of quaint details of many kinds. Something of the imperfection of humanity seems to cling about them, rather than the perfection of art. Hence, perhaps, the attraction they have for us. It can neither be explained nor justified. It is opposed to every rule of logic, or process of reason, but there it is. The sources of affection are ever hard to trace, and the result of modern restoration is so often the destruction of the human interest. It is like taking the soul out of a man and leaving the lifeless carcass, to see the empty, featureless appearance so many churches now present. I may be thought reactionary, but I would even retain the old box pews where they show any evidence of age ; and where the urgent need for space should call for their dismissal, I would say—" Do as your forefathers did, and add an aisle or transept in harmony with the church. Do not destroy its history."

The church is built on the edge of the brooklands, and from the marsh just north, with pool and rushes to form a foreground, and pine trees flanking the little spire, there is a pleasant picture.

One wonders whether the farm-house adjoining the church had an ecclesiastical origin, and formed one of a trio—with West Dean and Alfriston—of priests' houses ? I have not been inside, but

ALFRISTON CHURCH.
(By Frank Baker.)

there is a great deal of Caen stone in its exterior walls—a stone not often used for secular purposes, owing to its cost.

From Litlington you may reach Alfriston by either side of the river, both delightful walks. A bridge takes you over, and the path brings you out on to the road, by a red brick Georgian house, part of a larger building, whose name, " Burnt House," gives the agency by which it was partly destroyed. A view along the river, with Alfriston Church as the objective, is worth the walk to see. From here the road takes you into the village, past a delightful house (" Dean's Place "), that seems, to look at it from the outside, just what a country dwelling should be.

The Litlington side has the advantage of enabling you to reach Lullington Church more easily, and on the way getting an even more beautiful view of Alfriston across pools and river, where a gate leads down to a path skirting the road. Framed by over-arching boughs of trees, you see the whole village dominated by its church, and backed by the flowing line of Downs. This view is just north of Lullington Farm, an interesting homestead, with a square dovecote with shaped stone doorway at the corner of the farmyard.

Lullington Church has gained some artificial notoriety by being called what it is not—"the smallest church in England." It is the chancel only of a larger building and should be visited more on account of the view than anything else. This, and not its size, will be your reward. It shows little indication of style, except its Decorated windows, but like most Sussex churches its genesis was probably Norman. It lies up the hill directly opposite Alfriston causeway and bridge.

"STAR INN," ALFRISTON.
(*By Arthur B. Packham.*)

Alfriston is so well known that it should fall outside the scope of these papers. I am loth, however, to pass it without comment, because it also possesses among other attractions a clergy house, although of later date than that of West Dean. This is timber-built, and thatched, and has a fine carved roof to its central hall. There is no flooring to this, and it would probably be rush-strewn in olden days. There are two floors at each end of the hall, and the rooms, with chimney-corners and other quaint features, remain much as they originally were.

The fine church (these words sufficiently describe it without using, as is sometimes the case, a more pretentious title—"The Cathedral of the South Downs") is one of three which may have been designed by the same architect in the following order—Etchingham, Poynings and Alfriston. The last two are very similar.

The palm must, perhaps, be given to Poynings for its noble tower, windows of good design, and fine proportions generally; but Alfriston runs it close. It may be said of the former, that the exterior is the finer, and of the latter, the interior, owing to its greater length. Similarity is proved in several points. The east windows of both are practically identical in design as are the triple sedilia and two fragments of old glass in each north transept— the Annunciation and St. Alphege respectively. Here the concave pillars and capitals upholding the tower are unusual, and there is much more to be seen that will repay study.

ALFRISTON CROSS AND STREET.
(*By C. H. H. Burleigh.*)

In common with other churches in Sussex, Alfriston shares the legend of supernatural intervention during its erection, the stones being removed nightly to the present site by angelic craftsmen. Except that our forefathers were rather careless in choosing sites, it is difficult to see where else the sacred edifice could have been erected other than on its present knoll, out of the reach of floods. At Udimore, the protest was not only confined to action. Voices were heard in the darkness crying " O'er the mere," of which Udimore is a corruption—if you are sufficiently credulous to believe it ! The builders of Alfriston Church, however, provided a much more lasting and useful lesson in the work of their hands than in this monkish legend. Let no one omit to take note of the exterior walls. They are built of that beautiful local mosaic, small squared flints, with greenstone dressings. Many Sussex churches show this flint-work, but none in greater perfection. It is a silent sermon in patience. Few operations are more laborious and require more skill, but the reward is great. Time has little effect upon them, except to add a beautiful grey patina to the dark blue facets of the flint. There are various qualities of work, both large and small, but the latter is best, and is most in evidence here.

Another feature is the insertion of isolated square blocks of stone above the plinth all round the church. Are these the stones removed by the midnight angels, and thus singled out for special honour ?

The famous " Star Inn," with its carving more or less original, and its fearsome lion or dragon of blood-red hue " rampant " at the corner, was one of the religious hostelries—say the antiquarians. In design, it appears to me to be just what an inn should be. It seems to fall naturally into place in this old street of old houses. If the elaborate ironwork of its sign, and the blazon thereon were absent, the traveller would certainly mount its steps by instinct. Once inside all doubt would vanish !

A market cross once reared its sacred symbol over the ancient crowd of buyers and sellers to remind them of honesty and fair dealing. Only curtailed steps and a meaningless stump remain. If it were not so difficult to add new work to old, one would wish to see it renovated.

Beauty—but of another kind—was restored to it on the last occasion I passed through the village. Three little bare-legged girls—" summer children "—with wind-blown curls, were grouped upon its base, with that unconscious grace which is given only to children to assume naturally. Oh, for an invisible camera, to catch such loveliness when found !

It only remains to note the beauty of situation Alfriston presents. If the Cuckmere were less of a ditch than it is, and more in evidence, the view from almost any direction would make the little town a greater favourite with artists than at present.

There is a delightful path from here through Berwick to the station ; or the weary may avail themselves of a conveyance that plies to and fro from Alfriston, in correspondence with certain of the trains.

# CHAPTER XXXIII

## PEVENSEY TO HURSTMONCEUX AND ETCHINGHAM
### (About 24 Miles)

#### BY RAIL TO PEVENSEY

#### With Illustrations by the late Joseph Diplock, Conrad Leigh and A. S. C.

I AM very loth to take you to Pevensey without making more than a passing reference to its famous castle, probably the oldest Roman relic in England, the fine churches of Pevensey and Westham, not to mention the Mint House, with its beautiful panelled rooms, and other timbered and ancient houses.

To pass by the place where English history may be said to have begun requires courage, but it is neither " off the track," nor unknown, and does not come within the scope of this book. My aim is to get you to spend a day in the Pevensey Marsh, even if you get to an equally well-known spot—Hurstmonceux—in the end.

I know that these great bare stretches of earth with greater sweep of sky, which so attract certain temperaments, repel those whose mental outlook is prescribed, or who prefer limits to thought and sight in a more definite horizon. I have spoken with many, both hillmen and lowlanders, in my wanderings, and have come to the conclusion that the dweller in marshes is generally the more silent man ; and if " silence is golden," he should also prove the wiser ; but here the individual supervenes, and character, that most difficult and complex of studies, begins. If the moods of a landscape, under the varying light, are many, be sure that there is more in most men than they care to show to every casual inquirer ; but that the marshes engender silence, at least, may be conceded. At most, the area of land to be seen is small, and the immense dome of blue is that which meets the gaze more frequently, and this illimitable void inclines man to commune with himself ; and the sky at night, by its very vastness, invites contemplation rather than speech. Perhaps this is why those whose lot it is to live in these solemn spaces are more tolerant of a troubled

Herstmonceux Castle.
The Gateway.

HURSTMONCEUX GATEWAY.

*(By the late Joseph Diplock.)*

sky than most people. It is the chief source of movement. The pageantry of clouds gives the diversity denied them in their sur-roundings. It takes the place of moving shadows and waving trees, and by influencing the light supplies more rapid effects and changes than colour makes in the appearance of the hills. It is the heavens rather than the earth they study. This is why the lowland folk are more weatherwise than most.

And marshes do not, any more than men, unfold their character at a glance. If they have fewer moods than the hills, they have many more than one would think, and these are not less beautiful for those who have " eyes to see." It cannot be denied that they also have fewer lovers, but these are faithful admirers, and find beauty enough to repay their devotion.

As most good things are said to come from above, so does beauty descend from the heavens on to Pevensey Marsh. No spot on God's earth responds more quickly to the changes and intensity of light, for it must not be forgotten that there is no bar to diffusion in these levels. The ray, whether large or small, strong or weak, finds its full fruition on grass or pool, and travels as fast as it may. There are more rapid changes from grave to gay in marshland than elsewhere. The life that light gives is made more vivid by the grassy surfaces of the pools or the ripple of the streams and back-waters. This is the chief glory of these otherwise sober levels. Only the sea, on summer days, can claim the palm of brightness, but it is brightness only, not the contrast which heightens the effect of sunlight itself by glooms and flashes, as from a mirror held awry.

But, except for that tremulous, palpitating quality of air that heat always gives, it is not under a cloudless sky and summer sun that marshland reveals itself to those who look for its charms. To return to a previous simile, quiet natures attract most by the moods they are capable of showing when their placid temperaments are stirred into action. Then, to our surprise, much that is entirely unsuspected comes to light. It is eminently so with marshland. To me it is least interesting in the height of summer, and not even in April, when the play of light would seem to be most varied, and cloud forms at their best, are these levels most attractive. It is rather in the fall of the year, when the sky is lowering and clouds and rain are contending with sunshine for the mastery. It is then that the most surprising, nay, superb effects are to be seen ; but the very conditions are against there being many be-holders. October rains, like the tears of the hopeless, are heavy and long of duration, and shelter is an unknown thing. But the artist is not easily deterred, and great is his reward. Pevensey Marsh lends itself, more than most levels, to the play of light and shade. It is by no means " an unending plain." Willingdon Hill and the range of Downs are prominent on the south-west, and to the north the land rises rapidly at Hurstmonceux.   The only outlets are along the sea and westward.   The particular characteristics of marsh, as such, lie east of Pevensey.   Here there is little relief. Only the Martello towers break the line between land and sea, but westward the watercourses begin to be fringed with low bushes, developing at last into trees with here and there a coppice and farm.

I was through the marsh last October on such a day as I have described.   The rain threatened, yet mercifully did not come my way ;  the constant changes were wonderful to behold.   Sometimes the sea shone like a scimitar from under the low pall of cloud, an intense gleam at the edge of the dark plain.   Then it failed and only the Martello towers stood white against a sea as black as ink, while the marsh began to lighten, and the sky frowned less heavily.   The clouds lifted to the south and Willingdon Hill gave the first touch of colour to the sombre view.   In a few moments it had faded again, and as if to fight against extinction, the river caught the sunlight, and became a moving, shining thing as the rays followed the rift across the marsh, driving the grey cloud-webs before them, and the trees slowly changed from dim shadows to warmth of late autumn tints, while the oxen and the gates across the dykes took definite shape :  then, glowing with a dull fire, the wooded hills—" studded with windmills, oast-houses, and church steeples, in beautiful opposition to the southern line of Martello towers."*   Finally, the recurring gloom over the whole marsh, and all things merge themselves into one plane of purple-grey, as if the very life were fading with the light :  only the sea, far away south, giving promise of breaking clouds.

For less marked contrasts, April brings most beauty.   The vivid green of the newly-sprung grass is tempered by the cool shadows of the clouds, and the sweeping showers here and there about the marsh are like gauzy curtains drawn aside to reveal the sunny distances.   Only the gates and an occasional bush suggest the perspective, except the cattle dotted about, and these give just that note of colour wanted to break the monotony of the level green. They vary from black and rich brown to grey and white, and the sunlight that quickens the surface of the marsh with streaks of brilliant green, in like manner lightens the hue of their coats until colour is lost in distance, and they become inanimate dots of darker tone merely.

Artists, of course, are among those who love the marshes, perhaps because the difficulties appeal to them of portraying the subtle details of the distance on half an inch of space, while the foreground

* Coventry Patmore.

and sky between them take, by comparison, yards of the canvas! No other scenery has quite the attraction, unless it be the mud-flats of an estuary. I was once arranging a sketching trip of some artists, and was besought to " take them where there were muds " ! The secret, of course, is to be found in the suavity and grace of line presented by sand and mud at every ebb of the tide, and in the sneaking regard artists always have for grey tones.

Pevensey itself, as its name implies, was once an island or eyot, before the marsh was fully formed by silting or accumulation. The river is wider above the bridge, as if a barrage kept it up, but lower down " the Haven," as it is called, it " peters " out, and gains the sea somewhat ignominiously through iron pipes under the shingle. The castle itself probably had quays at which

PEVENSEY FROM THE MARSH.
(*By A. S. C.*)

the ships of early days could moor, and the distance it now is from the sea is eloquent of the process which has made Pevensey Marsh.

You may wander at will, but there are several branches of the river, besides innumerable dykes, and should you be brought up by a watercourse too wide to jump, make for the nearest gate. These give access from field to field, but you will find your progress very quaint and crab-like. You will probably " box the compass " many times if you are bent on thoroughly exploring the marsh. It is tiring, also, the grass being coarse and deep, and the surface rough and trodden into holes by the cattle when the ground is soft after the spring floods.

A road leads north to Wartling, which is pleasantly situated at the crossways well above the level. It is a tiny place, and its church has overmuch " Churchwardens' Gothic," but not therefore

THE DACRE MONUMENT, HURSTMONCEUX CHURCH.
*(By the late Joseph Diplock.)*

to be dismissed as in some of the guide-books. The interior is simple, but the arches are not without elegance. The Pelham Buckle, which has been the badge of the family since Sir John Pelham shared in the honour of taking the French King prisoner at the Battle of Poictiers, a St. Catherine's Wheel, and a shield defaced, all in high relief, are to be found on the outer walls.

Dallington is some seven miles to the north, and the road to Hurstmonceux branches off to the left on your way. The castle and its history are too well known to be enlarged upon here, but

DALLINGTON MILL.

(*By A. S. C.*)

a good drawing of the beautiful gateway is given to make amends for the omission. The church, standing apart on the hill, is not so often visited, being overshadowed in fame, but not in situation, by the great brick mansion, which dates from 1440, while the sacred building is several centuries older. Like many another in Sussex, it marks the change from the sombre Norman to the lighter Early English style, and is mainly Transitional. It has fine arcading in its massive tower, and a lofty shingled spire. Enlargement probably followed very quickly, for the pillars and arches on the south side of the nave are of slightly later date than the others. The culminating achievement of Gothic architecture in the

Y

Perpendicular style, and the enthusiasm it seems to have evoked, resulted in nearly all the windows being replaced. But the chief glories of Hurstmonceux Church are the tomb to Thomas, Lord Dacre, 1534, and a fine brass to the father of the builder of the castle. The former is very elaborate, and, by will, was expressly dedicated as an Easter sepulchre. The Decorated font, two canopied recesses and the aumbry are also worth seeing. The stained glass is—" mixed " !

Retracing your steps to the high road and going north, the country you now traverse is noted for its beauty. Hilly it certainly is, but there is nothing of the plateau about it. Wide, deep valleys and steep ascents culminate in Brightling Beacon, which has a superb view in nearly every direction. The Weald, the Downs and sea, and a great part of Surrey and Kent lie stretched out before you. After Yorkshire (because of its great size) it is easily seen why Sussex is the most wooded county in England. You are looking over what was the great forest of Andred. Notwithstanding its primeval trees were mostly burnt in the iron furnaces, sufficient time has elapsed to enable fine oaks, ash and beech trees to take their place, and the " forest " is no mere name to-day.

Dallington is a pretty village, and its church has one of the three ancient stone spires in Sussex. Both this and East Preston, like the majority of Sussex churches themselves, are of modest proportions. Only Chiddingly reaches any commanding stature (128 ft.). The nave and chancel have been rebuilt. It stands well on the hill-side, but lower than the handsome octagonal mill. Like many others, this is falling to decay.

The same charming road, over hills, into valleys, across bridges and streams, will bring you to Burwash, which has one of the prettiest village streets in the county. The view given here meets you on entering, and the rest of the houses fringe the road running along the top of the hill from Etchingham westward. There are some quaint, and at least one notable (Georgian) house, just west of the church. It is, to my mind, a beautiful design. The building line of the street is pleasantly broken, and the type of houses varied, while the foot-walks are bordered by pollarded trees. There is a well-to-do air about the whole place.

The church tower is probably early Norman, but has two-light belfry windows divided by balusters, which are usually considered Saxon, and a shingle spire. The interior underwent restoration and enlargement in the sixties. The most interesting things are the cinque-foiled low-side window, the old chalice and paten, dated 1568, and the cast-iron slab to the memory of " Jhone Coline." It is not only considered the oldest specimen of Sussex iron slabs, but the foliated cross in relief is both beautiful and appropriate to the material, and the Lombardic lettering could not be improved upon.

The Rev. John Coker Egerton, the author of that quaint collection of stories, *Sussex Folk and Sussex Ways*, was rector here.

A path through the yard of the " Bear Inn " will bring you, out of your way, to " Batemans," where Mr. Kipling lives. It is a charming Tudor house set in a valley among wooded hills. That

THE ENTRANCE TO BURWASH.
(*By Conrad H. Leigh.*)

the poet loves the surroundings his " Puck of Pook's Hill " shows, yet I cannot quite think of him living out of sight of the sea—let alone the Downs! These, perhaps, can be seen from the neighbouring hills, but the sea——! Doubtless, in these days of rapid transit, it is not far off, but for me, living by it all my life, no rural prospect can take its place. A restless man myself, I pine for its restless companionship—its living, moving presence. No man can be dull by its shores, and our poet (who has " Sussex by the Sea " nearer his heart than her own gifted singers ever had), hidden behind his inland hills, seems lost to us until we hear his voice in song. A foolish fancy, may be, seeing that "Batemans" is in Sussex, if not by its shores. The sea, however, claims one sacrifice from all who love it. Boundless itself, it cuts off half the points of the compass to a landsman!

A pleasant but "ower straight" road of two and a half miles brings you from Burwash to Etchingham, beautifully situated near the Rother, in a valley surrounded by wooded hills. It is subject to floods at times, and this may account for the "moat" that used to surround the church. An almost universal legend is told of Etchingham also. Deep in the water of its one-time moat lay

BATTLE ABBEY GATEWAY.
(By the late Joseph Diplock.)

a mighty bell, which could only be brought to the surface by six yoke of purely white oxen. Alas for tradition, the moat is dry now, yet no bell has been found!

The church itself is of greater moment. Built by Sir Wm. Echingham, of that famous family, in 1376 or thereabouts, it is a gem of late Decorated architecture, in one style only (a rare thing in our county) except for an earlier doorway in the chancel and the font. Albeit somewhat short for its massive tower, internally it is quite beautiful. There is a fine brass to its builder, but the whole church is the best monument to his name and bounty. The windows throughout have old stained-glass shields of his own and other noble families connected with him, and even the copper vane, fashioned like a pennant, is pierced with " an escutcheon fretty of six pieces for the arms of Echingham "—in heraldic parlance. Of old glass also is a chain of angels playing on harps and viols, in the chancel and north aisle windows. I cannot help expressing wonder that, with such beautiful examples to imitate, those in authority consented to such poor, weak stuff side by side, coloured like the chance combinations of a kaleidoscope, without its saving grace of pattern. Indeed, the stained-glass windows in most country churches are among the greatest trials the present-day pilgrim has to bear. Seeing that in most cases a faculty is required to get rid of these well-meant but unhappy gifts, the absence of this particular form of decoration is a positive

BATTLE STREET.
*(By the late Joseph Diplock.)*

advantage to be thankful for. The art is now better understood and practised.

The windows are mostly different in pattern, and the tracery is unusual. They have not quite the simple beauty of those at Isfield, the most unique examples of pure Decorated in the county —but are nevertheless elegant. The east window (almost identical with Lindfield) shows the influence of the Flamboyant style, which never took the sober fancy of our people, as it seems to have fascinated our neighbours across the Channel, or else it was followed too quickly by the essentially English style of Perpendicular.

Poynings, built about the same time, is in the latter style, and how late in the Decorated period Etchingham is, can be seen by comparing the two.

There is much to see inside, the oak screen and stalls especially, massively carved, so unlike much modern work. The tombs and four fine brasses, and a coat of arms of 1623 in the south aisle, over the infant son of Sir Giffard Thornhurst, are attractive. The old tiles in the chancel have again failed to influence the restorers. The spirit of the old work is entirely wanting in the new examples.

The little pent-house of a porch is original, of later date than the church, and the effect seen from the gateway of the churchyard is undeniably quaint. It has a roof of shingles and is moss-grown with age. Another interesting feature is the double set of flat voussoirs over the west door, which is only slightly moulded. A tomb with a floriated cross was found on excavating on the north side of the chancel. There was evidently a chantry or chapel, as the corbels for its roof and a broken piscina remain in the outer wall. To accommodate it the buttresses are out of angle.

There is much that is interesting in the history of the Echingham family and of the place.

On your way home you may alight at Battle and see the fine parish church, and the remains of the Abbey, of which a view of the gateway is given. The story of Battle lies outside the scope of these papers. It is worthy of a volume by itself. I make only one remark on the great event which has made it for ever famous. Perhaps too little attention has been drawn to the remarkable fact that Sussex was not only the scene of the great tragedy of " might made right " in the Norman Conquest, but also of that other great battle above Lewes, which was the beginning of freedom for the people of England—an instance of poetical justice without parallel in our history. Here is a subject for a poem, indeed !

# CHAPTER XXXIV

## HARTFIELD TO BOLEBROKE AND HOLTYE (7 MILES)

### BY TRAIN TO HARTFIELD.

#### WITH ILLUSTRATIONS BY WALTER PUTTICK AND A. S. C.

" I will go north about the shaws
And the deep ghylls that breed
Huge oaks and old, the which we hold
No more than ' Sussex weed.' "
—KIPLING.

IF you are not quite among the " deep ghylls " at Hartfield,
you are certainly among the " Sussex weed." The oaks
in Buckhurst Park are a sight to gladden the eyes. A New
Forest man tells me that some of them are sixty or seventy
feet " in the straight "—before boughs are found. But not in Buckhurst Park only. The whole district teems with them, and what
is perhaps noteworthy above all else—the hugeness as distinct
from great age. They are not youthful, of course, but in the
very prime of life, and mighty indeed they are, despite the comparatively poor soil. Oaks require less water than most other
trees. My forester said they do not grow so well in the immediate
proximity of a stream. Seeing its almost universal growth throughout the Weald, it is little wonder that it should be used for so
many purposes, even to spires of the churches, while many a dwelling
has frame and beams enow in the ceilings to recall the matted
boughs of the oak itself—except that here there is ordered riot in
their disposition.

Hartfield lies just south of the Medway, for which river Kent is
indebted to Sussex. It rises at the back of Forest Row. The
village is pretty and its church is worthy of a small town. Its
fine tower and shingled spire catch the eye from many a rise both
south and north, for this is indeed a land of " deep ghylls."

The Crowborough range, with its many ridges stretching right
and left, continues on through Ashdown Forest, and north lies
another eminence running westward to East Grinstead and beyond,
and between the two, rising from the deep valley through which
the Medway winds, there are " ups and downs " enough to delight
the eyes—and tire the feet.

THE GATEWAY, BOLEBROKE, SUSSEX.

THE GATEWAY, BOLEBROKE, SUSSEX.

*(By A. Stanley Cooke.)*

Hartfield Church is a fine Perpendicular structure, with a Decorated south aisle.   The earlier style probably gave way to the later, the nave being slightly wider than the chancel.   The tracery of all the windows is good, especially the east window in the aisle, also good modern oak stalls and pulpit ;  and a glass screen of chaste design, to protect worshippers from draught, separates the tower from the nave.   There is evidence of loving care throughout the church, which is spotlessly clean.   A trophy of flags surmounts some tablets to military men—one belonging to the " Church militant "—and there is a good (1640) canopied monument of alabaster and black marble in the aisle.   The font and piscina are

HARTFIELD VILLAGE.
(*By Walter Puttick.*)

Perpendicular, and the stained glass is fine in colour, but lacking in simplicity of design.

Altogether it is a typical Sussex church, not the least interesting adjunct of which is the simple but charming cottage over the lych-gate.   This has an entrance from the churchyard, and was probably used for one of the priests.   It is timber-framed, with cement panels impressed with geometrical patterns.   These panels are of recent date, but may have replaced similar ornament.   The lettering of the date (1520), however, is manifestly a specimen of " the modern antique."

The nearest way to Bolebroke is by a footpath to the left, taking off across a field a mile north on the main road ; but the lover of natural beauties recks not the most direct route. Owing to the scarcity of roads hereabout, the field-paths are many and lead to scattered farms through charming scenery. For want of a better simile, I can only liken them to the jewelled chain taken from the neck of some fair chatelaine, and laid loosely across the soft inequalities of a richly-coloured cushion. You know the beauty of these necklaces, with stones of fine tint, large and small, breaking the line of delicate filigree-work at short spaces. They are much in favour among the fair sex now, and to me, at least, are more adorning in their simplicity than richer necklaces of set pattern, with jewels of greater size. I liken our footpaths to these jewelled strands, winding in beautiful freedom across the fields and slopes. Here and there, the colour of the cornelian, they have the orange-red roofs of the farm and oast-houses set amid the green, precious alike to the artist or wanderer ; and now the greater jewel of such a mansion as Bolebroke, with its semi-castellated gateway of bygone days, to gladden the eyes of all, be they artists, antiquarians, or roamers merely. So I do not scruple to take you by the longer route, taking in many farms, very picturesque, and together with Bolebroke, all, alas, bearing witness to dwindled prosperity.

Whatever may be the remedy for the decay of industry in rural England, it is none the less apparent, and sad, indeed, in its effect. Cornfields and hop-gardens turned to rough pasture, mainly of thistles, the oast-houses falling to decay, the mill-wheels silent or broken, everywhere on the farm ill-kept hedges and gates in bad repair tell the same tale of shrunken means. Except coarse hay, little else is grown, and the country-side seems deserted of folk. The pity of it !

Leaving Hartfield by the path which crosses the cricket field into a lane, you descend to the banks of the Medway. The valley might be a park, so studded is it with fine trees, amid which the rippling stream, suggestive of trout, meanders. It is " plain sailing " by the bridge and up the cart-track to Chartnes Farm, so named after John Chartneis in bygone days. A characteristic of this part of Sussex is the rising of springs high up, or on the very apex of the hills, due to the uptilting of the shaly strata. Such a spring, filling first the pond and then a fine pool in the wood close by, rises here. Across the pond the oast-house rising out of the water gives quite a French aspect to the farm-yard. The house is a good specimen of a yeoman's dwelling, with fine beams upholding the floors.

The road winds through the yard and leaves by a gate on the west side into a shady lane, gaining the road to Bassett's Farm. Three hundred yards to the left a stile and a path through more pasture leads straight to the place, which is in sight on the rise beyond. Here again is the shadow of bad times apparent in the poor condition of the farm buildings. The house is a large substantial structure of the eighteenth century, and its sunken roof-tree bears witness to the weight of the Horsham stone, which it originally bore.

At the entrance of Bassett's yard, a lane on the right leads into the fields and on to a stile in the margin of the wood beyond. The central path winds through this into other fields, and from these the outbuildings of Bolebroke can be seen.

Bolebroke, or Bolebrook,* probably takes its name from the little stream which fed the pool or lake originally filling the dip to the north of the house, still called the Pond Meadow; the broken bay which once held up the water can yet be traced. Whether it supplied a moat for the house can only be conjectured, although the slot for the drawbridge chains can still be seen above the door in the gateway. This door is largely original and has a smaller wicket gate in the centre. The knocker, hammer shaped, still adorns its ancient panelling.

Our sketch gives an exact representation of this interesting gateway, almost unknown to the majority of Sussex folk. The chimney-breasts on the outer walls on both sides point to a whole range of buildings, of which the oast-house is now a part. Much of the house itself remains, and Bolebroke in its prime must have been a miniature Hurstmonceux. It is built of similar materials, thin hand-wrought bricks, evidently of local manufacture, hard and deep in colour, and not too exact in shape. The stone of the mullions is of the most lasting quality. Despite its exposure to the weather for three hundred and fifty years, the edges are wonderfully sharp.

The gateway, although now detached, formed part of a much more extensive building, probably enclosing a courtyard. The design is characteristic of the period when the " alarums and excursions " of less peaceful times had ceased, and only petty marauders were to be guarded against ; and the castle became the mansion with some of the warlike features of the fortress retained. Whether the cupolas crowning the tower represent the original covering or not is a moot point. Certainly they existed in 1785, when Lambert sketched them. If so, the original material may have been lead or copper. From the interior of the towers, it may be seen that they are domed with brick. These domes may have been faced with the yellow stucco used on other parts of the building. The secret lies beneath the present zinc cupolas.

---

* The name of this mansion is curiously like the cry given by the cock pheasants as they seek the woods at night.

The house itself, although but half its former size, has large, lofty rooms and the original staircase, with finely-turned balusters and solid oak steps. Although at present somewhat dilapidated and uncared for, better times, I understand, are in store for it, when its fine windows, plastered up since the days of the window-tax, may again admit the full light of day. Bolebroke has been acquired with a view to complete restoration, and it certainly represents what a friend of mine calls " an eligible ruin," with unbounded possibilities for the expert in sixteenth-century architecture. For a man of taste and means, I can conceive no more congenial task. Such a man prefers an untouched building, even though the walls be covered with modern papers, the ceilings plastered, and the oak staircase painted that uninspiring tint beloved of the Victorian era—stone colour ! What may not lie hidden behind these fustian surfaces ? Only a few weeks ago, the friend above mentioned found—in a delightful old house called " Basings," just over the Kentish border—the original Elizabethan or Jacobean wall fresco, with two quaint rhyming couplets, hidden behind panelling of much later date. Probably many such discoveries await the restorer at Bolebroke, but the panelling of one of the principal rooms will not be found—it was removed some years ago to adorn the chapel at Buckhurst.

One use for the abundant wealth of these days is found in the restoration of the fine stone and timber-framed houses which are hidden in many a secluded spot throughout the forest.

Historically, Bolebroke is first mentioned in 1272. It was held by John, the father of Sir Walter de la Lynde, Knight, whose daughter married John Dalyngrigge, father of the Sir Edward Dalyngrigge, who built Bodiam Castle. But who built Bolebroke is not known, nor the date of its decline. It has been used as a farm-house since the beginning of the eighteenth century. The manor passed through many hands, the Sackvilles, Lewknores, the Earls of Thanet and the Dukes of Dorset holding it at various periods.

A cart-track on the left of the gateway leads straight north-west along a hedge into a wide green way, which may well have been chosen as a vista by the builder of Bolebroke for the fine bay windows of the house to face. Certainly it makes a charming view either way. It leads up and through the wood. In this woodland path I saw, day after day, a magnificent specimen of the dragon-fly range up and down in search of prey. His hunting ground was a hundred yards of this alley, where the sun shone most warmly. No sentry on his beat could have observed the limits more rigorously. Another incident in the bird life of the country was very common this torrid summer ; the starlings perched on the noses of the bullocks grazing in the fields, engaged in relieving their eyes of the tormenting flies. The great animals not only suffered their attentions, but appeared to welcome them.

" Chantlers " is the next farm, and is owned by the trustees of St. George the Martyr in the Borough of London ! It has chimney-corners of vast size, with fire backs and dogs, still used by the good-wife of the house.

Near to " Scraggs," the neighbouring farm, a stile leads to an almost obliterated path down to the stream and across rough pastures to the little inn, the " White Horse," at Holtye Common. Mine host, John Gulliver, has held it for forty years. He was the then Lord de la Warr's trusty forester until his death, having had charge of that work, and much else, and yet his heart is in the New Forest, whence he came. He was a " Queen's Forester " there. Few men know more of trees, deer, sport or country life than John, and, although sixty-seven, he is a dead shot.

The lawn at the back of the inn, approached by a gate in the hedge, is famous for the beautiful view across the forest to the Crowborough ridge—a prospect only surpassed by that from " Ghyll's Lap " on the ridge itself, from which the greater portion of the South Downs are visible, and the sea beyond.

Half a mile below the inn, at the bridge crossing the stream lies the Sussex border-line. Two miles beyond, passing through the pretty Kentish village of Cowden, there is a station on the South Coast railway system, which will bring you home again.

# CHAPTER XXXV

## HEATHFIELD STATION TO MAYFIELD AND ROTHERFIELD (7½ MILES)

### BY RAIL TO HEATHFIELD

WITH ILLUSTRATIONS BY FRED DAVEY, ARTHUR B. PACKHAM, AND THE LATE JOSEPH DIPLOCK.

I GIVE the above route to avoid the row of modern villas between Mayfield Station and the village, which quite destroy the glamour it wields when approached from the south, as in our sketch. Not that you will see Heathfield *en route*, for that village lies two miles to the south-east of its station. (Its church has a fine Early English tower, built of hard chalk faced with stone, with a shingled spire. It bears date 1445 in Arabic numerals, said to be the earliest use of these figures in England. There is a squint, a fourteenth-century crypt, and some thirteenth-century work in the south door and windows, but the heavy hand of the restorer passed over the building on two occasions in the sixties ; consequently, it is uninteresting. The village lies high and the view is superb.)

A mile nor'-east of Heathfield Station, a road runs north to Mayfield. " By using the tongue in your head," in Sussex phrase, a path can be struck in the valley, crossing the stream, and ascending by fields and woodlands to one of the most delightful villages in Sussex. Like most of the forest towns it is " set upon a hill," and is a joy to the eyes long before you reach it. Coventry Patmore considered it irreverent to approach it in any other way. " You must traverse leisurely the spacious circular valley which Mayfield, with its great archiepiscopal palace, dominates, in order to feel the harmony and contrast of its surroundings, and to catch those distant and various views of it which are themselves half its beauty and the fitting preparation for a closer acquaintance with the rest." Patmore had all the fervour of a true pilgrim.

In situation, Mayfield runs every other place in the county very close in the race for beauty, if, like other beautiful things, human as well as natural, its surroundings did not lack variety. This is the only point in which the scenery of East Sussex comes short. Standing on any of the higher hills—and the whole district is a series of high hills and deep valleys—while admitting the fairness of the prospect, which includes the Downs and sea, yet one feels that with these eliminated, the view would be monotonously beautiful ; one ridge after another more or less clothed with trees, falling into valleys broken with fields and woods, in an unending sequence far to the west, over the great expanse of Ashdown Forest, or sloping eastward into the valley of the Rother. They are crowned with here a church and there a mill, and Mayfield does its best to supply what seems to be wanted on the central height of all—the towers and spires of a large town to break the tree-line of the recurring highlands. One seems to crave the effect that the keep of a great castle, gleaming in the sunlight, would give, surrounded by bastions, and flanked by the isolated towers and steeples of a mediæval town ; with streets of white houses with red roofs winding down into the valley, much as at Richmond in Yorkshire. But the Forest of Andred would seem to have been too deep and wide, and wanting in rivers and roads, with industries too restricted, to attract large populations and big towns. These are generally the growth of many years and much commerce. They thrive better in the open. Forest towns are seldom large ; elbow-room seems wanting. How secluded Mayfield was, is borne out by the fact that its name is only mentioned once before the end of the thirteenth century. The archiepiscopal palace, however, soon brought it into note.

Forest scenery is beautiful enough for most people. Not being forest-born, there is too much woodland for me, on the principle that one can have too much of a good thing. As Kipling sings—

" The Weald is good, but the Downs are best."

Mayfield, with the palace in its original glory, may have been as prominent a feature in the landscape as most castle keeps. Built traditionally by St. Dunstan a hundred years before the Conquest, the oldest portions now standing are thirteenth-century work. Simon Islip, the Archbishop of Canterbury in the fourteenth century, was the builder of the great " banqueting hall," the noble arches of which reared their unrivalled single spans gauntly into the air for so many years while the ruins were uncared for. Now the care expended is in the other direction. Restored as a convent, the rules forbid the entry of visitors—of one sex at least—and so it comes to pass that one of the most interesting and famous buildings in Sussex is invisible, even to the antiquarian.

I visited it before the inhibition, many years ago, and saw the mighty ribs of forty feet span which now uphold the roof.

ENTRANCE TO MAYFIELD.

(By *Fred Davey*.)

Originally they were supposed to have carried stone walls which formed a dormer or clerestory with a gallery opening into the hall, so that the ancient roof was loftier, with the centre span occupied by a fumorel for the fire on the central hearth. This feature—the dormer—is only known to have been employed in four other buildings—the original Guildhall of London, Conway Castle, Ightham Moat House, Kent ; and St. Miniato in Florence. The appearance of this hall in olden days must have been most dignified, with its raised dais, heavy oak settles and tables, and other furniture. Here King John and Edward I were feasted by the lordly clerics, and Queen Bess by Sir Thos. Gresham when the Reformation had handed it over to more secular uses. It is used as a chapel now, and an iron screen of fine workmanship separates the sisters from the lay congregation. The windows are of two lights, divided by a transom and surmounted by a trefoil exactly suiting the semi-ecclesiastical nature of the building. (Similar windows of later design—Perpendicular—are to be seen in the Palace of the Archbishops of Canterbury at West Tarring.) Indeed, the whole of the details proclaim, by their strength and character, the master-builder's hand.

In restoration, or adaptation, the magnificent staircase had to go, but the gateway, on the old lines, has been preserved and added to. The vaulted entrance hall is perhaps too crowded with new pillars and handsome capitals ; but " Queen Elizabeth's Room," with the Gresham grasshopper carved on the chimney-piece, is still the guest-parlour, as of old. It is beautifully wainscoted.

The building still contains the tongs wherewith St. Dunstan seized the Devil's nose when, in the guise of a fair lady, he tempted the churchman at his forge. His cloven hoofs below the gown betrayed him ! With a roar the Evil One burst through the roof, St. Dunstan valiantly holding on for three miles. No nose, good or evil, could withstand such treatment, nor could the Saint keep up the pace. The organ gave way and Dunstan came to earth near a bridge still bearing his name. The vanquished demon cooled his nose in Tunbridge Wells chalybeate spring, hence its sulphur compounds.*

Appropriation or theft was condoned as between religious houses, such acts proving the enthusiasm or fervour of the monkish burglar. The bones of the only female saint Sussex seems to have produced, St. Lewinna, were stolen by two Flemish monks from the monastery of St. Andrew at Seaford, on Easter Eve, 1058, after hearing mass in the chapel. One of them tells the story with much relish and self-vindication. The feelings of the outraged owners of the sacred relics, and the language that they used are not recorded—which perhaps is as well.

* A more plausible version says that St. Dunstan slaked his tongs in the spring, hence its taste of quenched iron.

You will turn from fables to view the beautiful houses the same mediæval times have bequeathed these later days. There are many half-timbered houses in other Sussex villages, but Mayfield easily carries off the palm. Besides a number of quaint buildings, Georgian and nondescript, there are at least four houses, each of a different type, which will bear comparison with any in the kingdom. Our sketch here gives the most beautiful of these (Middle House, 1575) ; but the Tudor house at the west end of the village, the one built of stone next to the " Star Inn," and that adjoining the palace gateway, if not so striking, are equally fine in their way.

MIDDLE HOUSE, MAYFIELD (1575).
(*By Arthur B. Packham*.)

The wide street with its raised footway on one side, and its old-time post and chains on the other, with trees here and there between the houses, render it quite as characteristically beautiful as Broadway in Worcestershire, although of a different order.

Much more might be written if space allowed. I have said nothing of the walks that may be taken in all directions, nor of the views. These will speak for themselves. Only the church remains. Of course it has its legend also. The ubiquitous St. Dunstan corrected its orientation, after completion, by a mere shove of his shoulder. No underpinning, nor more powerful hydraulic jack than this simple action was required. Alas, that destruction or decay could not be arrested in similarly easy fashion ! The work of the Saxon Saint has entirely disappeared. Fire, the medium with which he vanquished the Arch-Fiend, destroyed all but the tower in 1389. And the tower only dates from Early English days. It has a shingled spire. The rest is late Perpendicular, bordering on Tudor. The south porch is vaulted and has a chamber over it. Good carving on the remains of the chancel screen and stalls, a squint and two piscinæ are worth noting, and the elegant eighteenth-century chandeliers. Most fonts are earlier than the bulk of the fabric, but here it is Jacobean. The cast-iron slabs in the flooring will recall the time when Mayfield was one of the chief iron-smelting and iron-founding centres. Nothing else

MAYFIELD STREET, LOOKING WEST.
(By the late Joseph Diplock).

remains to tell of that day. That an industry, usually so devastating to a neighbourhood by reason of its sulphurous fumes and destruction of trees for fuel, should have left no mark upon the landscape or the village, is eloquent of the recuperative powers of Mother Nature. Some of these slabs, and others under the choir stalls, are very elaborate and finely cast, with coats of arms, etc. Others, by the poorness of the lettering—the numerals being reversed—show the decay of the industry.

To add to the old-time character of the place, the curfew is still rung from Michaelmas to Lady Day.

Rotherfield may be reached by road or rail; the one for ease, the other for beauty. The same deep valleys and hilly roads bring the wayfarer to a similarly situated village, also built upon a hill, if anything loftier. Its history begins at an even earlier date than Mayfield, as far back as 795, when a deed of gift, confirmed by Offa, granted it to the famous abbey of St. Denis, in France, after which saint it is called. Experts in black letter manuscripts say, however, that the document is a fabrication. The glorification of monasteries, by such means, was not unknown in those days. In any case, the later grant of the church to the monks of Rochester effectually disposed of the former claim.

The village itself, if not possessing such beautiful houses as Mayfield, is quite as pleasantly situated, and its church is the finer. It has a lofty spire visible for miles in all directions. It is a most dignified Early English structure, the interior being lofty and broad, with a chancel nearly as long as the nave. The rood-screen has disappeared, but the archway and steps remain. The restorer has been at work, and the chancel has a kind of dado of brilliant, smooth tiles of a pattern I can only describe as Scandinavian! It is intended, I understand, carefully to cover it up with oak panelling, a form of decoration far more in keeping with our simple churches. Unsuitability characterises, also, the alabaster reredos, otherwise a delicate, handsome structure.

Good work has lately been done in opening fine lancet windows, hitherto walled up. There is an iron slab with double cross of good design in the north aisle, and a stone with three finely carved brass shields to John Wickham, rector here in 1580–91, lies under the choir stalls. Remains of a "Doom" fresco are to be seen over the chancel arch, and other mural paintings. The Jacobean pulpit, the finest in Sussex, but rather over-restored, is well worth notice. As at Mayfield, the porch has a chamber over it. This does not end the list. The arches originally opening into a south chapel can be seen in the chancel wall, and sedilia with triangular headed arches, two piscinæ and two old seventeenth-century chests, the founder's tomb, and part of the old altar slab. The influence of the previous style is shown in the Transition arch in north aisle. Here again the north and south arcades of the nave are nearly two hundred years apart in age—thirteenth-century circular pillars in the former and fifteenth in the latter. Finally, the west door is very fine Perpendicular.

Yet with all these embellishments, the fabric remains of the same simple, heavy character such as nearly all our Sussex churches exhibit, of whatever age or style. In them we may read the character of the men who built them—solid and stable, even if slow and apparently unresponsive. These were the traits of a people wedded to their native soil "since time began for men." It has been pointed out that Britons and Saxons share Sussex between them.

The former were never driven out of the Wealden forests. One seems to see the union of these two peoples in the work of their hands—as in Rotherfield Church.

It is pleasant to record that all the stained glass is good, and some excellent. The east window is by Burne-Jones, and needless to say is very beautiful. Opinions will differ as to the small size of the figures, and the background of foliage of various greens, with white glass between the leaves. Of the beauty of the choir of angels in the Perpendicular tracery, and the seraphim with wings of ruby red—a daring note of colour—there can be no question. But I am inclined to think that neither floral backgrounds, nor too elaborate canopies, suit the rather solid architecture of our churches. I prefer to see the subject surrounded by simple quarries. These are of many patterns, and have the advantage of admitting more light.

Perhaps, as a whole, this window just fails of being great. Seen from the nave, it gives the effect of a jewelled expanse of very satisfying colour, but it is hardly large enough in detail for its position, probably due to the obstructive reredos.

Perfection being difficult of attainment, even by Burne-Jones, it is scarcely to be wondered at that the other beautiful window (the Annunciation by Mr. Pailby) should also fall short. There is so much detail above and below the subject, that the eyes cannot find rest in viewing it. Yet much of the colouring is superb, and the detail and texture of the robes beyond all praise. The faces are frankly modern and beautiful, and the mien of the angel in the act of benediction is full of reverence and awe. To secure detachment from worldly associations, the faces in much stained glass are often so unreal that the finely expressive face of the Virgin in this window comes as a surprise, and will be commended or condemned according to the weakness or strength of the mediæval tradition in the mind of the beholder.

There are three other good examples, and some old glass in the Neville Chapel, where the arms and cognisance of the Earls of Abergavenny, the portcullis, are blazoned on the roof.

This ends our day, unless you make your lodging for the night at the " George Inn," and wish to see the most characteristic scenery of this part of your county. If so, make for Crowborough, and then for Forest Row Station, ten or eleven miles away from Rotherfield. This will take you through the heart of Ashdown Forest, a tract of country of singular wildness and loveliness. Crowborough will not detain you long in passing—if it be not heresy to say so! It is merely suburban, of an attractive type, without the advantage of a city close at hand. The surroundings, of course, are charming, and the air superb.

# CHAPTER XXXVI

## WINCHELSEA AND ICKLESHAM (ABOUT 8 MILES FROM FAIRLIGHT)

### BY RAIL.

### WITH ILLUSTRATIONS BY ARTHUR B. PACKHAM AND WALTER PUTTICK.

THERE is another and far more interesting way of visiting Winchelsea than by rail merely. It is by taking an early 'bus or conveyance from Hastings to Fairlight Glen, and then following the cliff edge to its limit, called " Cliff-end." Before descending you have your choice of routes—by road to Icklesham, or along the old military canal to Winchelsea (about 8 miles).

I scarcely like to advise—which is only another way of saying that I am not familiar with any cross-country cut to Icklesham from half-way along the canal. You may try, and trust to Providence that you are not brought up short by waterways, and compelled to retrace your steps. Frankly, being on the horns of a dilemma renders me an unsafe guide. I want you not to miss the delightful four miles of marsh leading to Winchelsea's West Gate ; nor yet lose the sight of Icklesham Church, notable for many things. A glance at the map will show the problem. I will therefore leave you to solve it, and speak of what lies before you as you stand at " Cliff-end," and gaze across Pett Level.

Pett lies below and to the left. To destroy the chief link with the past in the fabric of one's ancient church, and build a new one as at Pett, is to court oblivion ; for neither Brabant's *Sussex* nor Harrison's *Churches* so much as name the place. Still farther to the left lies Guestling, which has suffered a similar fate ; but the scourge of fire was the cause of its most interesting Norman church being destroyed. I give a sketch of it here. Note the round-headed windows in the tower divided by a baluster, which are considered undoubtedly Saxon work. Only one Norman arch remains in the rebuilt church to connect it with the past.

" Guestling "—a pleasant name to associate with a Sussex village,

Winchelsea Ch.
East end.

Arthur B. Packham
24/5/98

Winchelsea Church.
(*By Arthur B. Packham.*)

not in sound only, but in meaning also : that is, if the Court of which it was the title hailed from here.

A " Guestling " was a sort of Parliament instituted by the Cinque Ports to arrange matters among themselves, and negotiate with other seaport towns, such as Yarmouth, where the herring was chiefly sent, to exchange its silvery sheen for the sombre glooms and fiery tints of the dees. These consultations were much needed in those rough-and-ready days. Yarmouth local history is racy of the sea, and as turbulent as the tossing of its waves. All sorts and conditions of fishermen resorted thither, and many and frequent were the feuds, often ending in bloodshed.

GUESTLING CHURCH.
(*By Arthur B. Packham.*)

We who dwell by the water-side—albeit fashion reigns in this favoured spot, Brighton—are not entirely unacquainted with the manners and habits of these " toilers of the sea." Their very language and tone are things quite distinct from the ordinary type of disputants. It is loud and must necessarily be so, or how could they make themselves heard over the howling of the storm ; and a quarrel among fisher-folk is a veritable tempest of vituperation— and among their women-kind an undoubted squall, in every sense of the word ! There is little need for a novelist to go into un- frequented corners of Scotland or Ireland for crank dialogues and sententious sayings in speech requiring a glossary to make it plain. Let him don the garb of a beach-loafer, and visit any fishing village or port. There is as rich a harvest of quaint phrases, strange oaths, and what Jack calls " lingo," as of herrings. Now and again single characters have been sketched, but there are many waiting portrayal at the hand of the writer, and more for the dramatist.

To return, this aptitude for dispute ending in quarrel, which is so strong a characteristic of the men who go down to the sea in ships, led to the institution of the " Guestling." Whether it had any connection with our village and took its name therefrom, or whether the two things are as far as the poles asunder, is immaterial now. Suffice it that one is a pleasant, peaceful spot, within hail of the sea, and the other was an institution likewise peaceful and therefore pleasant, and also not far removed from the interest which the sea has for those who get their living out of its waters.

The " Guestling " is older than either Parliament or the House

NEAR THE CHURCH, GUESTLING.
(*By Arthur B. Packham.*)

of Lords, and its methods were exactly those which obtain in our Commons now. It may have been the model upon which the greater Institution formed its procedure. There were so many members who had a right to sit, as representatives of the Cinque Ports, and there were others who were chosen from the neighbouring towns and villages interested in the fisheries and privileges of the Ports, and of the towns with which they traded.

It was no hole-and-corner assembly, this of the " Guestling." It met in Church, and sat in solemn and sober council at a long table covered with a red cloth. It always opened its proceedings with prayer, and the president, who sat in rotation for each Cinque Port, was called " Mr. Speaker." His powers were as unquestioned as those of the Speaker of to-day, or if questioned at all, were as strenuously upheld as they are now by the true men of the Court, who knew a good thing was worth keeping ; and although the need for the Court has passed away, it was no mean assembly in the days when the Navy of England was drawn chiefly from the Cinque Ports. As a custom it still survives.

It has recently met with many quaint observances to swear allegiance to King George, to secure the recognition of the claims of the " barons " of the Cinque Ports and their " links," to hold the canopy over the King at his Coronation, and to protest against decreasing the coast-guards. About a hundred mayors and barons paraded to Hythe Parish Church for a solemn service, and afterwards met at the Town Hall. Three blasts were sounded through the open window on the old mote horn, and decrees from the Black Book were read, such as a fine of forty pence for interrupting a baron while speaking, and a penalty of twenty pence on anyone leaving the meeting without notice. The first of these two would be welcomed to-day in Parliament.

*       *       *       *       *

At " Cliff-end " below commences the strip of marsh called Pett Level, the beginning of the flat land, bordered by yellow beach and blue sea, which widens out into the immense Romney Marsh, east of Rye. Our beach-loafer " on the find " may stumble across flotsam and jetsam of every kind all the way from this point eastward. Coventry Patmore noted the " cartloads of corks " which dance ashore where the Level begins, with other gifts of the sea, water-worn though they be—which are treasures indeed to children, and in their eyes make the seashore such a wonderful place ; and not to children only. I know one " grown up " who still fills his pockets when a half-holiday makes him a " long-shoreman " ; and there is no shore so prolific as that which begins at " Cliff-end " and stretches right away to Dungeness.

After a storm the fringe of beach above high-water mark is strewn with many a child's tiny argosy of cork, with a skewer for mast. True, the paper sail has gone, but it is the lot of canvas " to go by the board " in rough weather, and calms are almost storms to such frail craft. These, and quaint oddments of wood, toys perchance, from the wreck of some merchant vessel ; bits of drift-wood, light as touch-wood from years of immersion ; now and then a small keg or box—unlike Pandora's—empty, or wreathed with seaweed ; all these, and the inevitable basket are but a sample of the gifts of the sea.

As you walk along the canal bank eastwards, you may not see anything to give rise to thought but weeds and rushes in its still waters, so unlike the restless ocean but a stone's-throw away. Both are typical ; the sea of ever-present danger, and the canal of peace assured by preparation for war, for this great military work, now so neglected and forgotten, was, in conjunction with the Martello towers, carried out at great cost during the Napoleonic scare—an eighteenth-century agreement with Drake's earlier advice to guard the coast of Sussex !

All is peaceful enough now. A repose greater than is suggested by Landseer's lambs playing around the abandoned cannon in his picture emblematical of " Peace," broods over the scene. You *may* meet another human being, but it is quite unlikely. Cattle out to grass, and wild birds, gulls or even heron haunt the banks, and take but little notice except to flap composedly ahead or give you precedence. There is nothing of the illimitable flat about this tongue of marsh. Winchelsea bounds the distance, and on your left, at no great way off, the rising ground that was once the shore sweeps round to join hands with the rocky mound or islet on which " New " Winchelsea, which seems so old to-day, is built.

Here, rather more than half-way, I ought perhaps to tell its tale ; but Icklesham lies a mile and a half due north, and is worth the journey there and back, before we proceed to Winchelsea— always presupposing that you can reach Icklesham from here !

It is pleasantly situated among trees on the main road to Hastings, within sight of the sea, but its chief charm is its fine church, mainly built on the border-line of a change of style. In vol. xxxviii. of the Sussex Archæological Collection there is an exhaustive, and— except for an architect—an exhausting article on its fabric, and on the problems it presents. Such particularising is necessary, of course, but for you it will be enough to say that the early Norman nave and chancel were, before very long, endowed with aisles, tower and chapel, much in the order given and according to the prevailing taste. Thus, the nave arcades are fine Norman, while the tower suffers from the impending change, and although Norman too, is scarcely massive enough—an apparently imperative characteristic. It is singularly like the results generally obtained by modern architects in building in this style. The beautiful wall arcades above stone benches which adorn the north and south chapels are Transition or—as the writer of the article prefers to call them—Early Pointed ; somewhat of a distinction without a difference. Less technical folk will prefer the usual terms, and in the range given by these will find Icklesham Church most attractive.

The vistas opening up from the nave into the chancel and chapels are all varied and picturesque. The contrast between the round and pointed work is marked. Some of the former is almost archaic in its simplicity, while the nave arches remind one of Steyning, without their richness. The capitals of the pillars of both churches are almost identical. The carving on the corbels carrying the chancel arch is delightful in design and execution.

The windows are various, and run the gamut of simplicity, beauty and ugliness, from early Norman to elaborate Decorated. The east window is a beautiful example of Decorated, but those in the south chapel are boldly elementary, without tracery or relief. They probably represent the work of some churchwarden of post-Reformation times, and on the exterior remind one of the lack-lustre cavities of the eyes in a death's head, fitly foreshadowing the decay of beauty in architecture. They form, in the opinion of ninety-nine out of every hundred beholders, a blot calling aloud for remedy. And the unsightly " over-all " roof of the nave is a second eyesore.

If the restorer in 1847 had turned his attention to these two points, he would have earned a debt of gratitude. He actually came across traces of clerestory windows, small indeed, but quite sufficient to break the great expanse of roof, and yet elected to retain the ugly feature, whereby an elaborate and pretentious scheme of roof-beam and carved corbel has been erected, now seen to be quite out of keeping with the simple Norman work in the nave. This is how our churches are disfigured, by wrong-headed zeal for architectural features, excellent in themselves, but quite unsuitable in application.

Here was the opportunity for " the man greatly daring." I admit that the problem was not easy, the nave roof coinciding with the chancel, both fourteenth-century work. There are, however, considerations to which uniformity must bow, and in my opinion this was one of them. The style of which a building is mainly composed has the first claim. The exterior angles of the roofs might have been slightly at variance, but the reinstating of the original clerestory would have been the salvation of the interior, and would have broken the ugly expanse of the present nave roof.

There is so much to see in Icklesham Church, that you will be wise to spend both time and attention on it. There are points of detail, beauty of design and execution which only a close study can fully disclose. Some of the facing of the stonework is done with a " Norman axe " ! Think of it, ye who aim at the most deadly-dull of scraped surfaces—the character and play of light upon the one, and the monotony, the truly " dead level " of the other !

Between here and Winchelsea you will see " the Black Mill " on a knoll. It is quite unlike most others in Sussex, as it combines the characteristics of the " tower " and " smock " mills, with its quaint fan-wheel approached by an outer staircase from below, and perched on the top of the roof to obtain the leverage necessary to turn the whole of the great body. Frank Brangwyn has etched it in his own peculiar but attractive way.

Winchelsea is built on a plateau which falls precipitously on three sides, at least, and slopes down to the marsh on the western face. It represents the final defeat of man in the struggle with one of the forces of nature, the sea, whose ways are past finding out and uncontrollable. In its dealings with coastwise towns it laughs man to scorn.

This—although old enough as we count age—is New Winchelsea. Its ancient namesake lies under water several miles to the south-east, overwhelmed by an inroad of the sea. The remedy seemed both easy and possible, viz. to bow to the inevitable and build a new town on the cliff and a harbour at its base. Edward I, being Warden of the Cinque Ports, planned the new city on lines of regal splendour, with encircling walls and gates, and made full provision for the commerce of the port ; and the sea looked on with indifference awhile, then, tossing sand and shells into the harbour, it turned contemptuously aside, leaving ruin and an ever-extending bank of shingle behind it.

It is far better for seaports to have the sea an active, declared enemy, than a sullen, retreating foe. However it may rage, with whatever ceaseless sap and storm it may attack the defences of a port, it can be kept in check by dogged perseverance, even though the cost be great. But it cannot be pursued, and the earthworks thrown up to mask its retreat are insuperable. Ruin is as inevitable as the decrees of fate.

The first thought that strikes one in Winchelsea is the contrast between its present aspect, and the mediæval fame history has made you acquainted with. To you it seems just a country village within sight of the sea, possessing a finer church than is usually met with in so small a place. It seems impossible that it could ever have been a busy seaport. Its harbour at the foot of the cliff has utterly vanished, and the sea is nearly two miles distant.

The old town was destroyed near the end of the thirteenth century, the sea completing what its enemies began. Taking the part of the Barons against Henry III, Prince Edward stormed it " with great slaughter " in 1266. The new town was no luckier. The French sacked it in 1359, 1380 and 1449, and would have added a fourth triumph to their arms, had not the Abbot of Battle repulsed them in 1377. A great sea fight with the Spaniards was fought off the town by Edward III in full view of his queen Philippa and her attendants, and during the troubled years of the Plantagenets it was the chief seaport on the south coast. It was not only the rendezvous for the Royal Navy, but also a hornets' nest, from which issued a cloud of piratical vessels, the terror of both friend and foe in the Channel. The records of Winchelsea teem with cases of flagrant piracy, not confined to lawless freebooters. Its mayor, Robert de Battayle, was indicted for robbing two merchants of Sherborne.

In 1450 its decay began, and in 1545 there was " no Winchelsea ship" in the fleet which " anchored in the *roadstead* off the *new*

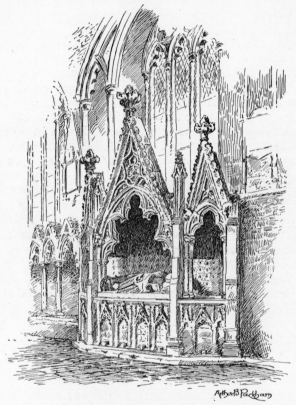

THE ALARD TOMB, WINCHELSEA.
(*By Arthur B. Packham.*)

Castle of Camber." This extract is eloquent of the ruin of Winchelsea city and harbour, and incidentally reads strangely in our ears by reason of the word applied to Camber, which seems of hoary age to us to-day. It was built by King Hal, and its " roadstead " is also a thing of the past. Sheep feed on the scanty grass which grows on the beach and sand thrown up by the retreating waves. The soil is only a few inches deep, and in places the shingle still prevails, while the castle is a ruin and deserted.

John Evelyn, during the Commonwealth, visited Winchelsea. He " walked over from Rie to survey the ruins of that ancient Cinq Port, which by the remaines and ruines of ancient streets and public structures discovers it to have been formerly a considerable and large Citty. There are to be seen vast caves (cellars) and vaults, walls and towers, ruins and monasteries, and a sumptuous church. . . . This place being now all in rubbish, and a few despicable hovels and cottages standing, hath yet a Mayor ! "

There is less to be seen to-day. The walls are almost gone, and the three gates only remain to tell of the great area the city was

RYE FROM THE STRAND GATE, WINCHELSEA.
(*By Walter Puttick.*)

intended to cover. It was built on the plan of a Roman town, with streets intersecting its thirty-nine squares at right angles. Most of these are green fields or wooded enclosures.

The church has but the shadow of its former greatness, yet is the finest of its style (Decorated) in Sussex. Whether it was ever completed can only be conjectured, or determined by excavation of its foundations. Certainly it had transepts, for the ruins of these are standing.

The interior requires intelligent restoration—indeed, calls aloud for it ; but there is still much to admire in the clustered and banded pillars, the beautiful natural foliage of the capitals and the tracery of the windows. The Alard tombs are celebrated throughout Sussex and with reason. They are exceedingly beautiful, as our sketch shows.

The Friars is an ivy-covered ruin in private grounds. It has a very graceful apsidal chancel of five windows, and a fine chancel arch.

There are several other old buildings of perhaps slight interest, and the three gates—the *Strand Gate* facing Rye, by which is a seat for the full beauty of the view to be enjoyed ; the *Land Gate*, built by one of Winchelsea's mayors in the reign of Henry V, bearing his name on a shield ; and the *New Gate*, far away in the fields, facing the marsh lying between Winchelsea and the Hastings Cliffs.

Thomas of Walsingham records " a miraculous escape " of the city's founder, King Edward the First, which is worth quoting :— " Whilst the King was dwelling near Winchelsea, he proposed to go one day to take a view of his fleet, and having entered the town, when he had just ridden over against the bulwarks, and was about to survey the fleet at the lowest station, it happened that he approached a certain windmill, of which there were several in the town, and his horse being frightened with the noise of the mill, and with the quickly revolving sails, refused to proceed, and leaped over the bulwarks ; upon which, out of the multitude of horse and foot who followed the King, or had assembled to have a look at him, no one thought but that the King had perished, or had, at least, been stunned by the leap. But Divine Providence so disposing, the horse fell upon his feet, even from such a height, into a road which from recent rains was softened with mud, into which the horse was able to slip for twelve feet, and yet did not fall, and being turned round with another bridle by the King, he ascended directly to the gate, through which he entered unhurt, and the people who were waiting for him were filled with wonder and delight at his miraculous escape."

This was evidently at the Strand Gate, and if you look over the wall here, you will see that the King's descent must have been much of the character of the feats at present indulged in by Italian officers on horseback.

If this was the scene of the incident, the harbour was close by. There is nothing but green fields now, and a belt of trees. What a transformation !

# CHAPTER XXXVII

## RYE

BY RAIL.

WITH ILLUSTRATIONS BY ARTHUR B. PACKHAM, WALTER PUTTICK
AND A. S. C.

FEW spots in this beautiful county of ours are better known
among artists than Rye. One can scarcely call it " off
the beaten track " for them, indeed, it may be said to be
almost over-painted—though not over-rated. Its situation
is so unique, standing as it does, like a sentinel at the verge of the
Romney Marsh, and having the beautiful level between itself and
Winchelsea to guard as a precious possession.

It has, like Chester, many quaint buildings among its crowded
streets, and much colour in its general aspect to charm the eye ;
and it fills the vision from whatever point it may be gazed upon,
filling it moreover with complete satisfaction to the artistic sense.
This characteristic, perhaps, accounts for the great affection so
many artists have evinced, and still show, towards Rye. It is not
merely in itself an artistic and unmatched jewel, but it is superbly
set and mounted, and borne in beauty by the landscape, like a
precious stone upon the bosom of a fair woman. Whether its
terraced houses and red roofs, surmounted in just the right place
by its noble church tower, be set against the tender flush of dawn,
or the deeper glow of sunset, blush to a fuller warmth beneath the
sunshine, or dream in velvety gloom beneath the moon's rays,
Rye is always charming, always fascinating to the painter.

But that it should contain much to interest is almost a wonder,
seeing that it has been burnt more or less to the ground four times
in the course of its history, with sundry other conflagrations and
fightings to give the townspeople employment. Fortunately these
fires happened between 1377 and 1448, so that there has been an
ample margin of antiquity for its buildings to become venerable.

The church, which also shows signs of having been partially
burnt, not only on its fabric, but in the medley of styles it presents,
is in many ways unmatched in the south of England. It seems
to belong to Rye in the sense of having shared its fortunes and

misfortunes, and to have become part of the domestic side of its
history ; so much so, that until recently there was almost as much
given up to secular uses as to prayer.   But this is past, and Rye
Church, which is almost a cathedral, is once more put to its proper use.

It is cruciform, and dedicated to St. Mary.   But it is as unlike

MERMAID STREET, RYE (WITH THE " HOSPITAL ").
(*By Arthur B. Packham.*)

the usual Sussex church as it is possible to conceive.   It apparently began by being a Norman church of fair dimensions.   Probably the various invasions and burnings brought ruin to parts of
the building, and the restorers deemed it better to replace the
worthy past by a more glorious present, and as the same thing
occurred again and again, Rye Church is like nothing else in the
county.   The nave is late Transition, and has a clerestory, but
not on a grandiose scale.   The embattled tower stands at the

intersection of the nave and the high chancel, and the transition from the narrow bounds of the former into the spaciousness of the chancel and chapels on either side is like passing from Rye Level to Romney Marsh. The total dissimilarity of the proportions is too great not to be noticed, and although the stickler for regularity might sniff, the manifold points of interest and the various vistas fully atone for the " big upon little " presented by Rye Church.

Then there are groined roofs, moulded ribs and flamboyant windows of the latest date set beside the earliest of Early English. One of the chancel chapels is dedicated to St. Clare of Italy, and the nuns, who were called Clarrises, had a small establishment at Rye, and this was their chapel.

If one enters by the west door, the view extends 159 feet to the east wall, a sufficient distance to merit comparison with some cathedrals. There are five bays of tooth-moulded arches on each side of the nave, and the transept has a pure Norman arch leading into it, and Norman arcading with triplicate and chevron mouldings adorns both walls. This arcading, which contrasts forcibly with the Perpendicular windows, shows also how much of the building must have been consumed for the styles to be so far apart.

The window over the high altar is magnificent, and a counterpart to that at St. Mary's, Oxford. On the flooring within the communion rails is the brass of Thomas Hamon, six times mayor and twice or thrice burgess for Parliament, and was probably a descendant of Fitz-Hamon, one of the Conqueror's followers, five hundred years before. This brass has the worthy man in the civic gown of the day, with all the bravery of a ruffled collar.

The windows lighting St. Clare's Chapel, have a small gallery or ambulatory in the thickness of the wall, which leads along, up, and across the north transept, and traverses the clerestory of the nave to the west door. Cathedrals often have these communications from west to east (used among other purposes for the repair of the glass), but parish churches very seldom.

The pillars and capitals throughout the east portion of the church are of various styles, some being late Perpendicular and others Early English. Oak screens separate the chancels of St. Clare and St. Nicholas from the transepts. That which adorned the entrance to the chancel proper has disappeared, all but some panelling in the south porch. The stained glass is of various quality. Burne-Jones's last design, " The Adoration of the Magi," is sumptuous in colour, and there are some good windows by Kempe. The east window is poor.

The mixture of styles is very marked at the north entrance, where the Norman arch and fillet moulding has a Perpendicular window above it, three centuries later : whilst the belfry gallery close at hand is such as one finds in St. Alban's Abbey.

In the parish chest, I was told there were two old brasses and a curious flagon of lead, which is the only remaining memorial of the French Huguenots, who worshipped in the church, when

RYE CHURCH.
(*By Arthur B. Packham.*)

driven out of France. It has two eagles' heads forming part of the handle, but, if symbolic, they are of very poor workmanship.

With this we must leave the fine fabric. Of its exterior, with the beautiful flying buttress, a visit is necessary to realise how completely it seems part of the ancient town, over which it broods like a hen over her chicks, a simile not original, perhaps, but absolutely expressive of the situation of Rye Church.

To see the town is to understand why artists love it. Its streets encircle the hill and church, and in that fact may be traced a great part of their picturesqueness and charm. Of the mediæval buildings only five are left, but there are others, notably, the " Hospital," the " Mermaid Inn," and the quaint brick Grammar School. Indeed, the whole town, delightfully irregular, both in plan and variety of structures, appeals irresistibly to those who love old things. Built on its one small hill, a situation unique among

OLD COURTYARD AT RYE (MERMAID INN).
(*By Arthur B. Packham.*)

English towns, it must have been, in the Middle Ages, just such a fortified city " set upon a hill " as one sees in the background of old paintings.

Of its old walls very little remains, excepting the Land Gate, with its bold round towers and fine machicolations. These were built by Edward III, but do not appear to have resisted the onslaughts of the French. Even less, or to speak correctly, none of the more ancient walls, for which Richard I granted a charter, exist above ground.

The early history of Rye shows that it must have been a very

unenviable dwelling-place. All " the ills which man is heir to,"
and those the Fates in their wrath or caprice inflict, fell on the
devoted town. The peace and quietude which now brood over it
in the sunlight is the calmness usually associated with old age.
But in its youthful days it passed through fiery trials indeed.
The coastwise towns of the Channel were peculiarly at the mercy of
warlike chances, and in those turbulent days peace was seldom
long assured ; and even if great causes were not at issue, filibus-
tering and piratical descents and forays kept men on the alert.
But all their care did not prevent Rye being burned in 1377 and
1448, and doubtless there were many " alarums and excursions "
besides. Pestilence—and what hotbeds of disease these crowded,
unsanitary towns must have been !—again and again ravaged it.

If Rye is to display all its beauty, it must be seen from without.
This is what the artists have discovered, and they seldom weary
of its charms. The subjects within are chiefly quaint or antiquarian
in character ; but from either Level or the hills to the north there
are no lack of views, with cloud effects innumerable ; sunrise
or sunset glories ; moonlight mystery or grey of dawn ; against
all the irregular buildings, roofs and towers of the ancient town,
crowned with its church, glows or glooms in answer to their mood.

But the views which are the peculiar possession of Rye itself
must not be overlooked—or, to be paradoxical—must be overlooked, if full enjoyment is to be ours. These are the prospects
stretching east, south and west, over the vast expanse of Romney
Marsh, the sea and the smaller Level, which has Camber Castle,
like a huge tortoise basking in the sun by the sea, and Winchelsea
at its western limit. I cannot resist quoting Coventry Patmore
anent these outlooks. For most of us, he says the first and last
word about them—" The glory of the town lies in its command of
so many great views of the marsh, which stretches for miles on every
side of it. The beauty of these views is beyond all description,
and has never been expressed even in painting. What strikes me
as being most characteristic and least noticed in these views is
the effect of sunshine. The sun, said to shine with double lustre
upon Rhodes, certainly seems to do so here. On a bright day, you
look down from these walls on something like a hundred square
miles without a shadow, except, perhaps, from the dark down of
Fairlight ; and the endless peaceful glory, organic and alive in
every inch of it, is doubled in effect by the continual presence of
that other bright, but barren and restless, plain of sea."

He notices also—as you will see for yourself—the singularly old-
world character of the streets, the most precipitous of which are
paved with boulders. Not a house less than a hundred years
old—most of them four hundred, as the mouldings of the cornices,

barge-boards, door-posts and window frames testify ; everything—
except the costume of the people—being ancient. In comparing
Rye with Chester, which has finer half-timbered houses of the same
early date, he speaks of the " unpublished character about everything " in our little Sussex town, whereas " Chester knows its
picturesque and antiquarian value."

In one of these old houses in Rye, once known as the " Old
Flushing Inn," and probably formerly an old religious house

MILL ON THE TILLINGHAM, RYE.
*(By Walter Puttick).*

(built in the reign of Edward IV), " a remarkable fresco, probably
unique in England," has lately been discovered. The house itself
is very quaint and interesting, and has chimney corners in all the
rooms. The fresco is 16 feet long by 6 feet high, with a frieze
15 inches in depth. Just under the frieze are three panels, the
first containing, in five lines of Early English black lettering, the
opening of the " Magnificat " ; the central, the second part ;
and the third the words " Glory be," the rest being obliterated.
The panels are supported by cherubs. The fresco is richly coloured

and beautifully designed, the motive being chiefly conventional scrolls and allegorical animals ; but there are three imposing oblique scrolls cutting through the groundwork, and on each is boldly inscribed " Soli Deo honor."

The "Mermaid Inn" and the Hospital should be visited. Although the former is no longer a tavern in the ordinary sense, it still provides housing and hospitality for visitors. The ground floor is a good specimen of mediæval architecture. The massive beams and oak panelling, the fine fireplace of the old kitchen (now used as a club-room), which has a flat arch reaching almost across the room, and the quaint little courtyard, will do much to transport you to old-world days. Originality is, of course, claimed for it, and in the main with truth ; but, as with all these tourist-haunted resorts, some of its antiquity is introduced. The general effect is, however, charming.

Among other attractive buildings, is the frowning little tower-fortress built by William of Ypres in Stephen's reign, and called after him. Seen from the river bank, it gives a touch of romance to the view.

The Land Gate does the same for the entrance of the town. It was built by Edward III, and is practically complete, with fine machicolations to its massive round towers. The open place just outside, in conjunction with the old gateway, makes a very attractive picture.

There are the remains of two monasteries : the chapel (wrongly attributed to the Carmelite Order) near the church on the south, which has been too carefully restored ; and that on Conduit Hill, with blocked-up windows of flamboyant character.

If you would see Rye as it should be seen, stop in it for a few days in summer. Although the days are hot, the nights are cool owing to the light mists rising from the marshes and the breath of the sea ; while your slumbers will be none the less sound for being lulled by a song you little expect to hear in a seaside town— the song of the nightingale. Nor are your waking hours less pleasant because the cuckoo, like yourself, also visits Rye in the summer.

THE END

CAMBER CASTLE (page 374).

(*By A. S. C.*)

# INDEX.

377